Covenantal Conversations

Covenantal Conversations
Christians in Dialogue with Jews and Judaism

Edited by Darrell Jodock

Fortress Press
Minneapolis

COVENANTAL CONVERSATIONS
Christians in Dialogue with Jews and Judaism

A study guide to this book may be found online at http://www.fortresspress.com.

Photo © Brandon Harman / Photonica / Getty Images
Cover design: Designworks
Book design: Jeremy Keller

Library of Congress Cataloging-in-Publication Data
Covenantal conversations : Christians in dialogue with Jews and Judaism /
edited by Darrell Jodock.
    p. cm.
 Includes bibliographical references and index.
 ISBN 978–0–8006–6275–2 (alk. paper)
 1. Judaism—Relations—Christianity. 2. Christianity and other religions—Judaism.
 I. Jodock, Darrell, 1941–
 BM535.C73 2008
 261.2'6—dc22   2007045380

Manufactured in the U.S.A.

To my many mentors—
including Rabbi Herbert Brockman,
Rabbi Martin Beifield Jr., and Dr. Franklin Sherman—
who have graced me with their understanding and their friendship.

CONTENTS

Contributors

Barry Cytron, director, Jay Phillips Center for Jewish-Christian Learning, St. Paul. (Conservative) Rabbi.

Elliot Dorff, Rector and Distinguished Professor of Philosophy, University of Judaism, Los Angeles. (Conservative) Rabbi.

Sarah Henrich, professor of New Testament, Luther Seminary, St. Paul. ELCA Pastor.

Darrell Jodock, Drell and Adeline Bernhardson Distinguished Professor of Religion, Gustavus Adolphus College, St. Peter, Minn., chair of the ELCA Consultative Panel on Lutheran-Jewish Relations, and member of the Region 3 Task Force on Lutheran-Jewish Relations. ELCA Pastor.

Isaac Kalimi, National Endowment for the Humanities (NEH) Senior Fellow at W.F. Albright Institute of Archeological Research in Jerusalem.

Ralph Klein, Christ Seminary, Seminex Professor of Old Testament, the Lutheran School of Theology at Chicago. ELCA Pastor.

Eugene Korn, Associate Executive Director, Center for Christian-Jewish Understanding of Sacred Heart University, Fairfield, Conn. (Orthodox) Rabbi.

Esther Menn, professor of Old Testament, the Lutheran School of Theology at Chicago, and member of the ELCA Consultative Panel on Lutheran-Jewish Relations.

Peter Pettit, Director of the Institute for Jewish-Christian Understanding at Muhlenberg College, Allentown, Pa., and member of the ELCA Consultative Panel on Lutheran-Jewish Relations. ELCA Pastor.

Richard Sarason, Professor of Rabbinical Literature and Thought, Hebrew Union College, Cincinnati. (Reform) Rabbi.

Frank Sherman, formerly Associate for Interfaith Relations, Department for Ecumenical Affairs, the Evangelical Lutheran Church in America, and previous chair of the ELCA Consultative Panel on Lutheran-Jewish Relations. ELCA Pastor.

John Stendahl, pastor of the Lutheran Church of the Newtons, Newton Center, Mass., and member of the ELCA Consultative Panel on Lutheran-Jewish Relations. ELCA Pastor.

Krister Stendahl, formerly dean of Harvard Divinity School, Cambridge, Mass., and Bishop emeritus of Stockholm, Sweden.

Karla Suomala, assistant professor of religion, Luther College, Decorah, Ia., and member of the ELCA Consultative Panel on Lutheran-Jewish Relations.

Mark Swanson, Harold S. Vogelaar Professor of Christian-Muslim Studies and Interfaith Relations, the Lutheran School of Theology at Chicago. ELCA Pastor.

Introduction

Darrell Jodock

Sixty years ago, in many parts of the United States, it was possible to be a church member and a citizen and have no contact with Jews or Muslims and no reason to ponder Jewish-Christian or Muslim-Christian relations. It is much less likely the case today. Clergy and laity come into contact with people of other faiths through their work or in their neighborhoods and want to understand more fully the theology of interfaith relations. There is a time and place for discussing the broader topic of "Christianity and all the other religions," but the non-Christian religions are different enough so that there is also a need to think more specifically about each individual religion and its relationship to Christianity. This book focuses on Christian-Jewish relations.

The relationship between Judaism and Christianity is special. No other religion shares so much with Christianity as does Judaism. Except for a different order of books and for the extra material in Roman Catholic Bibles (the Apocrypha), the two religions share a common Scripture. Jews call it the "TaNaK" (often spelled Tanakh) and Christians the "Old Testament." Both religions affirm the same God. Both religions see God active in history, working toward a goal of *shalom*. Both regard God to be a God of justice and mercy, who makes covenants and is faithful to them. Jesus and all the apostles were thoroughly immersed in Judaism. Biblical Israel provided a common background, out of which rabbinic Judaism and Christianity developed. Those two grew up side-by-side, growing from infancy to maturity between (roughly) 70 C.E. and 500 C.E.[1] By 500 all the main doctrines of Christianity had been defined, the structure of Christianity had been developed, the liturgy had been worked out, the Christian Bible had been canonized, and Christianity looked pretty much as it does today. By 500 Judaism had adopted its canon (not completed until 90 or 100 C.E.), worked out its synagogue structure, developed a prayer book, finished the Talmud, and looked pretty much as it does today. Christians defined their identity over against rabbinic Judaism, and to some extent rabbinic Judaism did the same vis-à-vis Christianity. At the same time Christians borrowed freely from Judaism, and somewhat less frequently, Jews borrowed from Christianity.

The disagreements between Jews and Christians may be important, but they occur in a shared vocabulary and a shared framework, a common understanding of God, the world, and human beings.

1

The special relationship between Christianity and Judaism is not limited to beginnings. The interaction has continued from 500 to the present. Yes, during the Middle Ages many Jews lived in Muslim lands, but as time went on larger and larger numbers lived as "guests" or "aliens" in Christian Europe. Sometimes their presence was mutually advantageous, but often Jews faced misunderstanding, special restrictions or hostility, pogroms, and even expulsion. So, even though the relationship was often an unhappy one for Jews, the interaction continued. Christians continued to define themselves over against the Jews, and the two communities interacted in one way or another.

During the past sixty years, several things have happened to introduce a new chapter in Jewish-Christian relations. The first of these developments was the shock of the Holocaust. When contemplating this state-authorized, deliberate, organized annihilation of some eleven million persons, one-half of whom were Jews, Christians asked how there could have been so few rescuers and resisters and so many perpetrators and bystanders in a population so deeply influenced by Christianity. One answer was that Christian teaching had included anti-Judaism, the view that Judaism was either of no value or in league with the forces of evil. This anti-Judaism had tilled the soil in such a way that racial antisemitism could more easily take root and grow.[2] With the significant exception of annihilation, almost all of the anti-Jewish measures instituted by the Nazis were copied from earlier actions of the church. All of the initial stages seemed very familiar. By the time the annihilation began in the summer of 1941, Nazi power was so entrenched that resistance had become very costly. For Christians, what all of this prompted is a nagging question. Is anti-Judaism an inherent part of Christianity? Can Christianity be interpreted authentically in such a way that it does not perpetuate anti-Judaism and does not prepare the way for antisemitism?

When contemplating the Holocaust there was a second realization—namely, that the two communities had been isolated and that such isolation contributed to the vulnerability of each. Many of the measures put in place by the Nazis during the 1930s were designed to increase the isolation. Jews and Aryans could not work together; they could not do business with each other; they could not intermarry, they could not attend the same school or live in the same neighborhoods. These measures undid the integration that had developed in western Europe during the nineteenth century. For many, the result of this second realization was a resolve to keep conversation alive. A not insignificant impetus for this was the recognition that Christians were also vulnerable. The experience of the churches under Stalinist-Leninist Communism made that evident. And there is considerable evidence to support the view that, had the Nazis retained power and made Europe Jew-free, their next target would have been Christians. Their brand of nationalism could not abide a rival loyalty, which placed God above the state.

Some developments in the United States contributed to a new chapter in Jewish-Christian relations. Soldiers in World War II were thrust together, and Jews and Christians came to know each other. The move to the suburbs after the war broke down ethnic communities and created a new mix of neighbors. The civil rights movement brought Jews and Christians together in common purpose. The Jewish commitment to public service prompted some to seek public office and become noticed. Increased mobility and ease of communication shortened the distances between diverse peoples. And on top of all of this, America's perception of itself changed. It endorsed religious pluralism. Instead of being hidden from view, non-Christian religions became noticed and talked about in schools and other public settings.

Still another development has been the creation in 1948 of the State of Israel and the ongoing conflict between Israelis and Palestinians. Throughout the Cold War, Israel was seen to be an ally of the United States in an area where, it was feared, the Soviet Union could readily exercise its influence. During that period Israel and its Jewish supporters were on the "right side" of geopolitics. Since the end of the Cold War, Christians have faced the question: In a volatile Middle East, in an ongoing conflict that often pits Jews against Muslims and Muslims against Jews, where do Christians stand? Where do their religious loyalties lie? What are their ethical obligations?

Partially as a result of the above the professional study of religion has become another factor in the emergence of a new chapter in Jewish-Christian relations. Today Jewish and Christian scholars belong to the same Society of Biblical Literature and read and interpret the Bible together. Jews and Christians belong to the same American Academy of Religion and routinely exchange views on religious and theological topics. The developments of the first century have become an area of intense scholarly interest, and a good deal of new research has occurred. It is probably not too much of an exaggeration to say that we currently have a fuller understanding of developments during the first century than in any time since the 500s C.E.

Interfaith relations are often not high on the agenda of local church leaders. The people who gather in a faith community are already, to one degree or another, committed to that faith. As they wrestle with the day-to-day problems of that congregation, it is easy to let contemporary Jewish-Christian relations slide from view.

Yet the issue does not disappear. Members of the faith community routinely interact with neighbors and coworkers from religions other than their own. What are they to think about religious views that seem so surprisingly

They have typically said that Christianity has displaced the old covenant. Chapter 2, "Covenants Old and New," examines biblical usage of the concept of covenant. In the New Testament, neither Paul nor the author of the epistle to the Hebrews disparages the old covenant; for both it is essential to the identity of Christians. In the Old Testament there is not a single covenant but six, each with its own specific promises. These multiple covenants are supplemented by the expectation of a "new covenant" that exists side by side with the others. This investigation suggests that there is a biblical foundation for an alternative, nonexclusivistic understanding of covenant.

Another troublesome topic has been the typical Christian usage of "law." It is often viewed in negative terms and then associated with Judaism and the Old Testament. Chapter 3, "Law and Gospel," contrasts this typical usage with the far more positive understanding of "Torah" found among Jews. Recognizing and appreciating the biblical foundation for Torah as "instruction" or "teaching" and recognizing that the Torah (the first five books of the Bible) includes far more than commandments can prevent Christians from misinterpreting Judaism. This recognition can also prompt Christians to appreciate the importance of instruction in their own religious tradition.

Christians have assumed that the new covenant is a fulfillment of prophecies found in the old and that Jews do not recognize that fulfillment. Chapter 4, "Promise and Fulfillment," takes a careful look at the relationship between fulfillment and prophecy within the Bible. It observes that promises often have multiple fulfillments. And an immediate partial fulfillment often leaves God's people crying out for a more ultimate one. Both Jews and Christians see evidence of God's presence and the fulfillment of God's promises in their lives. And both faith communities yearn for fuller fulfillment of God's promises. That yearning is present in the New Testament. The chapter suggests a more nuanced understanding of promise and fulfillment, one that draws Jews and Christians together in waiting rather than setting them apart.

Another troublesome topic has been the presence in the New Testament of passages that seem to disparage Jews and Judaism. Chapter 5 takes a look at these "difficult texts," especially those found in the Gospel of John. It emphasizes the importance of giving attention to the historical context within which each New Testament book was written and its influence on terminology. It also suggests interpretive strategies for communicating this awareness to church audiences.

One dimension of Judaism that Christians have had difficulty understanding is its allegiance to the land. While Christians have honored the "Holy Land" as the geographical site in which biblical events transpired, they have not, at least for the most part, regarded the promises of land to apply to themselves, as Jews have done. The attachment to the "promised land" has been important throughout Jewish history but taken on special significance during the last century. Chapter 6 has two parts. Together they seek to explain the role that "the land" has played and continues to play in Jewish identity; they ask Christians to understand that attachment; and they explore some of the complexity involved in Zionism and the contemporary relationship of Jews to the state of Israel.

Contemporary Christians and Jews have often found convergence in their motivation to serve society. The shorthand expression sometimes used by contemporary Jews to express their responsibility is *tikkun olam*, "to mend the world." Chapter 7, "Healing the World and Mending the Soul: Understanding *Tikkun Olam*," explores the history of that expression. Its present usage turns out to have a complex relationship to traditional terminology and traditional Jewish thinking, but this does not undermine the centrality of Jewish concern for the world. An analogous idea in Christianity is vocation—that is, one's calling to serve the world. *Tikkun olam* and vocation provide a fruitful area of overlapping concern, to be explored by Jews and Christians. Within this commonality of concern, the differences between the two religious traditions turn out to be mutually enriching.

Chapter 8 first describes the changing face of pluralism in America and makes some general suggestions for interreligious dialogue. Then it goes on to explore two questions. First, given all that has been said about the topics covered in this book, how should Christians regard Jews? Where do Jews and Judaism fit in the outlook of Christian theology? The chapter identifies some similarities and differences. With regard to questions of salvation, it suggests a form of religious agnosticism, which reinforces the need for actual dialogue. Among the benefits of Jewish-Christian dialogue is a deeper appreciation of aspects of the Christian tradition, such as a more corporate sense of redemption, a deeper appreciation of deliberation, and a greater emphasis on human participation in changing the world. And second, to what extent can Christian-Jewish relations serve as a model for Christianity's relationship to the other religions of the world? Though there are important differences between Christianity's relationship with Judaism and Christianity's relationship with other religions, the same religious agnosticism applies, as does the same acknowledgment of the reality of their experience of the sacred.

At the end comes a case study on the Arab-Israeli-Palestinian conflict. The purpose of this case study is to explore what the principles found in this book, particularly the first six chapters, might mean when applied to the ongoing conflict in the Middle East. The purpose of the case study is not to suggest a strategy for ending the conflict or a solution to each of the issues on the table but to sketch a framework within which Christians can think about their relationship to developments in that area of the world. The argument is essentially that American Christians seek both to understand the people and issues on both sides and then not to become the spokesperson for either side. Rather, they should be a third voice, working for reconciliation and peace.

One purpose of this volume is to introduce readers to themes and issues in the contemporary conversation between Christians and Jews. But there is also a second purpose. Taken as a whole, the chapters seek to suggest ways to think about Christianity that open its members to a more constructive engagement with our Jewish kin. The result will not be a diminishment of Christian vitality but an enrichment of it. From a more truthful portrait of the other, a fuller vision will emerge of Christians' own calling to participate in the mending of this fractured world.

1

•

Judaism Then and Now

Darrell Jodock
in Conversation with Rabbi Barry Cytron

To understand contemporary Christian-Jewish relations, it is not enough to rely on what the Bible says about Israelite religion and Jewish practices. One needs to understand the character and the development of postbiblical Judaism.

The purpose of this chapter is to introduce rabbinic/postbiblical Judaism. The brief discussion found here will serve as a starting point or as background for the other chapters in this volume. It will distinguish between rabbinic Judaism and biblical Judaism, survey a few of the first-century developments out of which rabbinic Judaism arose, describe briefly some of its features, explore common misunderstandings, and characterize the four branches of Judaism that can be found in the United States.

BIBLICAL JUDAISM AND RABBINIC JUDAISM

Judaism traces its roots back to God's covenant with Abraham. Remarkably, it has been a continuous community throughout at least three millennia. However, a major transformation in the first century altered Judaism in significant ways. In order to have a vocabulary to speak about this transition, we must distinguish between "biblical Judaism" and "rabbinic Judaism."

At the risk of using generalizations that deserve many qualifications, we can illustrate the distinction in the following ways:

- Biblical Judaism was the religion of a gathered nation. In contrast, rabbinic Judaism has been the religion of Jews in diaspora—that is, of Jews scattered among the nations of the world. The diaspora began before

9

the transition to rabbinic Judaism was complete, but rabbinic Judaism was tailored to life in the diaspora.

- The worship center of biblical Judaism was the Temple (and before that, the tabernacle). Prior to the destruction of the Temple in 70 C.E., as many Jews as possible came to Jerusalem from their homes outside of Israel three times a year for one of the pilgrim festivals (*Sukkoth* or Tabernacles, *Pesach* or Passover, and *Shavuoth* or Pentecost). In contrast, the worship center of rabbinic Judaism has been the synagogue. There was only one Temple; there can be and are of course many synagogues. Again, synagogues existed as places of study and prayer prior to the destruction of the Temple, but after 70 C.E. they became the center of lived Judaism. The sacrifices associated with the Temple were abandoned, the priesthood ceased to function, and the synagogue became a place of study, prayer, and social gathering.

- Through much of its history, biblical Judaism was an oral religion. By means of public gatherings and instructions passed on from parent to child, its stories and rituals were preserved and celebrated. Not until about 400 B.C.E. did it have a religiously authoritative set of writings, or Scriptures, consisting of the first five books of the Bible, the Torah. About 150 years later, the second section of the Hebrew Bible, known as the Prophets, was accepted as Scripture. (This section includes not only what Christians would call the prophets—Isaiah, Jeremiah, Amos, Micah, and the like—but also Joshua, Judges, 1 and 2 Samuel, 1 and 2 Kings.) Not until fifty or sixty years after the death of Jesus and twenty or thirty years after the destruction of the Temple was the third section of the Hebrew Bible, the Writings, canonized. In contrast to biblical Judaism, rabbinic Judaism has been focused on the Scriptures, especially the Torah. The Scriptures have an important advantage for Jews living in diaspora—namely, they are portable. Wherever there were ten or more adult males, a synagogue could be established as a place to study the Scriptures. To symbolize the significance ascribed to the Torah, the focal point of the worship space in a synagogue is the ark in which the Torah scrolls are kept and from which they are removed to be read during services.

- The distinctive offices of biblical Judaism were prophet, priest, and king. The distinctive office of rabbinic Judaism is the rabbi, who is a teacher, especially of Torah. When the Temple existed, priests were necessary in order to perform some of the sacrifices; only the priests knew how to do the ceremonies. In contemporary America, rabbis often lead public worship services, but, strictly speaking, in rabbinic Judaism rabbis are not needed for any of the ceremonies. Any adult Jew can lead the services. Traditionally, the primary role rabbis have played is as teachers, not worship leaders.

As is evident from the above, the four elements of dispersion, synagogue, Scriptures, and teachers are all interrelated and mutually dependent—that is, the use of synagogues, Scriptures, and rabbis were well adapted to life in the diaspora.

FIRST-CENTURY DEVELOPMENTS

In order to understand more fully the transition from biblical to rabbinic Judaism, it is important to take a quick look at first-century Judaism.

The Maccabean revolt in the 160s B.C.E. ended about 150 years of rule by the Greek generals, the Seleucids, who ruled Israel after the death of Alexander the Great. Following the success of that revolt, Israel enjoyed about a century of independence. The governance of independent Israel was in the hands of the Hasmonean family, whose legitimacy was questioned by some, because that family was not of the proper royal or priestly line. The Sadducees, Pharisees, and Essenes likely all arose during this period. By 63 B.C.E., Israel was once again under foreign rule—this time, by the Roman Empire.

At the time of Jesus, the religious situation was very dynamic. There were a variety of parties within Judaism. Among them were the following:

- *The Sadducees.* Drawn largely from the upper classes of Jewish society, the Sadducees were Temple-oriented. They accepted only the written Torah and did not accept the interpretations and amplifications known as the oral Torah. Since there is no reference to resurrection in the written Torah, they did not accept this idea. Generally speaking, they endeavored to accommodate themselves to Roman rule. They feared rebellion and wanted to preserve worship at the Temple.

- *The Zealots.* This was a cluster of groups who regarded Roman power in a significantly different way. For them, foreign rule was not simply a political tragedy but also a religious scandal. God alone was to be their ruler. They felt it to be their religious duty to strive for Jewish independence. In some cases, they were the freedom fighters, the rebels, of their day. They were active enough to provoke a Roman governor, such as Pontius Pilate, to be especially cautious whenever the crowds gathered in Jerusalem for a pilgrim festival. Recent interpretations of the historical Jesus (such as that by John Dominic Crossan[1]) have argued that the plight of the poorer people was largely ignored by the Jewish leaders in Jerusalem, who took office only with Roman approval. Under those circumstances many were ready to listen to the Zealots.

- *The Essenes.* They opted for religious community and set themselves apart, perhaps in an effort to establish a purer form of Judaism than they saw practiced by either the leaders or the populace during the Hasmonean and Roman periods. Some Essenes lived in the wilderness areas of Israel; others lived in the city. They shunned pleasures and practiced self-control in an effort to prepare the way for God's coming—an event that would bring with it the triumph of good over evil and the fulfillment of Israel. It is likely that some, at least, saw their communities as models of what the larger society should be.

- *The Pharisees.* Drawn largely from the middle class, the Pharisees wanted to improve religious observance in Israel. They did so by teaching the Torah, interpreting it, and applying it. Unlike the Sadducees, they accepted the "oral Torah" and the resurrection of the faithful once the messianic age arrived. They either tried to stay away from politics in order to concentrate on the religious and the ethical, or they were more "middle of the road" than the Sadducees or the Zealots.

- *The followers of Jesus.* For the sake of clarity, let us distinguish between "Christianity" as a separate religion, as it emerged after 70 C.E., and the initial movement within Judaism, which we will call "the followers of Jesus." The followers of Jesus were Jews who considered themselves members of the Jewish community, were circumcised, worshipped at the Temple and/or local synagogue, and accepted Jesus as the Messiah. Like the Pharisees, they tried to stay away from the political extremes of the Zealots or the Sadducees. Like the Pharisees they were interested in enriching the religious lives of ordinary people. Like the Pharisees they made use of the written Scriptures (Torah and Prophets) and of their own additional oral teachings, drawn from Jesus. Compared with all the other parties in Judaism the followers of Jesus were more like the Pharisees than they were like any other.

In 66 C.E. the Zealots succeeded in fomenting a revolt against Rome. With a significant show of its military power, the Romans crushed the revolt, destroyed the Temple, took its contents to Rome, and laid waste much of Jerusalem. With no Temple, the Sadducees disappeared. Having caused so much turmoil, the Zealots were somewhat discredited but retained enough strength to spark another revolt in 132 to 135 C.E. Then they disappeared. For reasons that are not understood, the Essenes disappeared. Two groups survived: the Pharisees, who formulated rabbinic Judaism, and the followers of Jesus. After

70 C.E. the followers of Jesus gradually gave shape to Christianity, a religion separate from rabbinic Judaism.

In 70 C.E. a Pharisee named Johanan ben Zakkai received permission from Vespasian (the Roman general who became emperor) to found an academy in Jamnia (Jabneh). That academy worked to educate religious leaders and to keep Judaism alive. With the academy and the Great *Bet Din* ("Court of Law"— successor to the Sanhedrin) there, Jamnia replaced Jerusalem as the center of Jewish life, and its sages oversaw the transition from Temple Judaism to rabbinic Judaism. One result was greater uniformity of practice and outlook than had characterized the Judaism of Jesus' day. As part of the ongoing effort to preserve and to educate, Judah Ha Nasi (Judah the Prince), in about 175 C.E., started gathering together and writing down the oral Torah. His compilation became the Mishnah, the core of the Talmud. (Later the Gemara would be added.) Its authority in rabbinic Judaism is second only to the Scriptures. But it is an authority not so much in the sense of providing answers as in establishing the framework for an ongoing discussion that continues to this day. The Talmud records not only the outcome of the debates among the rabbis regarding the proper interpretation and application of the Torah but also the arguments themselves. (Rabbi X argued thusly, while Rabbi Y countered by saying thus and so.) Even within the Talmud, major figures from the past are cited, so that its debates are already intergenerational. The conflicting interpretations sometimes reflected established traditions. Already in Jesus' day there had been two rival schools of interpretation: the school of Shammai, who interpreted the provisions of the Torah very strictly, and the school of Hillel, who interpreted its provisions somewhat more liberally and humanely. When the Gospel accounts mention a disagreement between Jesus and the Pharisees, his disagreement is usually with members of the Shammai school. Hillel and Jesus had far more in common. In order to place the Gospel accounts in proper historical context and accurately identify the differences and similarities between rabbinic Judaism and Christianity, it is important to note that the outcomes of about 65 percent of the debates recorded in the Talmud favor Hillel rather than Shammai. More often than not, rabbinic Judaism did not endorse the positions held by the opponents of Jesus.

After 70 C.E. a divorce[2] occurred between the followers of the Pharisees and the followers of Jesus, the two main parties that endured after the destruction of the Temple. (The pain of this divorce is reflected to some extent in the Gospel of Matthew—from the 80s C.E.—and even more so in the Gospel of John—from the 90s C.E.) Synagogues were split. One religion became two. The two sides argued about the interpretation of the Scriptures—that is, the Torah and the Prophets. One group regarded Jesus to be the primary revelation of God; the other regarded the Torah to be the primary revelation of God. The followers of Jesus redefined the meaning of "Messiah" as a nonpolitical figure who would establish a religious kingdom by fulfilling the hitherto unconnected prophecies regarding the suffering servant and the Son of Man. They regarded Jesus to be this Messiah (= the Christ). The followers of the Pharisees, working with a more traditional understanding of "Messiah," pointed out that the anticipated reign of peace and justice known as the messianic age had not yet arrived; thus the Messiah had not arrived, and Jesus could not have been the Messiah. These debates were possible, because the hopes for a Messiah were suitably vague; there had been no single, accepted definition of the expected one. The struggle was more or less a "fair fight" until the 300s C.E. when Christianity was adopted as the official religion of the Roman Empire. From then on, Christianity enjoyed a privileged position in society and the support of political power, whereas those Jews who lived in Christian lands eventually came to be seen as "outsiders," sometimes welcomed and at other times harassed or expelled.

SOME FEATURES OF RABBINIC JUDAISM

Under the leadership of the early rabbis, Judaism developed into a vibrant religion. It developed a prayer book that outlined services of prayers, songs, and Scripture reading. It adopted the practice of reading the Torah through each year.

It continued to worship the God of the Bible, viewing God as creator and sustainer of all that is, viewing God as a just and gracious redeemer. It developed a strict monotheism, taking seriously the biblical prohibition against any graven images. Thus, rabbinic Judaism has not allowed artistic portrayals of God in its synagogues, nor has it allowed pictures of human beings in the sanctuary. (Affirming that Jesus is the revelation of God, Christians, by contrast, have used the human form freely in religious art and architecture.)

Judaism continued to see itself as an elected or called community—that is, as a community chosen by God. This choosing had nothing to do with their virtue or status. The purpose of the call was understood in different ways, but it was always an election to obligation more than privilege. To the Jewish community God had entrusted the Torah, the divine guidance regarding how to live, and the members of that community were its custodians. The rabbis expected that the teachings of Torah were important not just for the Jews but also for the world. In many cases, they had to do with authentic humanity.

Unlike Christianity (and Islam), Judaism, throughout most of the last millennium, has been a nonproselytizing religion. The Christendom of the Middle Ages allowed no public teaching of religious ideas other than those approved by the Catholic Church. Conversions to Judaism put both the convert and the Jewish community at serious risk. In part because earlier developments during the Roman Empire had already inclined Judaism in that direction, Judaism eventually adopted as its own the nonproselytizing stance that necessity had required. Accordingly, the Jewish teaching has been that a human being does not need to be Jewish in order to be right with God. There can be and are righteous Gentiles. The non-Jew needs to avoid idolatry, blasphemy, murder, cursing judges, sexual misdeeds, stealing, and eating flesh with the blood still in it—in other words, to obey the seven laws of Noah that are meant for all people. There are all sorts of advantages to being Jewish, in terms of access to revelation, richness of worship, and belonging to a strong community, but being Jewish does not itself "save" a person or give that person a privileged status unavailable to others. Instead, Jews simply have higher obligations. Tradition has numbered the commandments that a Jew is expected to follow at 613 (rather than the seven that apply to others). Converts are, of course, accepted and to be regarded as full members of the community once they go through instruction and join, but they are not to be sought.[3]

The word *torah* means instruction or teaching or guidance. It has two common usages in Judaism. The first is the narrower sense of the first five books of the Bible, which include both a narrative account of Israel's election and guidelines for living as the people of God. The second is the broader sense of the whole of Jewish instruction that has grown up over centuries of reflection upon and deliberation about the content of the biblical Torah. It is important to underline that Torah is regarded as a gift. After God chose Israel, the community asked what it means to be the people of God, and God graciously provided some instruction for their guidance. Torah is a gift because it prevents utter confusion, it enriches rather than diminishes human life, and it takes seriously human dignity and human responsibility.

Unlike the Christian community that marked membership by a profession of faith (originally, the profession was likely "I believe that Jesus is Lord"—words that, to prevent misunderstandings common at the time, were eventually expanded into what today is known as the Apostles' Creed), the Jewish community did not develop a profession of faith. It thus has no creeds to which members subscribe, and it allows for a fairly wide diversity of theological opinions, so long as they are rooted in the Jewish tradition. The emphasis in Judaism has been on participation in the community. To be in the community, either through birth or conversion, and to consider oneself a part of the community makes one a member.

Closely associated with the last point is a strong emphasis on education and on debate. Decisions have been made through reasoning and deliberation—conducted within a common framework of Jewish tradition.

The Jewish view of salvation is communal. Salvation is understood as the achievement of wholeness and peace. No individual can be whole apart from

the severity of his rule. A contemporary would not have had to say very much to convince him to condemn a Jewish subject to death. Moreover, the Jews who, according to the Gospels, were involved were the chief priests; as persons in office through Roman appointment (and in some case "appeasers"), they did not speak for all the Jews in the land of Israel, much less the even larger number of Jews living elsewhere. It is thus *not* appropriate to blame the crucifixion of Jesus on the Jews then living, much less on subsequent generations of Jews. The essential theological teaching of Christianity has instead made two claims: (*a*) that the powers of evil, under whose influence we all unfortunately operate, were at work. Those powers include political and economic as well as ethical and religious forces: for instance, injustice, political tyranny and collaboration, economic greed, aversion to intense religiousness, and the like, none of which characterize only one group of human beings or only one epoch. And (*b*) that "we all crucified Jesus." The religious impact of this essential message is undercut whenever the crucifixion is blamed on someone else.

Yet another common misunderstanding is to assert that Judaism is a relic or fossil of the past. This idea comes from different sources. One source is a strain of New Testament scholarship that has, since the nineteenth century, asserted that the distinctiveness of Jesus can be identified if one locates something new. This criterion of novelty automatically downplays the significance of the Jewishness of Jesus. The more this latter topic has been studied during the last sixty years, the clearer it has become how thoroughly Jewish were the teachings of Jesus and Jesus' self-understanding. Contemporary Jews have no trouble calling Jesus a profound Jewish teacher. A second source of the view that Judaism is a relic is far older than the first. It is a viewpoint known as supersessionism, which says that Christianity replaced, or superseded, Judaism. If replaced, then Judaism is out of date, a mere relic of the past, and not something one would want to endorse. But there is little or no evidence in the Bible that God abrogated God's covenant with the descendants of Abraham—that is, the Jews. The evidence is rather that God, in steadfast love, has exhibited remarkable fidelity to that covenant, upholding it through all sorts of difficulties and for long periods of time. So, it is quite possible for a Christian today to acknowledge that God's covenant with the Jews is a viable, ongoing covenant, and that members of that covenant community are involved in a lively, ongoing relationship with God. God's covenant with Christians then becomes a second covenant (or a second form of the covenant), a way God graciously and generously opened for the Gentiles, the non-Jews.[7] If God has not abandoned the covenant with Abraham and if Judaism continues to be a dynamic contemporary religion, then Judaism is hardly a relic or a fossil.

A final misunderstanding is that Jews are legalists. This assertion often comes from the one-sided portrayal of the Pharisees in the Gospels. (It is always a good idea, for the sake of historical accuracy, to interpret the passages in the Gospels where Pharisees come in for criticism as applying to *some* Pharisees—usually the followers of Shammai, as mentioned above.) If one were to mean by "legalist," someone who values rules for correct behavior, then it would be possible to apply that term to Jews, for, just as Christians have put a great deal of effort into defining their doctrines, so Jews have put a great deal of effort into codifying appropriate behavior. They have combed the Scriptures and collected the best of human wisdom and put it all together into guidelines for behavior. But "legalist" usually means something quite different—it means obeying a rule even when it is not appropriate. It means letting the specific provisions of a rule overshadow the purpose of the rule. In this sense, Jews are not legalists—or, if some are, it is not because of the teachings of their religion. The purpose of studying Torah, the purpose of deliberation, the purpose of education, is to achieve a clear sense of the reasons for acting in a particular way. Such understanding helps a person decide when following a rule is appropriate and when it is not. For a legalist a rule is a rule, but the rabbinic tradition provides recommendations regarding the relative importance of various prescriptions and prohibitions. One can break the rules to save a life. One can break the rules to achieve peace, and so on. The general recommendation is to perform a *mitzvah*—that is, any act that preserves or enhances life. Such ethical guidance is hardly legalistic.

It is probably important to add one other consideration. Americans have a proclivity for interpreting rules as automatically restrictive or limiting on human freedom. But obeying some rules can have the effect of enhancing human freedom. For example, in the Jewish tradition, observing the Sabbath is a gift. *Shabbat* (the seventh day of the week) is to be a happy day in which work ceases and humans can be recreated. It makes space for family. It makes space for leisure. It makes space for remembering God. Contemporary American society has abolished the observance of a Christian version of a Sabbath (on the first day of the week). One can say that the result has been an impoverishment of life, because the 24/7 pace of modern life provides no break. And if one tries to observe a private Sabbath, it is but a shadow of a genuine Sabbath, for only when the community stops does an individual have full permission also to stop. Every July 4, St. Peter, Minnesota, a town of 9,700, hosts a big parade. According to newspaper estimates, some 10,000 people come to watch it. It is a community celebration, and virtually everyone (except for police officers, nurses, and the like) is socially and communally authorized to participate or to observe and not to work. Such an observance is the closest equivalent one can find in our day to a communally observed Sabbath. Only when a community stops does an individual have *full freedom* to stop. Observing a Sabbath can be a gift; it can enhance life. In this sense a rule that safeguards a beneficial activity can be the source of freedom. Such is the intention of Jewish Torah.

BRANCHES OF RABBINIC JUDAISM

What, then, are the differences among various branches of Judaism? First, it is important to remind ourselves that the four main branches of Judaism can be found only in the United States and that only Orthodox Judaism (albeit in either an Ashkenazic [Germanic] or Sephardic [Spanish] form) existed prior to the nineteenth century. Second, it is helpful to observe that three of the branches, Reform, Conservative, and Orthodox, disagree primarily in their interpretations of human responsibility. They all accept the idea that God established a covenant with Israel and that humans are called, in one way or another, to obey God. The fourth branch of Judaism, the Reconstructionist, differs in that it tends to regard Judaism as an identity-forming community. Humans are to perform the rituals and to obey the commandments primarily in order to pass the heritage on to their children and grandchildren. That is, one studies Torah and one performs a *mitzvah*, not in order to obey God but in order to serve the community and keep it alive.

- *Orthodox Judaism.* Orthodoxy regards the written Torah and the oral Torah as both having been given by God to Moses on Mt. Sinai. Generally speaking, Orthodox Jews do not accept historical criticism of the Bible and think a commandment should be obeyed even if one does not understand why it was given. They are expected to keep kosher. None of the foods prohibited in the Torah are to be eaten, only meat that is slaughtered in kosher ways is permitted, and milk products and meat products are not served at the same meal. Indeed, two sets of dishes are maintained, one for each food group. Orthodox Jews are expected to walk to the synagogue. Once there, men sit in one section and women in another. Only males may be rabbis or cantors. No musical instruments are used to accompany singing, and the music is traditional in style. The worship services are mostly in Hebrew. When new moral issues come up, they are decided by rabbinic scholars. The child of a Jewish mother is considered to be Jew. Generally speaking, Orthodox Jews participate with other groups in community-service projects but are reluctant to engage in interreligious dialogue with Christians.
- *Reform Judaism.* Throughout the Middle Ages and early modern period, Jews were not allowed to be citizens. Often subject to distinctive laws and governmental regulations, confined to certain occupations and required to live in a separate area of the city, they were to that degree

isolated from the mainstream. In the early nineteenth century, forces of emancipation—unleashed in part by the Enlightenment—encouraged Jews in western Europe (that is, excluding Poland, Russia, and the remainder of eastern Europe) to become full members of society. In response to their new social setting and in response to historical studies that provided more information about the development of Judaism, changes were introduced, and a new movement known as Reform Judaism developed. Reform Judaism acknowledged that the written Torah and the oral Torah had both developed over time. If one could figure out why a piece of the tradition developed the way it did, then one could decide whether it should be retained or changed. For example, in the ancient world a man covered his head as a sign of respect; when he entered the presence of a king, he did so with his head covered. In nineteenth-century Europe, a man removed his hat or tipped his hat as a sign of respect. Thus, Reform Jews recommended removing the traditional head covering, the *yarmulke*. Or to cite one other example, the Orthodox prohibition against eating milk and meat products at the same meal is based on a thrice-repeated passage in the Torah that says a person should not steep the meat of a young goat in its mother's milk. Reform Jews observed that the Scriptures prohibited this practice for a reason: as a ritual associated with a fertility cult, the practice had held religious significance at odds with Israelite beliefs. Since no such fertility cults were around in nineteenth-century Germany, the verse did not have the same weight as it had once had, and the practice of not mixing milk products and meat products could be suspended. Thus, their understanding of the past allowed Reform Jews greater freedom with regard to deciding what traditions could be changed.

Reform Jews also considered themselves citizens of the lands in which they lived and wanted to be understood by their neighbors. Thus they translated part of the service into the vernacular. Following the example of the Lutheran churches in Germany, they asked rabbis to deliver sermons in the vernacular and introduced Western music and a Western instrument, the organ, into their worship services. Men and women were allowed to sit together in the sanctuary. Eventually *bat mitzvah* (for young women) was added to the traditional *bar mitzvah* (for thirteen-year-old young men). In the twentieth century women were allowed to become rabbis and cantors, and the prayer book was revised to include references to women as well as men. Within contemporary Reform Judaism, a person who is the child of a Jewish parent and has been raised Jewish is considered a Jew. Throughout the last two centuries they have referred to themselves a "Reform" movement rather than "Reformed" Judaism, because reform is an unfinished and ongoing task. Each new generation can decide what needs to be preserved and what needs to change. Recently there has been a tendency to reappropriate rituals and traditions that were abandoned during the period of "radical reform" in nineteenth-century America, while at the same time Reform Judaism has continued to revise rabbinic traditions and to consider altering some traditional practices.

◆ *Conservative Judaism.* The Conservative movement began at the end of the nineteenth century in the United States. It was in part a reaction to "radical reform"—that is, to a version of Reform Judaism that "went too far" in disregarding the past—and in part a haven for Americanized Orthodox Jews who had arrived in the United States during the post–1881 migrations from eastern Europe. Put most simply, when changes are considered, Conservative Judaism allows previous generations to have a vote. In other words, the attitude is to go slow and to favor evolutionary changes. The endeavor is to maintain as much of the tradition as is possible, while still making those adjustments necessary to permit Jews to be participants in modern culture. Worship services use more Hebrew than Reform services but less than Orthodox services. Keeping kosher is recommended, but Conservative Jews can be flexible in their adherence when they eat with non-Jews. Wearing a *yarmulke* is optional in most Reform synagogues; it is expected in a Conservative synagogue. A family may drive to the synagogue if that is the only way they can get there. Men and women may sit together in the sanctuary. Women may become rabbis and cantors. Decisions about new ethical issues are made by rabbinical scholars with input from informed lay members.

◆ *Reconstructionist Judaism.* Reconstructionist Judaism developed in the United States in the twentieth century. Throughout its history the chief educational institution for the Conservative movement has been Jewish Theological Seminary in New York City. One of its professors, Mordecai Kaplan, began the Reconstructionist branch of Judaism. He had been an advocate of Jewish community centers, places where Jews of every persuasion could come together. He thought of Judaism as a civilization, with a distinctive language, a literature, social customs, and religious rituals. The services and customs of Reconstructionist Judaism follow the pattern of Conservative Judaism, but, as already indicated above, this branch adopts a different reason for following those traditions. One participates in order to keep the community alive.

The first Jews who came to this country (in 1656) were Sephardic Jews. Their settlements were very small in size, their members were involved in the shipping trade, and they settled in cities on the eastern seaboard. After that, the first major migration involved German Jews, almost all of whom ultimately favored Reform Judaism. For the most part they became merchants. By 1875 Judaism in the United States was Reform Judaism, and Jews were spread relatively evenly throughout the East and the Midwest. Then in 1881 a major pogrom occurred in eastern Europe, and a second wave of Jewish immigrants came from Russia, Poland, and the countries to the east of Germany. Some of these Jews were secular (nonpracticing), but mostly they were Orthodox, and even those who were secular were acquainted with only Orthodox Judaism. They settled in the Northeast; from that point on Jews have been disproportionally well represented in that region of the country.

Beginning about 1902, under the leadership of a Jewish journalist, Theodor Herzl, political Zionism emerged. Having witnessed the Dreyfus affair in France, he decided that if antisemitism could be so virulent even in the home of the French Revolution and Napoleon, then Jews in Europe would never be safe. They needed a political home of their own. At first its location was an open question, but gradually political Zionism focused on Israel, and during the 1920s and '30s some Jews started to move there and to buy land. In 1875 Reform Judaism in the United States had been non-Zionist; it declared that the United States was its homeland. But many of the Eastern European immigrants were Zionist, and by 1937 Reform Judaism itself had adopted Zionist principles. Once Hitler put into motion his plan to expel or annihilate the Jews of Europe and succeeded in destroying two-thirds of their number, virtually all Jews in the United States became Zionist.[8]

One of the ongoing problems of the U.S. Jewish community is intermarriage. Two things make it problematic. First, so much of Judaism is practiced in the home—for instance, the observance of the Sabbath, the lighting of Sabbath candles, the Passover Seder meal, and so on. Second, for a relatively small, nonproselytizing religion, the loss of too many members, whether from intermarriage or indifference, can spell the end. A Jewish philosopher, Emil Fackenheim, has formulated his concern this way: do not, he advises, give Hitler any posthumous victories. Hitler's purpose was to rid the world of Jews; hence, giving up on Judaism contributes to Hitler's success. Fackenheim recommends that after the Holocaust Jews continue to wrestle with God and continue to practice their Judaism—in other words, it is their responsibility to survive *as Jews*. He calls this the 614th commandment.[9]

What Fackenheim's concern suggests can be stated still more plainly— that the Holocaust has been a defining experience for contemporary Jews. It has caused them to worry about the dangers of antisemitism. It has prompted them to value allies. For some, it has changed nothing theologically, because it is only another in the series of catastrophes that Judaism has endured. For others, it has challenged the tradition and required that it be rethought. If God did not come to the assistance of God's people during this horrific catastrophe, then what does it mean to believe in a gracious God and in a covenant? For a few, such as Richard Rubenstein,[10] reflection on these questions has meant abandoning faith in the God of history; for others, such as Elie Wiesel, it has meant preventing another Holocaust by defending any oppressed people, wrestling with God, and using stories as a way to mend the world; and for still others, it has involved reaffirming the cocreatorship of human beings. It was, after all, not God who failed the Jews, but humans who perpetrated it and stood by while it happened. When Jews call upon us all to remember the Holocaust, it is primarily to remember our responsibility as God's creatures to each other, so that no group will ever face a similar ordeal.

CONCLUSION

The purpose of this chapter has been simply to introduce postbiblical or rabbinic Judaism and thereby provide some background for the chapters to come. "Overly sketchy" may be the most accurate way to describe it. Much more could and should be said about any one of the points covered. Any good book on Judaism will begin to fill in the gaps.[11]

What is important is this: to understand Christian-Jewish relations, it is not enough to rely on what one finds in the Bible; one needs to understand and appreciate the development of rabbinic Judaism and the dynamic way in which, alongside of Christianity, the Jewish community continues to live out God's call to be stewards of healing for the world.

Response

Barry Cytron

"Works do not belong to the gospel; for it is not law, but faith alone, because it is nothing whatever but the promise and offer of divine grace."[2] That's how Luther sums up the gulf between his view of the proper religious life, and that of his adversaries. One common label assigned to this theological chasm is "law vs. gospel." While Luther's words here appear aimed at his Catholic opponents, his criticism goes to the heart of the divergence between Lutheran Christianity and rabbinic Judaism. Is religious life about faith *and* grace, *as Luther would have it, or about* obligation *and fulfillment, as Jewish thought came to envision it?*

This debate might seem quaintly theological to some, the sort of argument in which only religious sophisticates engage. Over the centuries, though, this dispute had dire consequences. Deprecation by many Christian writers of the traditional Jewish category of "obligation and fulfillment" ultimately led to denunciation of all of Judaism to, as Jules Isaac called it, "the teaching of contempt." One of the most stirring parts of modern Christian scholarship has been a renewed appreciation for the classical forms of Jewish thought, including the way in which its deepest religious and ethical values are embedded in the mitzvot, the commandments, of Jewish life. Jodock's thoughtful and sensitive essay here not only joins a growing cadre of Christian scholars who have encouraged their coreligionists to this reexamination, but enlarges the conversation in significant ways.

For example, Jodock's essay sympathetically illustrates the way each of the streams of modern Judaism struggles today with the place of the mitzvot in its religious orientation. For the orthodox community, the goal has recently seemed increasingly about rigorous stringency in observance. As for the more liberal movements, their challenge has been to balance the call of the ancient command with the compelling demand of modernity. But no matter how they resolve the precise role of the mitzvot in their lives, as Jodock shows, none of these streams question the ultimate legitimacy of the mitzvot as the proper way to the Godly life. For all, the proof is in the "action" rather than any "creed."

Perhaps a teaching by one of the great twentieth-century Jewish thinkers, Franz Rosenzweig, can help make clear why the mitzvot occupy such a pivotal place in Jewish religious life, even among the more liberal streams of American Judaism. As he saw it, what was "revealed" to the people as the way to life was not law but command. "God is not a law giver," writes Rosenzweig, "but He commands."

This is how one of Rosenzweig's best contemporary interpreters, Neil Gillman, sums up this distinction: "God revealed himself [at Sinai] in relationship with Israel. This covenantal relationship was itself a commanding relationship, as are all intense relationships. In all such relationships, the partner feels obligated to respond, to live in terms that are appropriate to the condition of relatedness. . . . The task of the modern Jew is to recapture, today, the original sense of God's self-revelation, and with it the sense of being commanded to respond."

As modern religious Jews strive to live out their faithful life in a complex world, the way they understand the call of the traditional mitzvot remains central. The more strict among us will read those ancient commandments in a more literal way, insistent that God legislated, in precise scriptural words and authoritative commentary, how to act. The more liberal will seek to discern, behind, or even well beyond, the formal words, the correct way to heed the Godly command within the clamor and cacophony of modern life. Yet for both, being in the covenant with God—being faithful—means somehow living the "commanded" life.

2

◆

Covenants Old and New

Peter A. Pettit
in Conversation with Rabbi Elliot Dorff

When anyone opens a Christian Bible, one of the first things to notice is its division into two parts—the Old Testament and the New Testament. With only a cursory look into those parts, it becomes clear that Jesus and the early church appear only in the New Testament, while the great figures and moments of Israel's history are the focus of the Old Testament. Combine these observations with an insight about language, that the words *testament* and *covenant* translate the same Greek word, and the question of old and new covenants begins to come into clear focus.

When anyone attends a church service, these words from Jesus introduce Holy Communion: "This cup is the new covenant in my blood, shed for you and for all people for the forgiveness of sin." One observes during the service that the congregation sits for the reading from the Old Testament and stands, often with verbal acclamation, for the reading from the Gospel in the New Testament. Again, the relationship of new and old appears to be central to the Word and Sacrament of God's people in Christ.

Looking back on history, we can see that a sharp distinction between old and new is part of the church's anti-Jewish pattern of teaching. Beginning with the book of Hebrews in the New Testament, early Christian theologians often drew a systematic contrast between Jewish blindness, which entailed the failure of Judaism, and the clear promise and hope of Christianity under God's blessing. This was most evident in a group of essays written in the second and third centuries C.E. that are known collectively as *adversus Ioudaeos* ("against the Jews"—which is also the title of several of them).[1]

The *adversus Ioudaeos* writers used Israel's own scriptures—the church's Old Testament—in their arguments that Judaism had failed and the Jews were inferior. On the one hand, they pointed to the prophets' criticism of their fellow Israelites to show that Judaism emphasized the wrong things and misunderstood God's call. So they accused the Jews of wrongly focusing on law instead of gospel, letter instead of spirit, worldly things instead of the transcendent, form instead of substance, and so forth.

On the other hand, they affirmed the prophets' visions of redemption—God's faithful restoration of Israel—as being fulfilled in Jesus. So they taught that Judaism, which could not make the same affirmation, had been superseded by Christianity. The Jews therefore were perpetuating former blessings that had been rendered meaningless by the better blessings of Christianity—animal sacrifices instead of Jesus' one true sacrifice, Jerusalem and its Temple instead of the heavenly city with its temple, the halakhic system of commandments instead of Jesus' new command of love, and so on.[2]

This systematic denigration of Judaism in favor of Christianity became standard in Christian teaching. Understandably, it also became a familiar part of the Jews' understanding of Christianity. In medieval disputations; in the indictments of the Inquisition; in political debates about Jewish citizenship in modern nation-states; in histories of Judaism written by Christians according to the most modern, scholarly standards: everywhere that the Jews heard Christians speak of Judaism they heard this theme reiterated—what the French historian of antisemitism, Jules Isaac, cogently summarized in his 1964 book as "the teaching of contempt."[3] While the past several decades have witnessed a broad and consistent repudiation of these teachings by many churches,[4] their legacy remains engrained in much of the church's language and practice.

When we now take up the topic of "covenants old and new," therefore, we must respect the hesitation and suspicion with which our Jewish neighbors may greet the effort.[5] Even beyond the particulars of our troubled history, it can be difficult to have one's own heritage characterized as "old," while a seemingly competing tradition is "new."[6] Jewish tradition and the Jewish community have not been in a position to defeat Christian supersessionist thinking about the covenant, so the tendency has been to sidestep it, to establish the Jewish understanding of covenant on foundations that do not directly confront the Christian claims. "Covenant" has been a theological arena in which Jews and Christians by and large have gone separate ways in their understandings. The terms and dynamics of covenant as the Jewish community has developed its understanding do not line up neatly with Christian parallels, yet precisely in the divergence lie insights that will prove worthwhile for our consideration.

The long history of Christian supersessionism and the differences in meaning that Jews and Christians give to covenant can make any exploration of it uncomfortable. Yet that discomfort cannot justify avoiding the topic. Only radical surgery on the church's scripture, liturgy, and systematic theology—to say nothing of its hymnody and educational materials—could eliminate all reference to covenant. Thereby we might eliminate the need to address the old and new in our pattern of teaching, but we also would certainly change Christianity in ways that could make it unrecognizable. So we must face this contentious topic, seeking to draw from the encounter an understanding of God's work among Jews and Christians that neither dismisses the old nor undermines the new.

To begin our encounter, we will turn to the two principal New Testament sources for covenant language, Paul and the letter to the Hebrews. We will then look more closely at Jewish covenantal emphases and, recognizing the divergences that become clear, suggest a dialectical approach to covenant that we hope will affirm difference without engendering rivalry.

COVENANT IN THE "NEW COVENANT"

Almost the entire New Testament basis for Christian thinking on covenant comes from Paul and from the letter to the Hebrews.[7] The strong influence of subsequent theology may easily mislead us into reading these early works as expressions of a supersessionist approach, for their language and their imagery were used extensively in developing that theology. Both Hebrews and Paul's letters, however, were written in settings in which Judaism's legitimacy and value were well established, while the Jewish and Gentile followers of Jesus were still finding and shaping their way. Later challenges of an ascendant Christianity to its senior rival had not yet developed. The first readers whom Paul and Hebrews addressed in regard to covenant were caught up in self-doubt and uncertainty, specifically in relation to the proven tradition of the Jewish community.

In that setting, the New Testament writers endeavor to buttress the young Christian communities on the strength of the very Jewish tradition that seems to challenge them. The new covenant in which they live is grounded precisely in the established covenant of God with Israel. Its figures and images and language pervade the efforts of Paul and Hebrews to inspire faithfulness to the new covenant. The author of Hebrews draws the language of "new covenant" explicitly from the prophets, for whom Israel's covenant was constitutive of the community.[8] Paul's attempt to reassure his readers regarding Gentile freedom from Jewish observance stays entirely within the framework of the first covenant, struggling to find a model within it that would speak to the Gentile situation without abandoning the Jewish covenantal foundation. As we will see in both Hebrews and Paul, the challenge of understanding the new covenant in relation to the old does not center on a rivalry of supersession—which is inherently better?—but on the question of appropriate application of the covenant tradition.

NEW COVENANT IN THE LETTER TO THE HEBREWS

Chapters 8 through 10 of Hebrews comprise a homily that serves to make a particular point in the larger purpose of the book. Although there is no scholarly consensus about its first readers, at least "part of Hebrews' function is to inspire the faithful endurance necessary to meet [persecution]. Of equal importance [is] the possibility of apostasy and [our author] wants to prevent it by rekindling faith."[9] The portrayal of covenant serves the latter end—preventing apostasy—by contrasting the covenant mediated by Jesus with the "first" covenant established with Israel through Moses at Sinai (Heb 9:18-20),[10] so that the readers will "have confidence," "hold fast to the confession," and live out that confession in communal life (Heb 10:19-25). The author seeks to persuade the readers that the covenant in which they live is not invalid in comparison to the first covenant. Indeed, the author uses the criteria of the first covenant to affirm the legitimacy of the new.

A citation of Jer 31:31-34 opens the argument of this section at Heb 8:8-12. From within the covenantal tradition of Israel's scriptures comes the language of "new covenant" that will guide the writer's discussion. The writer of Hebrews develops four elements that characterize the passage from Jeremiah, each element contributing to the writer's purpose. By establishing the credentials of the new covenant in terms of Israel's long-held expectation of a new covenant, the writer of Hebrews shows the priority and significance of the first covenant on which that expectation had been grounded. Whatever may be said of the new covenant, then, as a matter of principle it cannot be antithetical to the first.

The first element highlighted by the author of Hebrews is the fact that the first covenant is one in which the ancestors "did not continue" (Heb 8:9). This is a crucial factor for one who writes to exhort steadfastness in the readers.[11] Loyalty and fidelity, endurance and perseverance are the point of the argument in Hebrews—just the opposite of the ancestors' portrait of failure to continue in the covenant. The defining contrast that drives the argument of Hebrews is the contrast between those who "abandon" their confidence and those who have "endurance," who will "receive what was promised" (Heb 10:35-36). The author exhorts the readers to be among the latter, rather than the former, and the dominant theme of contrast in the book derives its significance from this one.

Second, the new covenant will incorporate the content of the first covenant. Jeremiah's word of the Lord is that "I will put my laws in their minds, and write them on their hearts" (Heb 8:10; Greek Jer 38:33 [= English 31:33] translated "my Torah" as "my laws"). There are no new covenantal acts or expectations to distinguish adherents of the new covenant from those of the first. It is distinctive that the new covenant cannot be broken, but this is true neither because the terms have changed nor because its human participants have become more capable of obedience on their own. Rather, Jesus' atoning sacrificial death "has perfected for all time those who are sanctified" (Heb 10:14).

Third, the new covenant will not require a hierarchy of teaching authority or administration. From Jeremiah's prophecy the author of Hebrews quotes, "they shall not teach one another or say to each other, 'Know the Lord,' for they shall all know me, from the least of them to the greatest" (8:11). This emphasizes Jesus' distinctive role as high priest and sacrifice who "once for all" (Heb 9:12, 10:10ff.) effects what had been the benefits of the priestly system under the first covenant. At the same time, it underscores the continuity of the new covenant with the first one by which people were taught to know the Lord.

Fourth, the covenant will be connected to the forgiveness of sin (Heb 8:12). The sacrifices of the first covenant were, among other things, effective in restoring Israel's purity and relationship with God through the forgiveness of sin. For the new covenant to be equally effective and worthwhile apart from temple sacrifices, it must have a comparable capacity for forgiveness. This the author shows exhaustively in chapters 9 and 10, demonstrating the adequacy of Jesus' sacrifice—even asserting its superiority—in order to qualify the new covenant in light of the first.[12]

If the new covenant in Hebrews thus is not inherently better than the first, being in most respects identical to it and in others gaining virtue by living up to the model of the first, we must consider whether it is "better" because it proves out as such in practice. Both past experience and future expectation play a role in making that determination, as becomes clear when we look at the comments that frame the quotation from Jeremiah.

As to the past, the author introduces Jeremiah's accusation of Israel by saying, "he finds fault with them" (Heb 8:8). Yet the question of failure in the first covenant proves to be problematic, because the record of Israel's practice ill fits the accusation of fault that Jeremiah lodges.[13] The "better covenant" to which Hebrews refers is one mediated by Jesus' "more excellent ministry," or priesthood (8:6). But in relation to the commands of the first covenant Israel's priests were not at fault.

Daily sacrifice was divinely ordained and accompanied by the promise of forgiveness. To engage in the ritual for the purpose of obtaining forgiveness does not then demonstrate that "they did not continue in my covenant" (Heb

8:9), nor is a priest who presides over the ritual ipso facto deficient. Thus, although the author of Hebrews introduces Jeremiah's accusation by saying that "he finds fault with *them*," the reality of the priestly practice has already forced the author to acknowledge that the fault lay not in actual practice but somehow in the covenant itself (Heb 8:6-7).

Perhaps, though, the first covenant ultimately will prove its inadequacy in the future. The author says as much in a comment following Jeremiah's accusation: "In speaking of 'a new covenant,' he has made the first one obsolete. And what is obsolete and growing old will soon disappear" (Heb 8:13). If this refers only to the system of temple sacrifice, it has no particular bearing on Judaism as a whole, because Judaism has always incorporated much more than animal sacrifices. And if it means Judaism in contrast to Christianity, the vibrant and resilient history of rabbinic Judaism even into our own day disproves the premise that it was obsolete; clearly, it has not disappeared.[14] In either case, future expectation fails to indict the first covenant any more than its past practice had. In terms of history, neither its predicted deficiency nor its practical failure has been shown.

At the same time, the author of Hebrews is plainly struggling to encourage and inspire steadfastness and perseverance in those who are in the new covenant. All the promises of inviolability notwithstanding, the very rhetoric of the letter testifies to the vacillation and uncertainty of its readers. Their obedience, their endurance, is not to be taken as inherent in the new covenant; otherwise the letter would be unnecessary. The new covenant is as susceptible to abandonment as Jeremiah says of the first.

Thus far, we have shown that the letter to the Hebrews presents the new covenant neither as inherently superior to the first nor as proving out more effective in practice. What then does the author mean by referring to the new covenant as "better" and the first as "obsolete" and "abolished" (Heb 8:6, 8:13, 10:9)? In the dynamics of the letter, such language is hyperbole, reminiscent of the same prophetic literature that has been the author's point of orientation throughout; it serves to encourage the readers to "full assurance of faith," to "hold fast to the confession of our hope without wavering," not to "abandon that confidence" but to have "endurance" (Heb 10:22-23, 10:35-36).

Confronted with adversity on account of their life in the new covenant, the readers are considering the advantages of the first covenant; the author reassures them by this argument that the new covenant is in every regard the full measure of the first, indeed asserting its superiority. The arguments that support the assertion may in fact only underscore the priority of the first, as we have seen, but the language has its effect in redirecting the readers back to the new covenant and its sufficiency. In the context of the first readers, the author needs only to establish the virtues of the new covenant and its appropriateness.

she is free, and she is our mother" (Gal 4:26).[16] The analogy derives from the contrast Paul wishes to make between slavery and freedom, as a foundation for exhorting the reader, "for freedom Christ has set us free. Stand firm, therefore, and do not submit again to a yoke of slavery" (Gal 5:1). As in Hebrews and 2 Corinthians, the thrust of the argument in Galatians is to encourage the readers, rather than to contrast the two covenants in detail.

Paul's second cluster of references shares a pattern of comparing covenantal traditions from Israel's heritage. We have already seen Paul refer both to Moses and to Abraham as covenantal figures, and these texts bring them into comparison with one another. In Gal 3:15 and 3:17, Paul uses a linguistic convenience—the same Greek word refers both to a personal testamentary will and to a divine covenant—to argue for the priority of God's promise to Abraham over the Mosaic revelation. In his work with Gentiles, Paul had become convinced that the marks of Jewish life stipulated in the Sinai covenant were more than God would require of Gentiles who came to faith in Jesus. Yet it is still God's covenant with Israel into which the Gentiles are brought, so Paul argues that the covenantal promises are already present for Abraham, making the Sinai revelation appropriate for some of God's chosen but not for all.[17]

The same comparison underlies Paul's argument in Romans, which includes two references to covenant.[18] Both texts are part of Paul's extended consideration of the place that "Israel"—Paul's "own people," his "kindred according to the flesh" (Rom 9:3)—holds in relation to God and to the Gentile believers who are Paul's readers. At Rom 9:4, Paul affirms their many distinguishing marks, including "the covenants," without further specification. At Rom 11:26-27, Paul quotes the same phrase that the author of Hebrews did, Jer 31:34. He does so in order to establish his assertion that "all Israel will be saved; as it is written, 'Out of Zion will come the Deliverer; he will banish ungodliness from Jacob.' 'And this is my covenant with them, when I take away their sins.'"[19] The covenant renewal promised to Israel through Jeremiah's prophecy is the very vehicle through which God "may be merciful to all" (Rom 11:32).

Thus Paul, like the author of Hebrews, continues to affirm the old covenant as the basis for valuing what God has done in the new covenant in Christ. Comparisons between them are effective rhetorically in encouraging Christians to hold fast to their covenantal identity, but that identity would be undermined were the contrast to invalidate the old covenant in its essence. Rather, within Israel's tradition Paul finds a plurality of covenantal traditions that serve his teaching in their very differences. Sometimes one and sometimes another is appropriate to the situation he addresses among his readers, and Paul is willing to take what he can from each of them to achieve his point. Thus he demonstrates what he also said of himself explicitly, that he was well trained and ahead of his peers in his skill as a Jewish interpreter.[20]

THE LEGACY OF COVENANTS IN ISRAEL'S SCRIPTURES

In Israel's own scriptures, we find a trajectory of covenant language that lays the groundwork for understanding how Paul developed his. That is, "covenant" is a powerful and pliable term, filled out in different ages by content of widely varying character.[21] Within the Torah alone we encounter four major covenantal events, with Noah in Genesis 9, with Abra(ha)m in Genesis 15 and 17, and with all Israel at Sinai in Exodus 19–24. The dynastic covenant with David is recorded in 2 Samuel 7, and the postexilic reestablishment of the Sinai covenant is narrated in Nehemiah 9. In addition, there is the pregnant reference to a "new covenant" in two of the writing prophets, Jeremiah and Ezekiel.

It becomes evident in surveying these that the only fixed point in the covenant tradition is the fact that covenant connotes a relationship with God. It may be granted unilaterally by God without condition, as with Noah and Abraham,[22] or entail Israel's responsibilities and obedience as at Sinai (Exodus 19, 24). The signs of the several covenants vary widely, as do the specific promises attached to them. There is no singular portrayal of "the covenant" in Israel's scriptures. "Covenant" is a flexible category that can be formed in various ways and filled with content that is appropriate to the times.

We do not have space here to specify the historical circumstances and community dynamics under which the whole succession of covenant images developed. It is enough to note that Paul was following his own scripture's lead when he made reference to several different covenants, valuing them differently depending on the point he was making and the setting in which he wrote. The height of the covenant-language emphasis in the writing of Israel's scriptures came during the days of the late seventh and early sixth centuries B.C.E., just before the destruction of the Temple by the Babylonians. Even then, views of covenant diverged.

Those who wrote Deuteronomy, who set forth the values that shape the interpretative history that follows it in Joshua through 2 Kings, were leaning heavily on the Sinai covenant as the divine guide for Israel's obedience; by holding fast to it, Israel could expect that God would protect them from the Babylonian threat. By contrast, the prophet Jeremiah, in the text already familiar to us from its use in the letter to the Hebrews, declared the Sinai covenant obsolete or threatened to make it so—with its uncertainty about obedience and its reliance on a priestly hierarchy. This was a covenant that the Israelites had already broken; in days to come God would fashion a new covenant with the people Israel, putting the Torah in their hearts and imparting knowledge of God directly to every class of people (Jer 31:31-34). That God's Torah stands at the center of Israel's life is the common point of agreement; there is a relationship between God and Israel grounded in God's revelation. What is at issue is the nature of that relationship, and the category of covenant is the vehicle through which the dispute is pursued.[23]

Seen in this light, the differences among the major covenant texts and traditions in Israel's scriptures are instructive. "Covenant" has no monolithic, clear-cut, unchanging meaning throughout Israel's existence. It is a symbol of the relationship between God and Israel that bears many meanings over time and even simultaneously for different groups within Israel. To proclaim a "new covenant" in Israel—as Ezekiel does in terms similar to Jeremiah's (Ezek 16:60, 34:25, 37:26; note Ezekiel's emphasis on the Davidic covenant tradition)—does not challenge God's favor for the people; rather it emphasizes the divine desire to fashion ties with the people that will fit the times and their circumstances. *Whatever* is the relationship of God and God's people, this is what Israel's scriptures portray as covenant.[24]

ELECTION AND WITNESS AS COMPLEMENTARY COVENANTAL THEMES

In everyday usage, as in the *adversus Ioudaeos* tradition, it may be common to assume that there can be only one valid covenant and that therefore we face the unambiguous choice between a Jewish covenant and a Christian covenant in making sense of the encounter with God. The foregoing surveys have dispelled that assumption. The New Testament writers do typically frame their covenant language on the presupposition that theirs is more worthy than any other, especially their opponents'. Yet the themes and images of the castigated covenant still yield the standards of excellence for their own. So too in Israel's scriptures, "old" and "new" can be contemporaries. Moreover, successive, even contradictory, framings of covenant are incorporated into a single narrative structure—the five books of Torah—that accommodates them without forcing their confrontation. As long as "covenant" has named the relationship between God and God's people, it has come with the possibility of different forms and of change over time.

What does not change is that "covenant" distinguishes God's people in the world. This is not often taken as a situation of particular privilege but rather as being for the sake of the world; usually it entails a greater obligation as God's witnesses and partners in working for peace and justice. Among the primary marks of the covenant is circumcision, the sign of a covenant with Abraham, to whom God had said, "In you all the nations of the world shall be blessed" (Gen 12:3, 17:1-22). Circumcision also carries forward into later generations the ritual involvement of blood in establishing covenants, which was made most explicit for Israel at Sinai (Exod 24:4b-8).

Like circumcision, other elements of the covenant have served for centuries to mark those whom God called to be "a priestly kingdom and a holy nation" (Exod 19:6), to carry God's revelation in the world. Each age has had its own particular marks, and some have been central elements throughout Jewish history. So the observance of the *Shabbat* (Sabbath) as a day of rest has become emblematic of Judaism. Whatever particular emphasis has been given to it, the weekly day of rest has set this people apart from those among whom they have lived. The traditional blessing over wine and bread on Shabbat morning begins with a recitation of Exod 31:16-17, where Israel is commanded to observe the Shabbat "throughout their generations, as a perpetual covenant." Likewise, the distinctive food laws of *kashrut* (kosher), the patent refusal to offer sacrifice or any kind of worship to any but the God of Israel, and the practices of family and personal purity—witnessed by the presence of *mikva'ot* (ritual baths) in the archaeological remains of Jewish communities wherever they may be unearthed and from whatever period—all these have been symbols of the covenant that have made it easy to identify who it is that lives as God's people.

Equally important, if not always as evident to outsiders, has been the passionate expectation that God's promises one day will come to fruition in a new fulfillment of Israel's collective life, and that this will take place at the center of biblical Israel's life, the holy mountain of Zion. Here stood the temples, and here the people of Israel—having separated themselves for this purpose from those not of Israelite descent—renewed and accepted the covenant of the Torah read to them by Ezra in the days after their return from exile (Nehemiah 8–10). Having heard the Torah that had been given at Sinai, having confessed the sins of ancestors who had failed to live as God's people, and having acknowledged God's mercy in preserving the people despite those sins, they took this covenant upon themselves anew. The Torah itself told of the day at Sinai when Israel answered the Lord, "We will do, and we will be obedient" (Exod 24:7). Now the people, "all who have separated themselves from the peoples of the lands to adhere to the Torah of God. . . , join . . . to observe and do all the commandments" (Neh 10:28-29). For this is what it means to live as God's people in the world, to be partners with God in fixing the world and moving it toward the fulfillment for which God created it.

It is not the case that following the commandments, living life as it is given to Israel in the Torah, is a prerequisite to being God's people or that it qualifies Israel as such. Indeed, the recitation of ancestral sins in Nehemiah 9, as well as the harsh critique of many of Israel's kings by the writers of Samuel and Kings, makes it clear that keeping faith with the Torah was a difficult challenge for God's people. But, for all that, they never ceased to be God's people (Neh 9:31). The ground of the call to live as God's people rests instead on the act of God that brought the people out of Egypt in the exodus. This is the moment of redemption that established Israel as God's people, when, God said, "I bore you on eagles' wings and brought you to myself [to] be my treasured possession out of all the peoples" (Exod 19:4-5).

This is the redemption that grounds every Jew as part of God's people. Each year in the Passover Seder, as part of the fifth segment, *Maggid* ("Telling the Story"), the *haggadah*[25] states: "In every generation one is obligated to see oneself as one who personally went out from Egypt. Just as it says: "You shall tell your child on that very day: 'It's because of this that God did for *me* when I *went out from Egypt*'" (Exod 13:8).[26] Knowing oneself as a part of the people of God is the starting point of Jewish life and identity, recited and renewed every year in the Passover story. Then comes the choice, whether to live in the covenant, that distinctive pattern that belongs to God's people in the world. But even a refusal so to live does not undo the fact of the exodus or the reality that Israel is God's people. Over the centuries the covenant in Jewish life has taken on a shape that presupposes God's election of the people and then seeks to define a way of life that marks their distinctive witness in the world.

First-century Jews such as Paul and Peter proclaimed to Gentiles that they too could be brought to God and counted among God's people. In the words of Ephesians, they had been "far off" but now could be "brought near," specifically by "the blood of Christ" (Eph 2:13). For ancient Israel, it was Pharaoh and Egyptian slavery that had stood between God and God's people, and the liberating redemption was the exodus. What had stood between the Gentiles and God? Sin.[27] And what is the liberating redemption that brings them to God? The victory of Jesus, won on the cross, over the power of sin and death.

This is the key element in connecting Jeremiah's prophecy of the new covenant with God's act in Jesus, as both Paul and the author of Hebrews do. The covenant Jeremiah proclaims is one that entails the forgiveness of sin. In early Christian theology, sin is the slave-master from which Gentiles need to be redeemed in order to be among God's people. To be a Jew is to be redeemed by God at the Sea from slavery to Egypt. In like fashion, for a Gentile, to be among God's people is to be redeemed by God at the cross from slavery to sin.

The blood of the covenant that is Jesus' blood thus signifies for Gentile Christians the same two things that the blood of the covenant at Sinai signifies for Jews: God has redeemed them and they acknowledge themselves as God's people in light of that redemption.[28] As at Sinai Moses sought the people's affirmation of God's covenant when they received the blood of the covenant (Exod 24:4b-8), so the eucharistic tradition seeks the people's affirmation and reception of the blood: "Drink from it, all of you" (Matt 26:27).

While these twin covenantal themes of election and witness are evident in both traditions, Judaism and Christianity have given them quite different emphases in the course of their respective development. We have seen that the Jewish covenantal balance has been toward witness—distinctive practices that make a plain witness to the world and that seek to fix it according to God's design. In Christianity, by contrast, the emphasis has fallen more on the side of election, redemption, and reassurance of the individual's place in the people of God.

This is understandable in that the inevitability of sin represented a constant threat to one's status among the people of God. Christians differed from Jews in most eras in that neither ethnic continuity nor cultural animosity reinforced their identity as God's elect. The fact of redemption from sin was what made one a part of God's people, so relapsing into sin would risk that redemption and jeopardize a person's Christian identity. Hence, the covenantal emphasis fell not so much on the distinctive witness of one's life as a member of the covenant people as it did on becoming part of the people of God through Christ's sacrifice, the forgiveness of sin, and the blood of the covenant.[29] If the Jewish balance leaned toward the witness of a distinctive life, the Christian balance leaned toward the reassurance of election.

This difference in emphasis can mislead us in thinking about God's covenantal ways. Indeed, in the development of Christian theology *adversus Ioudaeos*, just such a misleading took place. Rather than seeing the two common themes as differently stressed, the church set them in opposition to each other, so that theology closed the door to covenantal pluralism which the author of Hebrews and Paul had opened with their exegesis. This has been intensified among Lutherans and others of the Reformation tradition who set the struggle for justification at the center of the spiritual life. With the heritage of anti-Jewish understandings from earlier centuries, it was a short step to a simplistic application of the law-gospel dialectic that would credit only the Christian understanding of the covenant with life-giving power. Thereby the "blood of the covenant" too easily became the blood of the covenant people spilled in insistence upon which covenant will prevail.

But we can see now that there need be no inherent contradiction between Christianity and Judaism in the matter of covenant. As in the New Testament texts, so among us: "new" and "old" can coexist fruitfully. Both Judaism and Christianity affirm both covenantal redemption (by God's free election) and covenantal life (as a living witness to God in the world). These two themes interact creatively in the religious life of both communities; they are not mutually exclusive. To be sure, Judaism and Christianity locate the key covenantal moment in different historical circumstances, but the continuity of God as the covenantal partner is affirmed, the pattern of covenantal engagement between God's people and God is consistent, and the biblical flexibility in characterizing the covenant in different ways at different times and in different circumstances

3

•

Law and Gospel

Esther Menn
in Conversation with Krister Stendahl[1]

Many Christians, perhaps most notably among them Lutherans, speak of the word of God addressed to humankind in terms of both "law" and "gospel." Law, in this formulation, expresses God's righteous demand that we live completely in accord with the divine will, while gospel expresses the good news of God's mercy and salvation despite our failure to live up to the law's just standards. The emphasis in Christian theology generally falls on the gospel, with its proclamation of God's forgiveness and justification of sinful humanity through Christ alone and not through any human efforts. In this understanding of law and gospel, the theological concept of the law is primarily accusatory, highlighting the need for the gospel.[2]

Certainly throughout history there have been Christians with a much more positive and robust understanding of divine law than the one that this negative view represents. The earliest followers of Jesus, including Peter and the community at Jerusalem, were Jewish and followed a traditional way of life based on Jewish legal traditions and religious observances. During the Reformation, John Calvin, Luther's younger contemporary, intentionally based his theocratic governance of Geneva on Old Testament law. In our own time, civil disobedience of unjust state laws by Christians is sometimes justified by appeal to God's higher law. Yet, within Christianity the theological concept of the law tends to be negative, associated with divine wrath, judgment, and even death.

How remarkably different from this negative Christian understanding of the law is the positive Jewish celebration of "Torah" (the Hebrew word often translated as "law," but sometimes better translated as "teaching"). Within Judaism, Torah is regarded as God's gracious gift of guidance for faithful living within the covenant community. Exuberant praise for Torah finds expression in the Scriptures, for example in the longest psalm in the psalter:

> Oh, how I love your law [Torah, or teaching]!
>> It is my meditation all day long.
> . . . How sweet are your words to my taste,
>> sweeter than honey to my mouth!
> . . . Your word is a lamp to my feet
>> and a light to my path!
> . . . Your decrees are my heritage forever;
>> they are the joy of my heart! (Ps. 119:97, 103, 105, 111)

Jewish joy in Torah continues to be expressed today, most visibly in the congregational dancing with the Torah scroll during the festival of *Simhat Torah* (literally, "the joy of Torah"), which marks a new beginning of the liturgical reading of the five books of Moses in the synagogue each year.[3]

What should Christians make of this striking disjuncture between the law as divine judgment in Christian theology and Torah as divine instruction for life in the Jewish community? It is tempting to conclude that these sharply contrasting attitudes toward an important aspect of our intertwining heritage mark an irreconcilable difference, best respectfully noted and left in God's hands.[4] Christians cannot be satisfied with this easy course, however. Compelling reasons lead us to reconsider the theological concept of the law in light of recent developments in Jewish-Christian relations. Much is at stake, including a more authentic understanding of the relationship between Judaism and Christianity, a new appreciation for our sister religion, Judaism, and even the ongoing reformation of Christian identity and mission in the world.

Exploration of three major topics may facilitate Christian reassessment of the theological significance of the law. The first involves the history of Christian caricature of Jewish law as a polemical point of division between Judaism as an outmoded religion and Christianity as its superior replacement. Christians must take care not to continue this shameful legacy through unreflective, negative evaluations of the law. The second moves beyond worn polemics about Jewish legalism and works righteousness into a sympathetic understanding of Judaism's very positive assessment of God's Torah as a source of blessing and life. If Christians are to enter into a new relationship of mutuality with Judaism, they need to recognize this central concept. Finally, the third proceeds to reconsider and clarify the positive significance of law as divine teaching for life within the Christian community itself. Christians can experience following God's gracious commandments not as a burden or an impossible duty, but as a response to the transforming love that we have already received.

Luther?

CHRISTIAN ATTITUDES TOWARD THE LAW AND JUDAISM

Negative evaluation of the law is connected to a long history of Christian argumentation against Judaism. A stark contrast between the law of the Old Testament and Judaism that brings judgment and death and the gospel of the New Testament and Christianity that brings salvation and life remains more pervasive and influential than might be expected, even at this late date.

Most Christians do not intend to denigrate and misrepresent Judaism as the inferior predecessor of a superior Christian faith when they frame their own religious experience and convictions in terms of law and gospel. Yet traditional theological formulations that carry anti-Jewish attitudes remain potent and harmful, perhaps especially when these attitudes are unconscious and therefore immune to critique. Selected moments in the history of Christian thought can illustrate how criticism of Jewish law has long served to demarcate the line between Judaism and Christianity. This type of argument is no longer appropriate. Knowledge of the past can open the way for repudiating a triumphal Christian identity based on a negative definition of Judaism in terms of an ineffectual, outmoded, and even condemning law.

How did Jews and Christians come to hold such contrasting assessments of the law given at Sinai, especially in light of the fact that Jesus and his earliest followers were all Jewish? The four Gospels depict Jesus and his disciples following a distinctive way of life based on Jewish law, which in its broader sense includes not only civil and criminal statutes but also ethnic customs, holidays such as Passover, and other religious observances, as well as ethical norms and teachings drawn from the Hebrew Scriptures. Even Jesus' controversies with Pharisees and representatives of other Jewish groups reveal internal debates about aspects of the law current within Judaism, not Jesus' opposition to the whole body of Jewish law.

One of the factors leading to the very different assessments of Jewish law within Judaism and Christianity was the intentional outreach to include non-Jews within the early Christian community. The earliest writings in the New Testament, the letters of the apostle Paul associated with his mission to the Gentiles, illustrate some of the dynamics of this development.

As a former Pharisee who acknowledged his deep knowledge of Jewish law and his blameless observance of it for at least some portion of his life (Phil 3:6), Paul never wavers from his positive evaluation of God's commandment as "holy and just and good" (Rom 7:12). Indeed, he claims that he continues to delight in the law of God in his inmost self (Rom 7:22). Paul's frequent citation of the first five books of the Bible, commonly known as the Law of Moses (or, in Hebrew, the Torah), and his deep concern with the moral law that leads to virtue within the Christian community show that this apostle by no means discounted God's law. In fact, one of Paul's major projects was a reformulation of the law for the Christian community. "Faith active in love" (Gal 5:6) is the rule for God's new creation of Gentiles and Jews in Christ, since Paul maintains that "the whole law is summed up in a single commandment, 'You shall love your neighbor as yourself'" (Gal 5:14, which quotes Lev 19:18).

But in his passionate letter addressed to pagan converts to Christianity in Galatia, Paul emphasizes that circumcision and food laws do not apply to non-Jews. This position would have been shared by most Jews of his time and certainly by the rabbis (or sages and teachers) of later rabbinic Judaism. What was distinctive about Paul's stance, however, was his assertion that Gentiles should remain Gentiles even as they become part of God's people through Christ. Paul argued that there was no reason for non-Jews to convert to Judaism, since within the Christian community righteousness before God for both Jew and non-Jew alike was through faith in Jesus the Messiah (Gal 2:16), not through adherence to the law.

Significantly, to support his arguments Paul chooses a figure from the Torah itself (here in the sense of "the Pentateuch"). Abraham trusted in God's promises long before the giving of the law at Sinai, and even before this patriarch was circumcised as a sign of the covenant (Rom 4:9-12); yet God considered him righteous because of his faith (Gal 3:6; cf. Gen 15:6). Paul envisions a new Abrahamic family of faith, consisting not only of Jews but also of many nations. Through Christ there is already "neither Jew nor gentile" (Gal 3:28), but rather a new, more encompassing creation. Gentile conversion to Judaism would therefore be misguided, since it would suggest that there is a competing way to a right relationship with God. In arguing his position, Paul adds a stern admonition to Gentile Christians already justified by their faith in Christ Jesus, that if they begin to observe Jewish law through circumcision they unnecessarily expose themselves to divine judgment, since they thereby become accountable for all of the law's provisions.

The question of whether Jewish law has an enduring status for Jews themselves is less developed in Paul's letters. Recently, some scholars have argued that Paul may have envisioned Jewish Christians more or less continuing their traditional way of life based on observance of Jewish law, much as Jesus and his companions did.[5] But Paul's new perspective of faith in Jesus as the Messiah does appear to qualify his understanding of the law's place in his own people's history with God. As Paul recounts it, Israel's story culminates in Christ Jesus as the promised seed of Abraham, through whom God brings salvation and life for Jew and Gentile alike. From this perspective, Jewish law from Sinai becomes a temporary provision, acting as a guardian against sin for the Jewish people before the coming of Christ. But now that both Jewish and non-Jewish members of the body of Christ have already died with Christ's death, they are no longer slaves under the written code binding only on those living. Instead, they have new life in the Spirit to bear fruit for God (Rom 7:4-6; cf., Gal 2:19).

Paul also qualifies the efficacy of the law in other ways. He notes, for example, that, although it was intended to curtail sin, the law has the paradoxical effect of heightening awareness of sin and even of stimulating the passions that give rise to it (Rom 7:7-11). Paul's arguments are clearly hyperbolic at times. If we take his words at face value, however, Paul attributes no saving function to the law for Jewish believers in Christ, nor apparently for the rest of the Jews. This view is actually not at odds with the dominant position on the law within Judaism, which does not regard Torah obedience as a means to salvation but rather as a response to God's gracious covenant.[6] Reflecting further about the matter of salvation, however, Paul adamantly asserts that God has not rejected his elected people. God's gifts and calling are irrevocable, and all Israel will be saved (Rom 11:11-36).

While during Paul's time the church was a mixed community of Jews and Gentiles, by the second century, Christianity had become primarily a Gentile phenomenon. With the demographic shift that paralleled the parting of the ways of Judaism and Christianity, the debates internal to a movement with Jewish origins and ongoing connections rapidly turned into verbal attacks by Gentile Christians against Jews. The roots of Christian anti-Judaism may be detected already in the New Testament, exemplified by the repeated negative references to "the Jews" throughout the Gospel according to John.[7] The church fathers continued in this tradition, with rhetoric often resembling the type of Gentile Christian boasting against which the apostle Paul cautioned (Rom 11:17-24)!

The extreme position that the Jewish Scriptures have no place whatsoever in the church championed by Marcion in the second century was rejected in official Christian teaching. Yet, unsympathetic contrasts between Christian gospel and Jewish law became part of the *adversus Ioudaeos* tradition (arguments "against the Jews") of the church fathers, which extolled Christian faith by presenting Judaism as a negative opposite. Christianity represented by the gospel was associated positively with the new covenant, the spirit, grace, freedom, faith, and life, whereas Judaism represented by the law was associated negatively with the old covenant, the flesh (although Paul himself asserts that the law is spiritual in Rom 7:14!), wrath, slavery, works, and death.

In point of fact, the church fathers did not consider all aspects of the law in what they called the Old Testament as equally outmoded. Typological predictions of Christ through certain ritual traditions (such as the Passover law, which prefigures the sacrifice of Jesus as the true paschal lamb) and moral teachings (such as those found in the Ten Commandments) remained in effect. Jewish religious and civil law, however, was deemed to be obsolete since Christ's coming. Continued observance of this law was considered a sign of Jewish stubborn rejection of salvation through Christ.

During the medieval period, Christians came to recognize that over the centuries since Jesus' life there had been an ongoing tradition of legal development within the Jewish community, represented by the Babylonian Talmud (discussed further in the next section) and by the ongoing adjudication of specific issues by local and regional rabbis. Judaism as a thriving reality with a living legal tradition was problematic for Christian theology, since it could not be dismissed as a relic based on antiquated and superceded Old Testament law. The response by Christian governments was to order public burnings of the Talmud and other Jewish literature, such as occurred in France in 1240.[8]

The sixteenth-century reformer Martin Luther deserves emphasis in this brief survey, since he is generally credited as the source for "law and gospel" as a principle of scriptural interpretation, used extensively by Lutheran preachers, especially since the nineteenth century. Luther's reflections on his personal failure to live a righteous life, his intensive study of the letters of Paul and the theology of Augustine, and his often adversarial relations with the church of his day, which he regarded as impossibly mired in legalism, led him to distinguish between the law that condemns even one's best efforts and the gospel that graciously imparts life. Although Luther insisted that law and gospel remain bound together in Christian faith, he, like Paul, asserted that God's law cannot be a means of salvation, since as fallen humanity we are in bondage to sin and cannot fulfill its demands, no matter how sincere our efforts. In the face of the judgment and condemnation that the law brings, however, the gospel assures us that God imputes righteousness to us through grace alone, received in faith and apart from human works associated with the law's demands.

Luther creatively used terminology from the missionary letters of Paul to address the very different context of late medieval Christianity piety. When Luther speaks of the law, he is generally not referring to actual traditions and practices within the Jewish community. Indeed, Luther did not write extensively about the Judaism of his time until late in his life, when he produced shockingly vitriolic and inflammatory anti-Jewish works, now repudiated by the ELCA in its 1994 statement, "Declaration of the Evangelical Lutheran Church in America to the Jewish Community."[9] Luther's theological arguments, rather, were mostly internal to the Christianity of his day, often directed against what he viewed as the errors and abuses of Roman Church authorities. Luther's influential legacy nevertheless gave new life to the negative theological concept of the law, which all too easily fuels the tradition of Christian anti-Judaism.

Strong prejudices against the law and alleged Jewish legalism have continued to characterize Christian thought until quite recently. For example, the biblical scholarship of the nineteenth and first half of the twentieth century commonly described the new forms of Judaism emerging during the post-exilic and Second Temple periods with the phrase "late Judaism," as if that was the last chapter in a Jewish history ending with the emergence of Christianity. Instead of recognizing the vitality and diversity of the Jewish community centered around the Temple and Torah, these scholars described the religion of that time as legalistic, degraded, fossilized, and even dead. By using terms such as these, Christian biblical scholars transported much of traditional Christian polemic from the *adversus Ioudaeos* tradition directly into supposedly "objective" scholarship. Even today, it is unfortunately not all that unusual to hear Christian sermons that castigate the Pharisees as representatives of Jewish hypocrisy and legalism in order to extol Jesus' contrasting way of grace and love.[10]

This selective survey of Christian perspectives on the law as a theological concept—often related to critiques of Judaism as an inferior religion of the law superceded or replaced by Christianity—illustrates one of the persistent dynamics of Jewish-Christian relations throughout the centuries. The question for our age is how to prevent the traditional contrast between law and gospel that remains meaningful for many Christians on the experiential level from encapsulating and extending a long history of Christian anti-Judaism.

When Christians speak of law and gospel, we need to make absolutely clear that the relation between these terms remains an internal dialectic within the Christian faith itself. We cannot project "legalism" or "works righteousness" onto our Jewish neighbors. We need to acknowledge that self-importance and excessive preoccupation with rules and regulations are dangers internal to every religious tradition, including Christianity. Christians should know that Jewish texts including the Mishnah and the Talmud also offer searing criticism of the foibles of moral hypocrisy and self-congratulatory attitudes, directed, for example, at certain Pharisees whose conscientious observance isolated them from the ordinary people.

Christians also need to reject any understanding of law and gospel as two chronological moments within salvation history, represented by two successive covenants, the Old Testament of the condemning law equated with Judaism, and the New Testament of the saving gospel equated with Christianity. The history of Christian doctrine provides resources that will assist us in this endeavor, including aspects of Luther's own understanding of law and gospel. Building on Augustine's formulation that "the law is given that grace might be sought; grace is given that the law might be fulfilled," Luther viewed the law as preparatory for the gospel. Unlike Augustine and many other Christian thinkers, however, Luther did not view law and gospel primarily as two stages in the history of salvation, represented by the Judaism of the Old Testament and the Christianity of the New Testament, respectively. Rather, for him, both law and gospel are found in both the Old and New Testaments.

Luther maintained, for example, that the Ten Commandments, the essential summary of religious and moral law in the Old Testament, themselves have a gospel side, since they begin with the declaration that God has brought his people out of the land of Egypt. Luther's interpretation of the Ten Commandments expands even the negative prohibitions into a positive way of life in right relationship with God and one's neighbor, within which the gospel may be experienced. The reformer's high regard for the Ten Commandments as both law and gospel led him to consider them as part of the essential catechetical teachings for all Christians. Conversely, for Luther the cross of the New Testament, the most potent sign of the saving gospel, itself manifests the law in its accusation of sinful humanity on whose behalf God acts through Christ. Also, in Luther's conception of the Christian life as a daily baptism, through which one dies to sin under the judgment of the law and rises to life in Christ through the grace of the gospel, the dialectic between law and gospel remains a central dynamic within Christian faith itself.

Luther's objection to the understanding of law and gospel as two distinct stages in the history of salvation and his insistence that law and gospel both operate within Christian life itself moved him toward a position with the potential to challenge the stereotypical contrast between Judaism as the religion of the condemning Old Testament law and Christianity as the religion of the saving New Testament gospel. Unfortunately, this potential has not been realized in the five centuries since Luther's time. Now, however, in our new era of respectful interfaith dialogue and changing perspectives on Christianity's relationship with the other religions of the world, we can move beyond the worn polemics of the past.

Educational work to further this goal has begun. Much still remains to be done in the local churches in order to eliminate uncritical and often unconscious projection onto Judaism and Jews of all the negative associations with the law within the history of Christian theology, including self-righteousness, futility of works, and condemnation for sin. In our time, we need to be intentional about setting aside ancient definitions of Christianity as a superior replacement for Judaism, in order to learn from our Jewish neighbors themselves about the significance of Torah within their religious tradition.

BEYOND OLD POLEMICS: UNDERSTANDING THE POSITIVE SIGNIFICANCE OF TORAH FOR JEWS

Stereotypes and misperceptions thwart the possibility of mutual understanding and respect between religious communities. As Christians abandon false characterizations of the law within Judaism that have marred Jewish-Christian relations for nearly two millennia, we can come to appreciate that for Jews Torah offers a way of life within the covenant community graciously established by God.

This positive understanding of Torah builds on biblical foundations, as evident from the earlier citation of Psalm 119. Similarly, at the end of the book of Deuteronomy, Moses, the great mediator of the Torah, himself assures Israel that the commandments given at Sinai are not too difficult to keep, but rather offer a way of life and divine blessing:

> Surely, this commandment that I am commanding you today is not too hard for you, nor is it too far away. . . . No, the word is very near to you; it is in your mouth and in your heart for you to observe. . . . If you obey the commandments of the LORD your God that I am commanding you today, by loving the LORD your God, walking in his ways, and observing his commandments, decrees, and his ordinances, then you shall live and become numerous, and the LORD your God will bless you. . . . (Deut 30:11, 14, 16)

In interpreting Scripture, the Jewish sages and teachers known as the rabbis similarly emphasized that Israel received the commandments (in Hebrew the *mitzvoth*) in order to "live by them" (Lev 18:5)—to live and not to die. Far from the pedantic scribes of Christian caricature, the rabbis sought to implement this basic principle by creatively applying Jewish law in ways that would support and enhance life. Rabbinic interpretation of the book of Proverbs stresses this same goal when it equates God's Torah with divine wisdom, described metaphorically as "a tree of life to those who lay hold of her" (Prov 3:18a). The continuation of this verse claims that "those who hold her fast are called happy" (3:18b). "Happiness" belongs to those whose "delight is in the law of the LORD" so that they meditate on it "day and night" (Ps 1:2).

Since many North American Christians today live in communities that include Jewish members, they can ask a local rabbi or Jewish leader to confirm that Torah is viewed positively as a source of life, blessing, and joy. This personal connection will have the additional effect of making anti-Jewish attitudes and expressions that persist within the Christian tradition more apparent and unacceptable, since they will no longer be abstract theological statements, but words directed against real people in the neighborhood.

As Christians try to understand the positive attitude toward Torah in Judaism, it may be helpful to recognize that the Hebrew word *torah* has a much broader meaning than the English translation "law," and in fact is used in a number of different ways by Jews. As noted previously, *torah* is often better translated into English as "teaching," since it comes from a verbal root meaning "to teach," and other words in Hebrew refer more specifically to legal realities such as laws, commandments, statutes, and ordinances. Certainly, Torah does include the law codes associated with the Sinai covenant placed centrally within the first five books of the Bible. The Greek translation of the Hebrew Scriptures known as the Septuagint, dating from as early as the third century before the common era, emphasized this aspect of the Hebrew word when it translated *torah* into Greek as *nomos*, or "law"—a translation with profound theological consequences.

Yet it is not just the law codes but the entire section of the Bible known among Christians as the Pentateuch (or "five books" of Moses) that is known among Jews as the Torah. This foundational collection of scripture occupies a pride of place within Judaism and is traditionally read in its entirety over the course of the liturgical year. A quick survey of Genesis through Deuteronomy reveals that the Torah includes many other types of material besides legal statutes, such as stories, poetry, genealogies, moral teachings, sermons, blessings, and much more. This diversity confirms the appropriateness of the more inclusive translation of Torah as divinely revealed "teaching" foundational for the covenant community.

Eventually within Judaism the concept of Torah became even more inclusive, with the emergence of the idea of the Dual Torah, including both the written Torah of Scripture and the oral Torah of its ongoing, authoritative interpretation. According to Jewish tradition, the oral Torah also originated through revelation on Sinai and was passed down by word of mouth through a chain of sages and teachers, beginning with Moses himself and continuing with the rabbis who decisively shaped Judaism over the centuries. The Mishnah (or teaching accomplished through "oral repetition") is a foundational collection of legal traditions edited by Rabbi Judah the Prince in Sepphoris (a city in the Galilee very near to Nazareth) around 210 C.E. This work received extensive commentary (known as the Gemara, from a verb meaning "to complete") in both in Palestine and in Babylonia, with the eventual result being the emergence of two editions of the Talmud (yet another Hebrew word for "teaching"). The Babylonian Talmud, completed around 500 C.E. was the longer and more influential of the two within the Jewish world, providing a basis for subsequent legal debate and decisions for community life.

A concrete example of this type of legal interpretation involves the *lex talionis* (or "law of the talons"), summarized by the expression "an eye for an eye, and a tooth for a tooth." For many Christians this phrase encapsulates the severity of Old Testament law. According to rabbinic interpretation, however, this biblical principle is not a literal mandate for maiming corporal punishment, but rather an indication that monetary compensation should correspond to the seriousness of the physical injury inflicted. Legal traditions and their reinterpretation over the centuries are known collectively as the *halakhah*, literally in Hebrew the way of "walking" the Jewish faith in everyday life. The combination of strong continuity and creative development from the Bible to current practice shows that Torah is far from a "dead letter of the law." It is rather a vital and responsive process within Judaism. Stem-cell research and preemptive war are among the issues treated by rabbis today in decisions and rulings that answer contemporary questions, collectively known as the responsa literature.

Since Christians often equate the Pharisees of the New Testament with Jewish legalism, it is important to clarify their role. During Jesus' time the Pharisees were a small lay group that attempted to bring the holiness associated with the Temple into everyday life, to make it accessible not only for priests but even for ordinary people. In many ways, Jesus had more in common with the Pharisees than with any of the other groups that comprised first-century Judaism. In the Gospels, he is frequently depicted engaging in discussions with them, and the conflicts recorded in the New Testament reflect serious inner-Jewish debates about important matter of the law, including the appropriate observance of the Sabbath, marriage and divorce, issues of purity, and ethical questions such as the identity of the neighbor that one is required to love as oneself. In Jesus' description of the Pharisees as sitting "on Moses' seat" (Matt 23:2), he acknowledges their authority to interpret Jewish law for the contemporary generation, even as he criticizes their execution of this essential task. The apostle Paul boasts that he himself had been a Pharisee, when he lists the credentials that authorize him to speak with authority about Jewish law.

The harshest criticism against the Pharisees in the New Testament appears to stem from a later period, when Christianity and Judaism were undergoing a bitter separation. Many Christians do not realize that their Jewish neighbors highly regard the Pharisees as the founding figures for rabbinic Judaism, which was the form of Judaism that gradually emerged after the destruction of the Second Temple in 70 C.E. This form of Judaism, with its emphasis on practices centered in the home and the local community such as the observance of the Sabbath, dietary laws, regular communal prayers, and Passover, has enabled the Jewish people to endure and thrive as a distinctive community over the last two millennia despite the destruction of the Temple, the loss of autonomous political government, and life primarily outside of the land of Israel often as a hated and persecuted minority.[11]

Today there are various perspectives on the significance and shape of Torah obedience within Judaism itself, with different branches emphasizing Jewish legal traditions to varying degrees. Reform Judaism offers the most flexibility for individual choice and Orthodox Judaism practices the most comprehensive communal observance, with Conservative and Reconstructionist Judaism somewhere in between. Nonreligious or secular Jews may retain some traditional practices as part of their cultural identity. But although there is no single Jewish perspective, all branches of Judaism recognize Torah as a way of life that includes more than the adherence to specific laws and practices. Within

Judaism there is also the goal of becoming a moral and righteous person and of living within a community established on justice and righteousness according to God's commandments. Laws are therefore always interpreted in the context of ethical principles, theological perspectives, stories of exemplary Jewish figures, and the like, all of which also comprise a part of Torah. Torah as a precious gift and way of life serves as the mediation between God and the Jewish community. More encompassing than any legal code, Torah is the divine wisdom present in the fabric of creation. It remains active in the ordinary structures of daily life, lived in harmony with God's intentions for the Jewish people.

It is worth emphasizing once more that within Judaism, Torah is not viewed as a means to earn salvation, as Christians have erroneously perceived it. Indeed, the idea of individual salvation earned by performing specific deeds is foreign to Judaism. According to the book of Exodus, the commandments were given to an entire community that had already experienced deliverance from slavery in Egypt and rescue from death at the crossing of the sea. God redeemed the Israelites from slavery and death well before establishing them in a covenantal relationship by giving the Torah. The central question for religious Jews is not how each person might earn individual salvation. It is rather how best as God's elected people to give obedient assent to a covenant relationship that sanctifies all of life, graciously initiated by God on Sinai and continuing to the present time.[12]

Judaism is realistic in its acknowledgment that human beings sin, but just as God has already graciously provided guidance for the community through Torah, so God readily forgives all who repent of wrongdoing and return to righteous ways. Psalm 51 articulates this confidence in divine forgiveness:

> Have mercy on me, O God, according to your steadfast love;
>> according to your abundant mercy blot out my transgressions.
> Wash me thoroughly from my iniquity,
>> and cleanse me from my sin. . . .
> Purge me with hyssop, and I shall be clean;
>> wash me, and I shall be whiter than snow. (Ps 51:1-2, 7)

The solemn holiday of Yom Kippur, or the Day of Atonement, provides the occasion for the entire Jewish community to fast and offer prayers of repentance, in order to begin each New Year afresh with God's forgiveness.[13]

Observance of a distinctive way of life based on Torah has ensured the survival and thriving of the Jewish people over the centuries. Especially in light of the recent threats to Jewish existence and identity with the Holocaust (or Shoah, meaning "catastrophe" in Hebrew) and with the rapid rate of assimilation to the dominant culture, it is a serious matter for Christians to continue thinking in theological patterns that denigrate Jewish law. We bear false witness concerning our Jewish neighbors and foster a climate of hostility when we repeat stereotypes that do not reflect Jewish self-understanding. Embracing a sympathetic and authentic understanding of the role of Torah within our sister religion Judaism is the only way toward a mutual relationship between our two religious traditions.

As Christians acquire and internalize a new understanding of the positive role of Torah within Judaism, they will find that they need to abandon self-definitions that extol Christianity as a superior faith through negative and false stereotypes of Judaism. Rather than relying on distorting contrasts, Christians may be free to articulate the uniqueness of the Christian faith in more mature and truthful ways. They may also be able to recover positive aspects of the law as God's gracious guidance for the Christian church itself in its life and mission in the world today.

THE LAW AS DIVINE GUIDANCE FOR CHRISTIAN LIFE IN THE WORLD

Negative associations with the concept of the law have sometimes obscured its more positive functions within Christianity itself. Interfaith dialogue with Jews concerning the vital role of Torah for life within the covenant community may inspire Christians to reconsider and affirm the theological significance of the law as God's gracious guidance for the Christian church. As a people already saved by the good news of Christ's life, death, and resurrection, we still yearn for empowerment and direction to become active partners with God in holy living as the salt and light of the world. God's commandments for Christians can become a source of abundant grace for the transformation of our lives, churches, communities, and all of creation.[14]

In light of conversations with Jewish partners who welcome the covenantal structures of life offered by Torah, Christians may wrestle anew with core questions: Is there something comparable in Christianity to the positive teaching for life and blessing that Torah provides within Judaism? How do Christians experience God's guidance concerning actions that are appropriate, commendable, and demanded as a redeemed people? What do sacred Scriptures and particular traditions of interpretation contribute to this divine pedagogy within Christianity? What are God's intentions for human life, as the contemporary Christian community discerns them through interaction with the essential resources of our heritage? Do all of the physical, emotional, spiritual, social, and economic aspects of our humanity have the potential to be transformed through God's guidance? How active a role does humanity play in our journey toward wholeness? What impact does the religious community's transformation through God's grace and guidance have upon the larger world?

Christians are not unfamiliar with the idea of commandments and grace working together. The sacraments of Baptism and Holy Communion illustrate this positive connection within Christianity. Jesus commissions his disciples, saying, "Go therefore and make disciples of all nations, baptizing them in the name of the Father and of the Son and of the Holy Spirit, and teaching them to obey everything that I have commanded you" (Matt 28:19-20a). Jesus takes bread, gives thanks, breaks it, and gives it to his disciples, saying, "This is my body that is [broken] for you. Do this in remembrance of me" (1 Cor 11:24; cf. Luke 22:19), and likewise after supper shares the cup, saying, "This cup is the new covenant in my blood. Do this, as often as you drink it, in remembrance of me" (1 Cor 11:25; cf. Luke 22:20).

Christians do not generally consider Jesus' institution of the sacraments in the New Testament as part of God's law. Yet, the New Testament tells us that Jesus issued a command—namely that we "do this"—apply water in the name of the triune God and share bread and wine in remembrance of his last meal and sacrificial death and in anticipation of the coming kingdom. In Christian ears these commandments sound like gracious invitations to newness of life, since the sacraments instituted by Christ become the visible means of an invisible grace. Through the sacraments God works in our lives, redeeming and transforming us into whom we are called to be as adopted sons and daughters of one heavenly Father. In the sacraments, law and gospel, command and salvation, are held together.

Significantly, both baptism and communion have roots in Jewish practice. Immersion in water for purification was a feature of first-century Judaism, and there are some indications that baptism as part of conversion rituals was taken up and given new significance in early Christianity. The Lord's Supper in the Synoptic Gospels (Mark, Matthew, and Luke) takes place during the Passover, and retains connections with this Jewish celebration centered in a ritual meal. Clearly we cannot ignore our dependence on Judaism, since even our sacraments have their origins in practices mandated by Torah!

Within Christian theology, exclusive emphasis on the gospel as what God has graciously done through Christ for the forgiveness and salvation of individual Christians may unintentionally lead to neglect of the role of the human being as a moral agent within the larger community. If Christians remain riveted on God's justifying work through Christ for us as individuals, it may become difficult to direct our attention outward to the neighbor and the world. The focus on justification by faith alone within Lutheranism, for example, is liberating in that it relieves Christians from the fear of not living up to God's high standards, and yet the corresponding deemphasis on human accomplishment may sometimes prove problematic. In light of God's all-sufficient work in Christ and of human bondage to sin, human efforts may appear futile or

Moral passivity and even cooperation with unjust systems of power may ensue when the love and mercy of the gospel consistently trumps the justice that God's law demands. The lack of enthusiasm for systemic justice among many North American Christians is a continuing weakness that needs to be addressed in our age marked by global poverty, the AIDS epidemic, preemptive war, racial discrimination, and ecological crisis.[17] Our understanding of Christian vocation needs to be more vigorous than conscientiously discharging one's duties within the family and society, since this understanding makes us vulnerable to perpetuating structural distortions, inequalities, and even violence. A larger vision of what makes for peace and justice needs to inform our action as Christians, and for this vision we need divine guidance. The two ideals of justice and mercy are not opposites in tension with each other, as is often supposed. To the contrary, for the marginalized and those denied fair opportunities in society, justice is grace.[18]

To transcend what appears to be a characteristic under-valuation of human moral agency and an ineffectiveness in addressing systematic injustice, Christians may draw on the same scriptural resources that have sometimes fostered a critical and active stance within Judaism. These include the Torah's narratives of resistance and liberation, as well as other scriptural calls to justice and wholeness found in biblical laws, wisdom literature, and prophetic writings. As Christians come to appreciate the Jewish understanding of Torah, they can recover valuable dimensions of our common biblical tradition that cultivate an active life of justice seeking, social critique, and community service.

Jesus himself builds on this scriptural foundation when he summarizes the essence of the Torah and the prophets with the dual commandment to "love the Lord your God with all your heart, and with all your soul, and with all your mind" and to "love your neighbor as yourself" (Matt 22:37-40). In this teaching, he quotes Deut 6:5 and Lev 19:18. Jesus gives substance to these overarching principles from the Torah at many points, such as when he states his expectation that his followers feed the hungry, give drink to the thirsty, welcome the stranger, clothe the naked, and visit the sick and those in prison (Matt 25:31-46).

In the Sermon on the Mount, Jesus emphatically asserts that he comes not to abolish the law and the prophets, but to fulfill them. Continuing in the tradition of Moses, he interprets the Torah in his ethical instruction of his disciples. He exhorts them to go beyond conscientious obedience to the commandments, including those against murder, adultery, and taking the name of the LORD in vain, so that not only in their behavior but also in their interior disposition toward their neighbor they will "be perfect, as your heavenly Father is perfect" (Matt 5:48). Jesus sharpens the demands of the Torah when he tells his followers that their righteousness must exceed even that of the scribes and even presumptuous attempts at works righteousness, since they suggest that something still remains to be done to achieve God's favor.

This negative attitude toward human initiative and endeavor is exceedingly discordant to the American spirit, which celebrates free choice, individual responsibility, and effective action. It also misses some of the most compelling aspects of Christianity. In point of fact, most Christians, including among them Martin Luther and the Lutherans named after him, have placed a high value on certain modes of charitable and ethical behavior in the world, not as a means to salvation but as a response to the gospel. As forgiven and justified sinners, acting freely out of gratitude and love and not merely out of a fear of punishment or the burden of duty, Christians in all walks of life are called to love and serve their neighbors. Christian vocation, or ministry in daily life within the family and community, is a blessed opportunity to give personal witness to the good news of God's active presence in our lives and in the world.[15]

Luther himself could hardly be charged with antinomianism, or being against the law, since he considered even the political law of governments also as divinely given to perform a variety of functions, including ensuring justice, preserving order, and securing peace. While Augustine emphasized that Christians are citizens of the City of God, Luther asserted that Christians are citizens of two kingdoms, the temporal and the eternal. Because of this position, Lutherans have not kept themselves separate from the larger society in which they find themselves, but rather have been actively involved in all occupations and institutions as possible contexts for Christian vocation. This involvement has many positive aspects, since it frees Christians to pursue God's will for altruistic and responsible behavior in interaction with the larger culture. Such involvement also requires vigilance, however. Sometimes respect for governmental authority as a God-willed check on antisocial actions has made Christians far too easy to govern.

Luther himself reminded rulers and citizens alike that they were to remain faithful to God's will and serve as instruments of that will. At times, however, uncritical obedience to state power by Christians has had appalling consequences. The most heinous case in the context of Jewish-Christian relations is of course the annihilation of six million European Jews during World War II. In this grim context there were instances of heroic resistance by Christians that deserve to be recognized. Yet the fact that the Holocaust was conceived and organized in Germany, Luther's homeland and a center of the Christian world, and that many European Christians remained silent or even became participants in this genocide compels us to reexamine how our doctrinal emphases shape our attitudes and behavior with respect to corrupt and evil power structures.[16]

Pharisees (Matt 5:20). This messianic heightening of behavioral norms can be observed also elsewhere in first-century Judaism. For example, the ascetic community responsible for the Dead Sea Scrolls found at Qumran similarly viewed itself as living in the end times before God's kingdom, and hence they required heightened moral standards.

In addition to ethical teachings such as these, Jesus also provides a model for Christian behavior through his own life and death. His encounters with the poor, the outcast, the foreigner, and the sinner show us how to treat each other. The cross itself most clearly exemplifies a life of transforming selflessness and refusal to return violence for violence. The love for one another that Jesus teaches and embodies goes beyond positive emotions toward the neighbor. It calls for a commitment of one's entire life to building up the community through concrete acts.

Christians do not need to surrender our traditional emphasis on the good news that even non-Jews have been called to be part of God's people, even as we endeavor to respond to Jesus' summons to become his disciples, to obey his commandments, to imitate his actions, and to embody the interpretations of the Torah that he imparted to his disciples and to the whole church. For Christians, Christ is a source both of salvation and of divine guidance for the Christian life. A post-communion prayer in the *Lutheran Book of Worship* captures the dual aspect of Christ the God's word: "Almighty God, you gave your Son both as a sacrifice for sin and as a model of the godly life. Enable us to receive him always with thanksgiving and to conform our lives to his; through the same Jesus Christ our Lord. Amen."[19]

Just as Paul and Luther reconsidered the significance of God's law within their own particular moments in history, Christians in the twenty-first century can boldly reconsider the theological significance of the law as divine guidance for human life in our global community. Ours is time of moral confusion and competing claims for how to live, in which concerns such as national security, the global economy, and personal comfort threaten to eclipse all other values. God's guidance can foster an alternative community with the power to address the ravaging effects of our age on individuals, societies, and the environment.

We cannot face these challenges alone, as individual believers. Christ himself clearly calls his followers to a distinctive way of being and acting as a community in the world that anticipates and manifests God's kingdom of justice, peace, and compassion. To speak of God's reign or kingdom as Jesus does is to use the language of government, so that Christian life involves not only individual salvation but also wider social and political considerations. Without doubt, in our many areas of common concern, Jews and Christians will find ample opportunities for cooperation.

New appreciation for the positive guidance that God provides does not mean that Christians should begin to observe all Jewish laws, festivals, and customs. In fact, such a development would be inappropriate and offensive to our Jewish neighbors. To take a concrete example, the practice of holding "Christian seders" is problematic, since our sacred meal is the Eucharist, not Passover. Judaism and Christianity have developed into two distinctive faith traditions over the centuries, and care should be taken not to trespass on each other's holy ground. Christians have a distinctive understanding of God's guidance for their lives, rooted in Israelite and early Jewish faith and practice, centered in the person, teaching, and example of Jesus Christ in continuity with those early roots, and evolving over centuries of discernment within the history and practice of a church in which the Spirit is still working. Christians are called to be a distinctive community, a people set apart for service in the world and joyful obedience to God's commandments, in a way that is different from the Jewish community. We have a unique witness concerning both God's salvation and God's intention for us as individuals and communities, so that we may be all that we are created to be in God's graciousness.

Reassessment of the Christian theological concept of the law in our time provides an opportunity to correct problematic aspects of our own tradition, to enter into a more respectful and appreciative relationship with our sister religion Judaism, and to clarify and revitalize our own Christian faith and witness in the world. Giving thanks to God for the potential of this particular moment in history with its unique promises and challenges, the Christian community can rely on the good news of God's forgiveness, salvation, and gracious guidance, given for abundant life and for the blessing of all creation.

Response

Krister Stendahl

Why do I think that the habit of interpreting Scripture in the pattern of "law and gospel" is the issue for Lutherans when it comes to Jewish-Christian relations? The long and tragic history of Christian contempt for the Jews has been driven by many different perceptions and slogans: Christ killers, or even God killers; the demonizing of the Pharisees; interpreting the fall of the Jerusalem Temple as God's punishment of the Jews for the crucifixion; and the like. That those are offensive to our Jewish neighbors is obvious, but when we speak and think in law/gospel language, our intentions are far from denigrating anyone. But intentions are less important than the unintended yet real effect: a not-so-subtle source for antisemitism.

How can that be? It is very simple. When the law is persistently seen and experienced in contrast to the trumping gospel, then the Jews become unavoidably Exhibit A of the wrong way to approach God. Jews must feel that as an insult, if not as a sacrilege. For, as this chapter reminds us, the law is the pride and joy of the Jewish community.

It has also become a habit among us to use "gospel" as a code word for Christianity. Then one forgets easily that our Bible is the whole Bible with its first thirty-nine books much more than the dark background to its second part's twenty-seven. (That is the downside to the recently introduced term "The Hebrew Bible.")

This chapter raises some warning flags, but it also suggests ways in which the precious insights, which our tradition came to popularize as "law and gospel," can be cleansed from implicit and explicit denigration of Jews and Judaism. We need to sharpen our ears to when and how that happens, and there is a safe way of doing that: now and then, check with the local rabbi how he or she hears what you are thinking or saying—especially what you are preaching or hearing in a sermon.

Come to think about it, there are many books in our New Testament that do not see the drama of our faith as one of sin-guilt-forgiveness-justification. They are composed in other keys. It is important to give them their due to receive the fullness of the faith. Take, for example, the Johannine writings, where we do not even find the word justification. *Here it is all about* life. *It is about the restoration of that full life that God wanted for us, even in his image—the image now so sorely tarnished but not destroyed. "I came that they may have life, and have it abundantly" (John 10:10); "I am the way, and the truth, and the life" (John 14:6); "In [the Word] was life, and the life was the light of all people" (John 1:4). And think of the final vision in the book of Revelation, "At the river of the water of life" stood "the tree of life . . . and the leaves of the tree are for the healing of the nations" (Rev 22:1-2). And to the preachers I say: Try now and then to preach in that key, and let it sound like John. It will enrich your theology and enliven the faith of our community.*

4

•

Promise and Fulfillment

Ralph W. Klein
in Conversation with Isaac Kalimi

Promise and fulfillment[1] are characteristic activities of the God of the Bible and are richly in evidence in both testaments of the Christian biblical canon. Promise and fulfillment are ways of talking about God's faithfulness and reliability, demonstrated in words and saving actions in the past, and hoped for and trusted in for the present and the future. Christians see fulfillment of God's promises in the life, death, and resurrection of Jesus and in the existence and preservation of the Christian church. Promise and fulfillment are ideas about God held in common by Christians and Jews, but they have also often been a source of division and offense when Christian claims for fulfillment give the impression that God's faithfulness and presence are not experienced among Jews and in Judaism. This essay will explore the theme of promise and fulfillment within the Old Testament[2] and how the theme of promise and fulfillment plays out in the relationship of the two testaments. It will do so in order to clarify the limits and the legitimacy of the New Testament claims. Such a clarification is important for Jewish-Christian understanding. I thank my Jewish colleague and friend Isaac Kalimi for discussing this essay with me and suggesting a number of ways for its improvement.

PROMISE AND FULFILLMENT IN GENESIS

Two promises dominate in the stories of Israel's ancestors, Sarah and Abraham: land and descendants. The LORD's first word to Abram is: "Go from your country and your kindred and your ancestral home [NRSV: 'father's house'] to the *land* that I will show you. I will make of you a great *nation*" (Gen 12:1-2).[3] Before Abraham and Sarah can become parents of a great nation they have to start with one child of their own, but this first promise is delayed for a long time and even doubted by them. Abraham and Sarah considered adopting their servant Eliezer in an attempt to help God out in fulfilling this promise (Gen 15:1-3), and Abraham actually engendered a child by the Egyptian maid Hagar in a dubious attempt to bring about the promise's fulfillment (Genesis 16). But Abram believed when God promised him as many children as the stars (Gen 15:5-6).[4] Sarah finally conceived and bore Isaac when both she and Abram were very old, beyond reproductive age. Through this birth the LORD did for Sarah as he had promised (Gen 21:1-2).

The promise of land is also delayed; in fact, its fulfillment lies on the other side of four centuries of servitude in Egypt (Gen 15:13-16).[5] The only land that the ancestors themselves owned was a burial plot, the cave of Machpelah, where Sarah and Abraham, Rebekah and Isaac, and Leah and Jacob are buried.[6] Each time an ancestor is buried in the cave of Machpelah is a kind of mini-fulfillment of the land promise and at the same time a reaffirmation of the land promise itself. Only after the conquest under Joshua and the distribution of the land (Joshua 1–21) can the narrator proclaim: "Thus the LORD gave to Israel all the land that he swore to their ancestors. . . . Not one of all the good promises that the LORD had made to the house of Israel had failed; all came to pass" (Josh 21:43, 21:45).

THE PROMISE OF A LINE OF PROPHETS . . . AND A FUTURE PROPHET

The book of Deuteronomy hails Moses as a prophet and accompanies that affirmation with a distinctive understanding of his prophetic role. At Horeb, Deuteronomy's name for Sinai, Israel found the divine voice that spoke the Ten Commandments unbearably frightening and begged Moses in the future to listen to the LORD himself and then hand on, or mediate, that word of God to the people (Deut 5:23-31; cf. Exod 20:18-19). The prophet, therefore, in Deuteronomy's view, is a person who hears the word of God and announces it to the people. This understanding of prophecy is put in the form of a promise in Deut 18:15, 18:18: "The LORD your God will raise up for you [again and again[7]] a prophet like me from among your own people; you shall listen to [NRSV: 'heed'] such a prophet. . . . I shall put my words in the mouth of the prophet, who shall speak to them everything that I command." The Deutero-nomic theologians in the seventh century no doubt thought that prophets like Moses could be seen in people such as Elijah, Amos, Hosea, Isaiah, Micah, and Jeremiah. These and other similar prophets were fulfillments of the promise made to Moses.

But a later writer[8] recognized a disjuncture: however good Elijah, Isaiah, and the rest had been, they were not quite up to the standards of Moses. He recorded his misgivings in Deut 34:10-11 (my translation): "Never since has there arisen a prophet in Israel like Moses, whom the LORD knew face to face. Moses was unequaled for all the signs and wonders that he did in Egypt, against Pharaoh and all his servants." This verse recognizes that the line of prophets was at best a partial fulfillment of the prophet like Moses, and therefore this verse gives the promise of Deuteronomy 18 a new, far more eschatological significance. If the LORD had promised to raise a prophet like Moses, and yet had not yet fully done so, the ultimate fulfillment of Deuteronomy 18 still lay in the future.

Postbiblical Judaism expected such an eschatological prophet.[9] When Judas the Maccabee restored the Temple after its desecration by Antiochus, the people tore down the polluted altar and stored the stones in a convenient place until "a prophet" should come and tell them what to do with them (1 Macc 4:46). When Simon the Maccabee was installed as high priest, they decided that his term should last forever, or at least until "a trustworthy prophet" should arise (1 Macc 14:41). The people who wrote the Dead Sea Scrolls expected two messiahs and an eschatological prophet. "They shall govern themselves using the original precepts by which the men of the *Yahad* [community] began to be instructed, doing so until there come the Prophet and the Messiahs of Aaron and Israel" (Rule of the Community 9:10-11).

Early Christians capitalized on this promise of an eschatological prophet and saw in Jesus a fulfillment of the prophet like Moses. When Jesus fed five thousand, the people said, "This is indeed the prophet who is to come into the world" (John 6:14).[10] The feeding of the five thousand resembled Moses' feeding Israel with manna in the wilderness. In a sermon in the book of Acts Peter proclaimed that God had raised Jesus from the dead and added: "Moses said, 'The Lord your God will raise[11] up for you from your own people a prophet like me. You must listen to whatever he tells you. . . .' When God raised up his servant, he sent him first to you, to bless you by turning each of you from your wicked ways" (Acts 3:22, 3:26). Early Christians tried to live out another prophetic word from the book of Deuteronomy when they held all things in common (Acts 4:32). After all, had not Moses said that there should be no poor among you (Deut 15:4)?[12]

PROPHECIES THAT "FAILED"

What if God promises something and it does not happen? Deuteronomy proposes this as one criterion for distinguishing between true and false prophets. "You may say to yourself, 'How can we recognize a word that the LORD has not spoken?' If a prophet speaks in the name of the LORD but the thing does not take place or prove true, it is a word that the LORD has not spoken" (Deut 18:21-22).[13] Many of the prophets whose words of judgment are now contained in the biblical canon were proved true by the Assyrian and Babylonian invasions of 722/721 and 587/586 B.C.E. Even in the best circumstances, however, this is not the most useful criterion for distinguishing between true and false prophecy since a person may need to decide what to do in the very near future and cannot wait to find out whether history will vindicate or falsify the word of the prophet.

When God or a prophet makes a promise, however, it is always a risky business since trying to tell how history will turn out is like aiming at a moving target. In 587 B.C.E. the prophet Ezekiel announced that Nebuchadrezzar would bring judgment on the island city of Tyre (Ezek 26:7-21). Some sixteen years later Ezekiel revised that prophecy. Despite a lengthy, thirteen-year siege, Nebuchadrezzar had little to show for his attack on Tyre. Now Ezekiel announced that God would instead give Nebuchadrezzar a victory over Egypt since Nebuchadrezzar had "worked" for God in bringing judgment against Judah and Jerusalem (Ezek 29:17-20). Walther Zimmerli described this as the faithfulness and freedom of the LORD: faithful to his word of reward to Nebuchadnezzar, but free to adapt it to the changed circumstances of history after Tyre's stubborn defense.

At other times prophecies may have a partial fulfillment that leaves an expectation that God will someday carry out the still outstanding details of his promise. The promise of a new exodus from Babylon in Second Isaiah may be a case in point. Second Isaiah opens with a divine address to the heavenly council, telling them to give comfort to Jerusalem that had already received twice as much punishment as it had coming (Isa 40:1-2). A second voice from the divine council gives orders to other angelic beings to build a superhighway from Babylon to Jerusalem, with leveling of mountains, filling in valleys, and taking out the "S" curves. God would make an appearance during that new exodus as a witness to all the nations (Isa 40:3-5). A related passage in Isaiah 35 announces a concomitant renewal of handicapped human beings and almost a new creation: the blind will see, the deaf will hear, the lame will leap, the tongue of the speechless will sing, and water will break out in the desert.

In the years following the Persian takeover of Babylon some Jews did return from Babylon, with Cyrus' permission and encouragement, and they even rebuilt the Temple, but the numbers were relatively small,[14] the new Temple was disappointing to many who had known Solomon's Temple (Ezra 3:12-13), and the community was faced with inner divisions (see Isaiah 56–66). There surely was no "interstate" from Babylon to Jerusalem, no revitalized desert, and no wholesale healing of people with handicaps within Israel.

The people who wrote the Dead Sea Scrolls saw a fulfillment of this prophecy of Second Isaiah in the establishment of their community. In the Rule of the Community we read: "They shall separate themselves from the session of perverse men to go to the wilderness, there to prepare the way of truth, as it is written [Isa 40:3]: 'In the wilderness prepare the way of the LORD, make straight in the desert a highway for our God'" (1QS 8:13-14). Their refuge by the shore of the Dead Sea was seen as a way of preparing a way in the wilderness.

Matthew, too, used similar exegesis in an attempt to understand the ministry of John the Baptist: "This is the one of whom the prophet Isaiah spoke when he said, 'The voice of one crying out in the wilderness: "Prepare the ways of the Lord, make his paths straight"'" (Matt 3:3).[15] Preparing the way is now interpreted as moral regeneration and not as building a highway through the desert. When John was later thrown in prison, he sent some of his disciples to Jesus and asked: "Are you the one who is to come, or are we to wait for another?" Jesus answered: "Go and tell John what you hear and see: the blind receive their sight, the lame walk, the lepers are cleansed, the deaf hear, the dead are raised, and the poor have good news brought to them" (Matt 11:3-4). Jesus' answer to John is "Yes, I am the one who is to come," but it is couched in words that see in his miracles of healing and in his identification with the poor a fulfillment of the promises in Isaiah 35 and 40.[16] Thus both some Jews and early Christians identified additional fulfillments of Isaiah's words in the things they had experienced, beyond those experienced in the immediate decades after the ministry of Second Isaiah.

In considering Old Testament promises, one must also consider the possibility that some promises from the beginning were meant metaphorically, and not literally. Ezekiel's vision of the new Temple in 40:1—44:3 seems to assign symbolic meanings to the various measurements of the Temple and the sacred area of the land, with the sealed east gate indicating that the LORD would never again leave the Temple. Similarly his description of the new boundaries of the land and the tribal portions in 47:13—48:29 stresses a separation from the territory of Transjordan that was always more vulnerable to apostasy. This metaphorical description of the land assigned equality of size and power to each of the twelve tribes, with some advantage to those tribes descended from the wives instead of the concubines of Jacob, and with the whole land centered on the temple and the regions of the priests and Levites. The stream that comes from the Temple and renews the Judean wilderness and brings a multitude of the fish to the Dead Sea in 47:1-12 is designed to show that when the LORD is present with his people there is nothing impervious to change. Such promises are open to multiple fulfillments. In the Gospel of John, the body of Jesus is identified with the Temple (2:19-21), and the stream of water flowing from his side at the crucifixion (19:34) could be seen as analogous to the stream of water Ezekiel saw.

THE PROMISED MESSIAH

Many Christians who undertake critical biblical studies are surprised at the relative infrequency of the messianic hope in the Old Testament[17] and how the initial significance of these passages in their Old Testament contexts is quite different from their interpretation in the New Testament and subsequent Christian theology. Study of the messianic motif in the Old Testament discloses a transition from an expectation of a new or better king of the Davidic line in the very near future, to the development of a more eschatological expectation of a messianic figure, and finally to further transformation of this hope in subsequent Jewish and Christian theologies.

At the base of all messianic expectations in the Old Testament is the oracle of Nathan in 2 Samuel 7. There the LORD turned aside on principle David's offer to build a house (temple) for the LORD, stating that he had been content to move about in a tent or tabernacle, only to authorize David's son (Solomon) to build the Temple. The LORD also promised to make David's house and kingdom sure and to establish his throne forever. In its final form the oracle of Nathan gives a ringing endorsement to the Davidic dynastic house. Even if individuals in that line would commit iniquity and require punishment, the LORD promised not to take his steadfast love from this dynasty as he had taken it away from Saul.

The theological and political power of this oracle played a major role in the preservation of the Davidic dynasty over a four-century period. But the surety of this promise also played a role in the dynasty's weakest moments, and especially when it ceased to rule, for prophets concluded that this promise was still valid and would lead either to a replacement king or eventually to a figure who might be called an eschatological messiah. While the noun *messiah* (מָשִׁיחַ—"anointed one") is used some thirty-nine times in the Hebrew text, it is never used as a technical term in the Old Testament "messianic" passages as a designation for the future king.

Space permits us to look at only a few of the Old Testament passages dealing with the Messiah.[18] Passages dealing with a future king in First Isaiah are of uncertain meaning, or of uncertain date—or both. In Isaiah 7 the prophet Isaiah attempted to get King Ahaz to trust in the LORD for deliverance from the invading Syrian and Ephraimite forces, but, as we learn from the narrative history of Ahaz, the king eventually ignored this advice and sent a bribe to Tiglath-pileser III, the king of Assyria, to persuade him to attack Damascus and force the withdrawal of Syria and Ephraim from their attack on Jerusalem

(2 Kings 16). Isaiah offered to give Ahaz a sign, apparently to indicate God's readiness to intervene on his behalf, but Ahaz declined and said that he did not want to put God to the test. Isaiah interpreted this as a hypocritical excuse and decided to give Ahaz a sign anyway: "That young woman [over there] is with child and will bear a son, and shall name him Immanuel" (Isa 7:14). It is generally agreed today that the mother-to-be in question was not a virgin, but which woman Isaiah had in mind is unclear and casts some doubt on whether this should be considered a messianic passage at all. While there are many proposals about this woman's identity, the two most common suggestions are that she was the wife of Isaiah or the wife of Ahaz. If the woman is Ms. Isaiah, Immanuel would be the third child she would bear with a role in Isaiah's ministry—see Shear-jashub ("the remnant will return") in Isa 7:3 and Maher-shalal-hash-baz ("the spoil speeds, the prey hastens") in Isa 8:3. Perhaps a majority of scholars believe that the woman is indeed the wife of Ahaz so that the child to be born would be of the royal line. In neither interpretation, however, is the child hailed as a future king with specific responsibilities, and the sign offered by Isaiah may be nothing other than the child's name, Immanuel, meaning "God is with us." This name itself could be good news or bad. It would be good news if God's presence would mean deliverance from the invading forces, or bad news if God were coming in judgment. The positive connotation appears in Isa 7:16 and 8:10 and the negative connotation in Isa 7:17 and 8:8.

A second passage in Isaiah seems to refer to a new son born in the royal household whose birth indicates the continued effectiveness and validity of the promise to David (Isa 9:2-7). The passage speaks of this king's authority and just rule, but the most significant thing about him is his name, traditionally translated as "Wonderful Counselor, Mighty God, Everlasting Father, Prince of Peace" (Isa 9:6). The name itself is unusual for at least three reasons: (1) Israelite kings normally do not have a series of four names; (2) Hebrew names are usually sentences and not attributes; and (3) it would be very unusual in the Old Testament to infer that the king had godly status. I prefer to translate the name, therefore, as two sentences: "The mighty God is planning a wonder; the everlasting Father is planning a captain of peace."[19] That is, this name, like that of Immanuel, points to God's support of the king, just as the last line of this pericope affirms: "The zeal of the LORD of hosts will see to it that this will happen." Strangely, this verse is not cited in the New Testament as a prophecy fulfilled in Jesus.[20]

A third messianic passage in Isaiah is 11:1-9 (cf. also a series of supplements to this promise in vv. 10-16). This passage seems to presuppose the end of the Davidic dynasty or at least it predicts that end. It speaks of the stump of Jesse, meaning that the dynastic tree associated with David has been cut down. From that stump of Jesse will sprout a branch or shoot, that is, a new

David will arise. This new king will be endowed with the divine spirit, as were the first two kings, Saul and David (Isa 11:2). All subsequent kings ascended the throne not by virtue of their being endowed with the divine spirit, but because they were descended from David. The new king promised in Isaiah 11 will be a righteous judge, an advocate for the poor and weak (Isa 11:3-5), and his reign will usher in an era of nonviolence, symbolized by wolves living with lambs, leopards with young goats, and the like (Isa 11:6-9).

Two passages from Jeremiah will round out this brief survey of the messianic hope of the Old Testament. I think Jer 23:5-6 is from the prophet himself, although there are many dissenters from this dating. Jeremiah speaks of the LORD's promise to raise up a "righteous Branch," perhaps better translated as "legitimate heir." If the latter translation is correct, this promised new king would be an apt replacement for Zedekiah, a puppet king installed by Nebuchadnezzar after his attack on Jerusalem in 597 B.C.E.[21] The new king's reign, as in Isaiah 11, would be marked by justice and righteousness. Again, the king receives a new name: "The LORD is our righteousness," or, perhaps better, "The LORD is the source of our vindication." Either translation shows, as in the three Isaiah passages, that divine aid is the basis for the king's real strength. The Hebrew for this name (יהוה צדקנו) would seem to be a pun on Zedekiah (צדקיהו) with the two elements in Zedekiah's name in reverse order. It seems likely to me that Jeremiah is talking about a replacement for Zedekiah in the near future and not yet about an eschatological figure.

A second messianic passage, in Jer 33:14-16, is secondary since verses 14-26 are not included in the Septuagint, the second century B.C.E. translation of the Bible into Greek. Its secondary character is confirmed by literary critical judgments, namely, that the territory envisioned in this promise is much smaller—Judah and Jerusalem instead of Judah and Israel—and because the name is applied not to the new king himself, but to the city of Jerusalem.[22] The longer pericope in verses 14-26 presupposes that alongside the unbroken Davidic line will be an unbroken line of levitical priests, and that God will have an unbreakable covenant with each line. This passage is especially interesting because it shows the further development in some circles of Jeremiah's idea of a replacement for King Zedekiah with the notion of a an unbroken line of Davidides and an unbroken line of levitical priests.[23] The promise continues—and changes.

Before turning to the New Testament, we need to note that some passages dealing with reigning Israelite kings came to be read in late Old Testament times with messianic significance. I am thinking especially of the royal psalms (Psalms 2, 45, 72, 89, and 110). These psalms originally dealt with issues such as coronation, the righteous rule of kings, the marriage of the king, or the theological consequences of the king's defeat. Once Israel no longer had a king, it seems likely that many believers read these psalms messianically, that is, as referring to a future king rather than a contemporaneous king.

JESUS AS CHRIST/MESSIAH IN THE NEW TESTAMENT

One of the central affirmations of the New Testament is that Jesus is the fulfillment of Israel's messianic hope. The Greek word *Christ* is a translation of the Hebrew word *messiah*. Before we look at specific passages, however, I would like to rephrase what I said in the first sentence of this paragraph. One of the central affirmations of the New Testament is that Jesus is the fulfillment, *and radical reinterpretation of,* Israel's messianic hope. I note four changes that are significant departures from the messianic hope that began in the Old Testament and had developed further in early Judaism:[24]

1. The New Testament makes the death of Jesus one of his most significant features. That death, of course, has multiple interpretations in the New Testament, but all of the New Testament writers find deep meaning in his death (and resurrection). There is not a single Jewish text, in or out of the Old Testament canon, however, that talks about the saving significance of the death of the Messiah. In fact, the only mention of the death of the Messiah occurs in 2 Esdras 7:2-30, where at the end of the age, we are told that all will die, including the Messiah, and then the end will come. St. Paul was well aware of this departure from Jewish thought when he wrote: "We proclaim Christ [Messiah] crucified, a stumbling block to Jews and foolishness to Gentiles, but to those who are the called, both Jews and Greeks, Christ the power of God and the wisdom of God" (1 Cor 1:23-24). Christians therefore should not be surprised if Jews have a different expectation of the character or even fate of the Messiah.

2. While there are varying Christologies in the New Testament, some higher than others, Jesus is widely identified as Lord, a figure to be worshipped, and he is identified, in one sense or another, as Son of God. Although the doctrine of the Trinity is not fully developed in the New Testament, there are clearly movements in that direction, specifically with regard to the role of Jesus as Son. Again the Old Testament totally lacks references to the divinity of the Messiah, and where it has been detected by some, as in Isa 9:6, I believe this is based on a faulty translation of the passage (see the discussion above).

3. The New Testament does see the new (messianic) age breaking in with Jesus. His miracles are the signs of that age, and Paul sees his resurrection as the first fruits of the new age (1 Cor 15:20). And yet the New

Testament also speaks of Jesus' second coming and affirms that the new age is "already and not yet." This distinction between already and not yet, between a new messianic age that is partially but not wholly present, is again a radical departure from the view of the Old Testament itself and early Judaism. This adjustment of the promise to fit the realities of history is not different in kind from adjustments we saw in the prophecies of Ezekiel and Second Isaiah as history changed.

4. The New Testament conflates a number of expected figures from the Old Testament in its depictions of Jesus. Jesus is Messiah/Christ, but he is also the prophet, servant, Son of Humanity, the incarnate *logos*, and even Melchizedek.

THIS TOOK PLACE TO FULFILL . . .

Christians from the beginning have seen in Jesus the "Yea and Amen" to all of God's promises (cf. 2 Cor 1:20). Also from the beginning they had to account for a number of features about Jesus that must at first have been very surprising, even offensive to many of them. Clearly, Jesus' closest disciples had trouble at first dealing with his death and interpreting the reality and significance of his resurrection. As decades wore on, the separation from mainstream Judaism and the separate existence of the church were theological issues in need of interpretation and justification. But it is clear that the early Christians saw the gospel of Jesus as continuing the redeeming work of the God of the Old Testament. They searched the Scriptures they had (= the Old Testament), as Jesus had urged them (Luke 24:27, 24:32), with the expectation that these Scriptures would confirm the message of Jesus and help them to understand who he was and who they now were. Their search was undertaken as first-century people, using exegetical methods at home in the world of Judaism. Their search was also undertaken in contentious, even polemical times as the conflict with Judaism increased. Their speaking of fulfillment was usually an attempt to affirm continuity with the Old Testament past and with full acceptance of its authority. The last thing they thought they were doing was starting a new religion. We need to keep this in mind as we discuss fulfillment in the New Testament, realizing that modern Christians might draw lines of continuity with the Old Testament in different ways and with more current methods of interpretation. This is not to say that the exegetical methods of the New Testament writers were wrong, but only that their methods were part of antiquity and need to be understood both sympathetically and critically by readers of the New Testament today. But it also means that Christians should not be surprised that Jews see the promises of their Bible, the Tanakh, fulfilled in different ways, or still waiting to be fulfilled.

SOME NEW TESTAMENT FULFILLMENTS

We have noted that early Christians sought to understand the significance of the life and ministry of Jesus by interpreting the Scriptures of their time (what we would call the Old Testament). Thus they often started with a tenet of their faith and moved backwards, attempting to find a promise in the Old Testament of what they had experienced and to interpret what they had experienced as fulfillment of that promise. Christians came to believe, for example, that Jesus was born of the virgin Mary, and that the child conceived in her was through the power of the Holy Spirit (Matt 1:20). They sought to explain this miracle by referring to the Scriptures. Matthew concludes: "All this took place to fulfill what had been spoken by the Lord through the prophet: 'Look, the virgin shall conceive and bear a son, and they shall name him Emmanuel,' which means, 'God is with us'" (Matt 1:23; the biblical allusion is to Isa 7:14).

This type of interpretation resembles in many ways that used in the seventeen or eighteen Pesharim (biblical commentaries) among the Dead Sea Scrolls. The Pesher on Hab 2:2 reads: "When it says, 'so that with ease someone can read it,' this refers to the Teacher of Righteousness to whom God made known all the mysterious revelations of his servants the prophets." Thus Habakkuk, who lived in the late seventh century, is understood as prophesying about the Teacher of Righteousness, who was a leader in the community responsible for the Dead Sea Scrolls in the second century B.C.E. The interpreters who wrote these commentaries assumed that prophetic proclamation dealt with the end times and that they themselves were living in the end times. Hence prophetic proclamation dealt directly with them and their situation. Matthew was apparently schooled in this type of exegesis. A passage written by Isaiah in the heart of the controversies of the eighth century B.C.E. was assumed to have significance about the end times, that is, the era of Jesus. It helped in this case that Matthew was reading the Scriptures in their Greek translation, where the word translated "young woman" by the NRSV was rendered by *parthenos*, the standard Greek word for "virgin." Matthew would also have been pleased that the child's name from Isa 7:14, Emmanuel ("God is with us") fit so well with his understanding of the significance of the birth of Jesus. The virgin birth of Jesus therefore was seen in continuity with the message of Isaiah and hailed as "fulfillment." Thanks to the comparison with the Pesharim of the Dead Sea Scrolls we can now understand better how and why Matthew wrote this way. But just as the Pesher on Habakkuk cited above does not determine the meaning of Habakkuk in the seventh century B.C.E., so Matthew's understanding of Isa 7:14 does not determine what the prophet was trying to say in his eighth-century B.C.E. context.

When King Herod's mad policies threatened the infant Jesus, Joseph was warned in a dream to take Mary and Jesus and flee to Egypt and to stay there until the death of Herod. Matthew observes: "This was to fulfill what had been spoken by the Lord through the prophet, 'Out of Egypt I have called my son'" (Matt 2:15).

Matthew refers here to Hos 11:1, but modern readers of Hosea soon learn that Matthew's understanding of this verse was not that of the eighth-century prophet. In Hosea, "Out of Egypt I called my son"[25] referred to the exodus of Israel from Egypt, which was taken as evidence for God's election of Israel as his child and God's support of Israel right from the beginning. The next verse in Hosea confirms this understanding because the prophet claims that despite this early benefaction Israel had proven to be disobedient and had pursued Baals and idols throughout its history. The original context in Hosea, therefore, takes the exodus as a starting point for a history of disobedience, surely the last thing that Matthew would want to say about Jesus! Modern readers of the Bible assume that context and original setting determine a text's meaning; that is not an assumption shared by Matthew or by the persons who wrote the Pesharim at Qumran. For Matthew the successful flight of the infant Jesus was evidence for the faithfulness of God to his promises, which led him to read Hos 11:1 in an eschatological context. In Matthew in general the life of Jesus often recapitulates the history of Israel. The Sermon on the Mount presents analogies to the revelations Moses received from God on Mt. Sinai.

Christians today can share Matthew's conviction that the rescue of Jesus provides evidence of the faithfulness of God, and Christians today can affirm that the faith of the Old Testament has continuities with the faith of Christians. If we were today trying to demonstrate this faithfulness or these continuities by allusions to the Old Testament, we would express them with exegetical methods appropriate to our time. A historical-critical understanding of Hosea 11 offers a possible resource for Christian theologians. As that chapter proceeds, the disobedience of Israel leads to divine exasperation. Despite lavish divine parental care, Israel seems locked in behavior designed to lead to judgment. But God in Hosea 11 wrestles with conflicted feelings. Disappointment in Israel's behavior comes into conflict with divine parental loyalty: "How can I give you up, Ephraim? How can I hand you over, O Israel? . . . I will not execute my fierce anger; I will not again destroy Ephraim; for I am God and no mortal" (Hos 11:8-9). The doctrine of retribution insists that sin must be followed by punishment, but the God of Hosea 11 states that he is not bound by the rules of retribution. The happy contradiction between God's anger and God's love, in which the latter wins out—so central to the Christian understanding of the faith—is also a central conviction of the prophet Hosea. A modern Matthew could hail this as promise and fulfillment or at least as a significant theological continuity.

PROMISE AND FULFILLMENT AS THE BOND BETWEEN THE TESTAMENTS

The earliest Christians had only what is now called the Old Testament as their Scriptures. Later the New Testament books came to have similar canonical authority for the church. Lines of continuity with the God and the faith of the Old Testament could be expressed in a number of ways, including promise and fulfillment. Promise and fulfillment is a time-tested and widely held understanding of the relationship between the testaments. Luke's picture of Jesus with the disciples on the way to Emmaus is a typical example of this approach: "Then beginning with Moses and all the prophets, he interpreted to them the things about himself in all the scriptures" (Luke 24:27).

Some Christians, even in modern times, have denied that continuity. The prominent New Testament scholar Rudolf Bultmann thought the Old Testament was a shattering failure and wrote: "How far, then, does Old Testament Jewish history represent prophecy fulfilled in the history of the New Testament community? It is fulfilled in its inner contradiction, its miscarriage. . . . [F]aith requires the backward glance into Old Testament history as a history of failure, *and so of promise*,[26] in order to know that the situation of the justified man arises only on the basis of this miscarriage."[27] In the same context Bultmann also referred to "the false way of salvation which we find in the law." Despite his many illuminating comments on the New Testament, Bultmann had a blind spot in his understanding of the Old Testament and did not adequately recognize the strong lines of continuity in the theological affirmations of both testaments.

Promise and fulfillment is a welcome way to express that continuity. But this assertion too is capable of misunderstandings. We have seen that prophecies in the Old Testament can have multiple fulfillments. Second Isaiah's word about the end of the exile had an immediate, partial fulfillment in the Jews who returned to Jerusalem in the early Persian period. But there were still aspects of that prophecy that cried out for more ultimate fulfillment, as seen for example in the Dead Sea Scrolls and in the New Testament's interpretation of John the Baptist. Christians need to recognize that Jewish sisters and brothers see evidence for the faithfulness of God, and therefore for fulfillment of God's ancient promises, in the oral revelation recorded in the Talmud, in the land of Israel, and in the ongoing presence of God in the lives of Jews and Judaism. What Christians and Jews hail as fulfillments refer back to the promises of the same God.

The New Testament is not only fulfillment. It also contains promises and prophecies that still cry out for fulfillment. From the beginning Christians have prayed, *Maranatha*, "our Lord come" (1 Cor 16:22), looking forward to additional fulfillments of God's promises in the return of Jesus in triumph. Paul's wonderful statement in Gal 3:28 is still in many ways more promise than fulfillment: "There is no longer Jew or Greek, there is no longer slave or free, there is no longer male and female; for all of you are one in Christ Jesus." And what might be the fulfillment of this prophecy of Paul, "And so all Israel will be saved" (Rom 11:26)? The second petition of the Lord's Prayer reads, "Thy kingdom come!" putting future expectation or fulfillment at the heart of the New Testament message.

Contemporary Judaism recognizes that many of God's promises were fulfilled in the life of ancient Israel and in the subsequent history of Judaism. Some of the promises that Christians have seen fulfilled in the life of Jesus, such as the dawning of the messianic age, are seen by them as continuing *and as yet unfulfilled* eschatological expectations.

Promise and fulfillment are indeed important talking points between Jews and Christians. We need to learn to wait together for God's future.

Response

Isaac Kalimi

Over the years I have known Ralph W. Klein I have honored and admired his loyal friendship and fine scholarship. I feel privileged, therefore, to read his paper and respond to it.

All in all, Klein's essay is top quality, and he expresses important and interesting points. I would to add a few notes and stress several further points related to this issue as well as some others:

1. *I would use the term "Hebrew Bible" rather than "Old Testament," at least when it relates to Jews, since the term "Old Testament" can contain negative theological connotations, though definitely Klein does not mean anything negative by using it in his writing.*

2. *From the Christian theological viewpoint, the entire Hebrew Bible/Old Testament is a sort of "promise" (Verheissung) that found its final fulfillment (Erfüllung) in the proper (from the Christian point of view, of course) part of the Scriptures—the New Testament.[28]*

3. *"Promise and Fulfillment" is obvious also in the story concerning the enslavement and exodus—and not only the promise of the land—as promised in Gen 15:13-16 and fulfilled in Exodus 1–15.*

4. *"Promise and Fulfillment" dominate some other stories in the books of Genesis and Exodus:*

   a. *The promise of Eliezer of Damascus to Abraham concerning Isaac's marriage and its fulfillment (Genesis 24).*

   b. *The promise of Joseph and his brothers to Jacob about burial of his body in the cave of Machpelah (Gen 47:28-31; 49:29-33) and its fulfillment (Gen 50:4-14).*

5. *Concerning the problematic issue of including the Old Testament in the Christian canon, see the discussion in Kalimi, "Hebrew Bible/Old Testament: Between Judaism and Christianity," chapter 7, in* Early Jewish Exegesis and Theological Controversy *(see note 28).*

6. *In contemporary times, many Jews believe that the reestablishing of the Jewish State, including the immigration of Jews to Israel from all over the world, is, in fact, fulfillment of the prophecy of Amos (Amos 9:13-15).*

7. *God is devoted to Israel as he promised in Deut 7:9; Isa 54:9-10; 66:22; Jer 2:3; the book of Esther; and as expressed later on in Passover Haggadah. Thus the Jews have continued to exist, in spite of two thousand years of horrible history and the Holocaust![29]*

5

◆

Difficult Texts

Interpreting New Testament Images of Jews and Judaism

Franklin Sherman
in Conversation with Sarah Henrich

Christians are morally obligated to understand the New Testament's harsh words against Jews and Judaism in their original contexts, without translating those polemics into antisemitism.[1]

Ask the average churchgoer whether he or she has ever emerged from a worship service feeling hatred or prejudice toward Jews and Judaism, and the answer will probably be "No." The typical worshipper experiences the Christian faith as a source of compassion toward others, not hatred. Yet a Jewish visitor to such a service might wonder how this could be, if it was a day on which texts such as the following were read out:

> And the doors of the house where the disciples had met were locked for fear of the Jews. (John 20:19)
> Isaiah prophesied rightly about you hypocrites . . . (Mark 7:6)
> All who came before me are thieves and bandits. (John 10:8)
> Then the people as a whole answered, "His blood be on us and on our children." (Matt 27:25)
> Pilate, wanting to release Jesus, addressed them again; but they kept shouting, "Crucify, crucify him!" (Luke 23:20-21)[2]

If such a Jewish guest attended a Bible study session, he or she might learn of yet other New Testament texts with a distinctly anti-Jewish ring. Even if not appointed to be read on a particular Sunday, these other texts also influence

76

the Christian mind. The eighth chapter of the Gospel of John would be an example, where a lengthy interchange between Jesus and "the Jews" culminates in the charge: "You are from your father the devil, and you choose to do your father's desires" (John 8:44).

A study of the epistles would hardly be any more comforting, if one focused on a passage such as 1 Thess 2:14-16, which speaks of "the Jews, who killed both the Lord Jesus and the prophets, and drove us out; they displease God and oppose everyone by hindering us from speaking to the Gentiles so that they may be saved. Thus they have constantly been filling up the measure of their sins; but God's wrath has overtaken them at last."[3]

Texts such as these have helped to form, in the Christian mind down through the centuries, a highly negative and even demonic image of the Jews. The Christian movement was, of course, originally a minority movement within the Jewish context. Once Christianity gained cultural and political dominance, however, starting with the conversion of the emperor Constantine, it did not hesitate to turn upon the faith from which it had taken its birth. As Abraham Joshua Heschel has said, "The children did not arise to call the mother blessed; instead, they called her blind."[4]

Jews, during this long period, were often tolerated and sometimes flourished, but all too frequently were vilified and persecuted. The vehemence of Martin Luther's writings against the Jews and the violence that he recommended be employed against them were, unfortunately, all too typical. The culmination of this whole "history of hate" was the Holocaust, in which Jews were sent to the gas chambers with cries of "Christ killers" ringing in their ears.[5]

In the face of this sad history and the possibility that such "difficult texts" may still be misused today to foster enmity against Jews, and indeed *are* so used by hate groups and propagandists of various kinds, what shall we do with these passages? Some have suggested that they simply be omitted from the New Testament. This, however, would not only contravene the Christian reverence for Scripture but also would violate the integrity of the New Testament, even viewed merely as a set of historical documents. The demons of the past cannot be exorcised so simply.

Another suggestion has been to assign these passages to a subordinate status. In a sense, this has already been done with some of the verses cited above, such as those from John 8 and 1 Thessalonians 2, in that they are not included in the official lectionary (that is, are not appointed to be read on a particular day). One New Testament scholar, Norman A. Beck, has gone further by publishing a translation of the New Testament in which such offensive passages are printed in smaller type, as a clue to the reader to consider them less authoritative.[6] While valuable as a goad to reflection about the issue, this approach, again, is too idiosyncratic to find widespread acceptance.

How, then, shall we understand such passages, and how shall we interpret them?

TYPES OF "ANTI-JEWISH" POLEMIC IN THE NEW TESTAMENT

Not all the language in the New Testament that is negative toward Jews or Judaism is at the same level. George M. Smiga, in his book, *Pain and Polemic: Anti-Judaism in the Gospels*,[7] has made some useful distinctions in this respect. He distinguishes between three types or levels of such criticism, which he calls "prophetic," "subordinating," and "abrogating" polemic. Of these, he notes that the first two are really forms of intra-Jewish self-criticism. Only the third type, Smiga believes, really deserves the name "anti-Judaism" in the sense of objectifying Jews as the "other."

The first type, "prophetic" criticism, is in line with the heritage of courageous critique of the ruling powers that characterized all the Hebrew prophets, a critique that they fearlessly addressed to both the religious and the political establishment, or in other cases to the people as a whole. Indeed, this capacity for criticism-from-within may be regarded as one of the most enduring contributions of the Hebraic heritage not only to Jewish and Christian history, but to secular culture as well. It is in this light that we can view Jesus' forceful denunciations of hypocrisy, self-seeking, and the misuse of power.

A study of Jesus' teachings from this standpoint reveals that a remarkably high proportion of them, whether expressed as parables, wisdom sayings, or connected discourses, are polemical in nature. That is, they have a sharp edge directed against someone. But these teachings are surely not anti-Jewish; indeed, Jesus was never more Jewish than when he engaged in this kind of strenuous critique of his own people and their leaders. It was an example of what would later be called "speaking the truth in love" (Eph 4:15).

"Subordinating" criticism, Smiga's second type, goes further in demanding not only *reform* within a commonly accepted religious framework, but *reformulation* of that framework. In the light of the "new" that is now at hand, everything "old" must be re-visioned. The centrality of Christ gives a new focus to everything that has gone before—but does not deprive it entirely of significance. Torah, Temple, and ritual practice are subordinated to the eschatological reality of the dawning of the messianic age. (The exact nature of that subordination will be grist for the mill of continuing controversy within the new community.)

The third type of criticism, Smiga's "abrogating" polemic, goes beyond a call for reform or reformulation to an outright condemnation of the inherited tradition and those who persist in adhering to it. This involves the kind of "we-they" dynamic that modern sociologists have described as the "objectifying" of the other, in which the opponent loses his or her human face and becomes merely the object of one's hatred. The road is then open for vilification—that is, verbal violence—and, if the power relationships permit, actual violence against the other.

STEPS TOWARD POLARIZATION

Although it is notoriously difficult to unravel the history of early Christianity and read it afresh from the beginning, it is possible that the sequence of developments followed just these three steps. One can surely envision Jesus in his lifetime as exercising an intra-Jewish polemic of the *prophetic* type, motivated by a "tough love" for his people and a divinely given sense of mission to call them to repentance. In the next stage, his death and resurrection provide the traumatic and paradigmatic events that recenter everything around this eschatological fulfillment. What went before may have been valid in its own right but is now seen as only preliminary and preparatory (thus Smiga's term, *subordinating* polemic). In the third and final stage, this contrast is seen as either/or, black or white; two communities are arrayed in conflict, each claiming to be the legitimate heir of God's ancient promises. Only here do developments reach the level of *abrogating* polemic.

In this connection, we need to underline the point that, though a reader of the New Testament might quite naturally assume that the four Gospels represent the earliest stage of development, the Gospels *as written documents* are among the later of the New Testament books. This is true even though they incorporate and build on the earliest traditions of Jesus' life and ministry. Thus they reflect both the first and the third stages of the sequence—Jesus' original "prophetic" polemic and the later "abrogating" polemic. It is in the Pauline letters, which postdate the life of Jesus but predate the composition of the Gospels, where we glimpse the transitional stage. Here we see the new community in Christ struggling to understand the elements of both continuity and discontinuity with its Jewish matrix.

Paul's letter to the Romans is especially instructive in this respect. The first part of the letter culminates in chapter 8, where Paul eloquently proclaims Christ's resurrection victory and its significance for the whole creation. But when he then turns in the next chapter to the question of the status, in the light of this climactic event, of "my own people, my kindred according to the flesh" (Rom 9:3), he refrains from drawing the conclusion that they are utterly condemned by their nonacceptance of Christ. He lovingly reviews the precious gifts that God has given them: "They are Israelites, and to them belong the adoption, the glory, the covenants, the giving of the law, the worship, and the promises; to them belong the patriarchs, and from them, according to the flesh,

comes the Messiah. May he who is God over all be blessed forever. Amen"
(Rom 9:4-5).[8]

"I ask, then," Paul writes, "has God rejected his people? By no means!"
(Rom 11:1). He does see them, to be sure, as having "stumbled" (Rom 9:32),
but they have not fallen (Rom 11:11). He admonishes the Gentiles to realize
their indebtedness to the lineage from which they have sprung, the vine into
which they have been grafted: "Remember that it is not you that support the
root, but the root that supports you" (Rom 11:18). "The gifts and the calling of
God," he declares plainly, "are irrevocable" (Rom 11:29).

Thus two things are equally affirmed by Paul: God's faithfulness to God's
chosen people, and the decisiveness of the new thing that God has done in
Christ. Paul has no perfect solution to the question of how these two relate to
one another, but is content to let it rest in "the depth of the riches and wisdom
and knowledge of God" (Rom 11:33).

By the time another generation has passed, however, and we come to the
period of the composition of the Synoptic Gospels, this sense of what might
be called a "benevolent ambiguity" has been overtaken by the rhetoric of conflict. Now the struggle of the new messianic movement to establish its identity
and its legitimacy is seen as taking place *over against* the Jewish matrix, rather
than within it. By the time of the composition of the Fourth Gospel, near the
end of the first century, this polarization had become even more radical. The
result is a virtual demonization of "the Jews," viewed collectively as enemies
of Jesus. The reader is left with the puzzle of reconciling this with the obvious
fact that Jesus and his disciples and most of the early converts were themselves
Jews.[9]

"THE JEWS" IN THE FOURTH GOSPEL

It is instructive to track the way in which the various Gospels designate those
who are identified as Jesus' critics and opponents. In the Synoptics, they are
identified as "the scribes and Pharisees, the chief priests and elders of the
people"—clearly a leadership cadre. The term "the Jews" hardly occurs, except
in the phrase "King of the Jews" as found in the passion narrative, and in its
anticipation in the Christmas story: "Where is the child who has been born king
of the Jews?" And in this usage, Jesus is poignantly identified with his people,
not set over against them.

In the Fourth Gospel, however, "the Jews," used in an undifferentiated and
therefore inescapably collective sense, has become the standard appellation for
those who oppose Jesus. The phrase occurs sixty-seven times in the Gospel of
John, as compared to only five or six each in Matthew, Mark, and Luke. And in

the majority of cases, John's usage has a negative and conspiratorial connotation, as for example in the following:

- Therefore the Jews started persecuting Jesus . . . (5:16)
- For this reason the Jews were seeking all the more to kill him . . . (5:18)
- Then the Jews began to complain about him . . . (6:41)
- . . . because the Jews were looking for an opportunity to kill him. (7:1)
- . . . no one would speak openly about him for fear of the Jews. (7:13)
- The Jews answered him, "Are we not right in saying that you are a Samaritan and have a demon?" (8:48)
- . . . the Jews had already agreed that anyone who confessed Jesus to be the Messiah would be put out of the synagogue. (9:22)
- The Jews took up stones again to stone him. (10:31)
- . . . but the Jews cried out, "If you release this man, you are no friend of the emperor." (19:12)
- . . . Joseph of Arimathea, who was a disciple of Jesus, though a secret one because of fear of the Jews . . . (19:38)

If we try to attach a specific meaning to the phrase "the Jews" in each of these instances, we see that in no case can it, from the standpoint of any kind of historical verisimilitude, refer to the people as a whole. Referring to the first citation, 5:16—surely it would be *some* Jews that started persecuting Jesus—Jewish authorities, clearly. Who else would be in a position to do so? *Certain* Jews (unspecified, but certainly not the whole population) were seeking to kill him (5:18). "The Jews" answered him (8:48)? Surely this would be "those conversing with him at that particular time." "The Jews" took up stones to stone him (10:31)? Which Jews, and incited by whom? Joseph of Arimathea kept his discipleship secret "because of fear of the Jews" (19:38)? But Joseph himself was a Jew, and a prominent one at that.

What has happened to permit such an ambiguous and—as we know from the later history of antisemitism—dangerously inclusive use of the term? For one thing, the historical distance between any piece of writing and the events it describes can cause a blurring of differences; the fine distinctions between various actors and their respective motivations can be lost. In this instance, however, much more was at work. The rivalry between the new messianic movement and those who did not accept its claims had continued for at least two generations, and as we have already noted, such conflicts lend themselves all too easily to stereotyping and vilification of the opponent. Moreover, while this had been originally an intra-Jewish controversy, the increasingly Gentile nature of the new movement fostered a "we-they" attitude, in which the "they" could become not just the unbelieving Jews but the Jewish people as a whole.

In the case of the Fourth Gospel, at least two further factors are at work. Historically, it is quite possible that the community of believers out of which this Gospel arose had in fact experienced the sort of expulsion from the synagogue to which John 9:22 (as cited above) refers. Especially after the failure of the rebellion against Rome (66–70 C.E.) and the destruction of the Temple, Judaism needed to reaffirm its identity, and in so doing, to clearly define its boundaries. Thus the anathema against the *minim* ("heretics") was probably added to the Jewish liturgy during this period. The Christians reciprocated with their own anathemas, as it were, expelling the Jews from continuity with their own covenantal history. The "new Israel" had replaced the old; supersessionism (to use a modern term) had set in.

A further factor special to the Fourth Gospel is the author's strongly dualistic view of both historical and transhistorical realities, expressed in terms of a mighty struggle between God and Satan, light and darkness, truth and falsehood, life and death. All too often, "the Jews" are identified with the latter term in each of these polarities. Such texts, again, proved fertile ground for the demonizing of the Jews in later Christian history.

WHO CRUCIFIED CHRIST?

One of the most fateful charges made against Jews, and one that has been applied—in an astonishing leap of anachronism—to those living as many as twenty centuries later, is: "You crucified Christ!" And this was not only true in Nazi Germany; even Jews in America today, with its so much more benign environment, can recall being harassed as children, on the playground or in the street, as "Christ killers." It would be comforting to be able to say that the New Testament offers no basis for such a notion of extending blame to persons who, historically, had nothing to do with the events in question, but in fact this tendency can be found there. We have already seen this in the way in which the Fourth Gospel uses the collective phrase "the Jews." The situation is similar in the book of Acts, where the word *Jews* occurs eighty times.

To be sure, in many cases the phrase is simply descriptive, as in the Pentecost story: "Now there were devout Jews from every nation under heaven living in Jerusalem (2:5)." But the situation soon turns sinister:

> After some time had passed, the Jews plotted to kill him [Paul] . . . (9:23)
> But the Jews incited the devout women of high standing and the leading men
> of the city, and stirred up persecution against Paul and Barnabas . . . (13:50)
> But the Jews became jealous, and with the help of some ruffians in the market-
> places they formed a mob and set the city in an uproar. (17:5)

He was about to set sail for Syria when a plot was made against him by the Jews . . . (20:3)

Again, as in the case of similar usages in John, one has to ask, if one seeks to envision the matter historically, "*Which* Jews would have been engaging in such plots?" Surely not every member of the Jewish community in Damascus (Acts 9:23), Antioch (Acts 13:50), Thessalonica (Acts 17:5), or elsewhere in Greece (Acts 20:3). A cadre of leaders, perhaps, or those most incensed by the new heresy. The obscuring of such distinctions by use of the general term "the Jews" opens the door for readers to assume collective guilt.

The theme of collective guilt is evident in the sermons or speeches in Acts, as well as in the narrative material. This is already the case with Peter's address, on the day of Pentecost, to the "men of Judea and all who live in Jerusalem" (2:14): "This man, handed over to you according to the definite plan and fore-knowledge of God, you crucified and killed by the hands of those outside the law" (2:23).

How many of the citizens of Jerusalem, one must ask—not to speak of the whole of Judea—would have been involved in these actions? Yet the language used implies that all are blameworthy. Similarly, in Peter's speech following the miraculous healing at the gate of the Temple (Acts 3), he addresses "all the people," again with the collective "you": "But you rejected the Holy and Righteous One and asked to have a murderer given to you, and you killed the Author of life, whom God raised from the dead" (vv. 14-15). A qualification is added, "I know that you acted in ignorance" (v. 17); but the sting still remains.

In interpreting such passages, we have to bear in mind that, from a scholarly point of view, the book of Acts must be seen as reflecting the time of its composition as much as or more than the time of the history it narrates. But this does not alleviate the problem with which we are grappling; in fact, it makes it worse. It might be plausible to castigate those who were at least somewhere close, in both space and time, to the blameworthy events, and who if not directly involved, might at least have done something to prevent them. It is another matter if the "you" is extended to mean any and all Jews anywhere in the Greco-Roman world two generations later. This is a slippery slope indeed, viewed from the standpoint of subsequent history.

THE PASSION NARRATIVES

We can direct the same sort of question to the Passion narratives, trying to unwrap the collective term "the Jews" to discern who might have been involved in each case. Who was it that shouted out, "Crucify him, crucify him!" or that uttered the infamous cry, "His blood be on us and on our children"? Surely not all the Jews then resident in Palestine, much less throughout the world. If we look closely at the text, we see that the Gospels are, in fact, often rather specific about who the actors were:

Plotting to have Jesus put to death

Matt 27:1	All the chief priests and the elders of the people.
Mark 15:1	The chief priests in consultation with the elders and scribes and the whole council.
Luke 22:66	The assembly of the elders of the people, both chief priests and scribes.

Making accusations against him

Matt 27:12	The chief priests and elders (before Pilate).
Mark 15:3	The chief priests (before Pilate).
Luke 23:10	The chief priests and the scribes (before Herod).

Expressing preference for Barabbas

Matt 27:20	Now the chief priests and the elders persuaded the crowds to ask for Barabbas . . .
Mark 15:11	But the chief priests stirred up the crowd to have him release Barabbas for them instead.

Shouting, "Crucify him!" (or, in Matthew, "Let him be crucified!")

Matt 27:22f.	All of them (the chief priests and the elders and the crowd, v. 20).
Mark 15:13f.	The crowd, stirred up by the chief priests.
Luke 23:13, 21	The chief priests, the leaders, and the crowds ("they," v. 21).

Uttering the "blood curse"

Matt 27:25	Then the people as a whole answered, "His blood be on us and on our children."

We see that, for the most part, the texts are clear in placing blame for the tragic sequence of events at the feet of particular, identifiable groups—a leadership cadre or cabal, representing the political and/or religious "establishment." Only in the last text cited (Matt 27:25), does the author, fatefully, insist on "the people as a whole" as the actor. The other texts use the much more delimited term "crowd" (*ochlos*) rather than "people" (*laos*). How many would this group, under either term, likely have included? The reference could only be to those who had gathered outside Pilate's headquarters, the praetorium,[10] at that particular time. Several hundred, perhaps, or even several thousand—but in any case, only a small proportion of the hundreds of thousands of Jews who had gathered in Jerusalem for Passover, not to speak of the millions who remained at home elsewhere in Palestine or in the Diaspora.[11]

And what of the chilling reference to his blood being "upon us and upon our children"? Does that doom all subsequent generations of Jews to be labeled "Christ killers"? Hardly. It is likely that this was simply a formulaic way of saying, "We take responsibility for our actions," with the "we" referring to those actually present. And note that even for them, if we take the text literally, the curse was to last through only one further generation, not in perpetuity. For the author of Matthew, this may well have been meant to signify the destruction that was, in fact, visited on Jerusalem just a few decades after Jesus' time, namely, in the failed rebellion of the late 60s.

The Second Vatican Council got it right when it stated, in its famous declaration *Nostra Aetate* (1965): "True, authorities of the Jews and those who followed their lead pressed for the death of Christ (cf. John 19:6), still, what happened in his passion cannot be blamed upon all the Jews then living, without distinction, nor upon the Jews of today."[12] Similar declarations have been made by many other Christian bodies, for instance, by the Episcopal Church in the 1964 statement by its House of Bishops on "Deicide and the Jews" (1964), which notes that, among other considerations, "Simple justice alone proclaims the charge of a corporate or inherited curse on the Jewish people to be false." Likewise, "Guidelines for Lutheran-Jewish Relations," issued by the ELCA in 1998, states: "Lutheran pastors should make it clear in their preaching and teaching that although the New Testament reflects early conflicts, it must not be used as justification for hostility towards present-day Jews. Blame for the death of Jesus should not be attributed to Judaism or the Jewish people, and stereotypes of Judaism as a legalistic religion should be avoided."

SOME LINGUISTIC STRATEGIES

We dealt above with some ways in which the collective term "the Jews" can be deconstructed to reveal the more specific actors involved. There is also a very interesting linguistic strategy for reducing the negative impact of this term, and that is to translate it differently. Malcolm Lowe, followed by some other scholars, has urged that the term *hoi Ioudaioi*, as used in the Fourth Gospel, should in many or most places be rendered not as "the Jews," but "the Judeans"— meaning the residents of the province of Judea. The hostility between the Jesus movement and *hoi Ioudaioi* then could be understood as reflecting the conflict between a charismatic, perhaps heretical and/or revolutionary "Jesus movement" that was centered in Galilee and the governing religious and political authorities in Judea, especially in Jerusalem. The Galilean movement felt a prophetic disdain for the Judean power structure, and the latter felt an anxious fear of the former. This conflict between north and south, which is at the same time one between rural and urban, between the peasantry and the power elite, culminates in Jesus' arrest (on flimsy grounds) and all that followed.

This proposal to give a geographical interpretation to the term *Ioudaioi* is appealing, especially with reference to passages such as the following (inserting "Judeans" where it normally reads "Jews"):

> After this Jesus went about in Galilee. He did not wish to go about in Judea because the Judeans were looking for an opportunity to kill him (John 7:1).

> Then after this he said to the disciples, "Let us go to Judea again." The disciples said to him, "Rabbi, the Judeans were just now trying to stone you, and are you going there again?" (John 11:7-8).

The idea of translating most or all occurrences of *hoi Ioudaioi* in this way has not met with broad acceptance, but it offers an intriguing possibility for making sense of some of the most difficult texts.[13]

Another linguistic strategy that serves to downplay the notion of collective guilt is to substitute for the general term "the Jews" more specific terms such as "the religious leaders," "those standing nearby," or whoever the context indicates may in fact have been involved. The Contemporary English Version (CEV) translation published by the American Bible Society in 1995[14] does this consistently. For example, in the very first occurrence of *hoi Ioudaioi* in the Fourth Gospel, the NRSV reads: "*The Jews* sent priests and Levites from Jerusalem to ask him, 'Who are you?'" (John 1:19). The TEV has: "*The leaders in Jerusalem* sent priests and temple helpers to ask . . ." Paraphrasing translations such as Peterson's *The Message*[15] take a similar tack. Even if the translation being used in a given situation, for instance, in the formal reading of the appointed lessons, does not incorporate this feature, a preacher or teacher may choose to do so. This can be done either by substituting an appropriate word or phrase in the actual reading of the text, or using it in an explanatory comment before or afterward. This practice has the advantage of both illuminating the meaning of the text by making it more precise, and avoiding the constant repetition of the phrase "the Jews," which the hearer can so easily identify with Jews today.

Another important strategy is to provide a more nuanced interpretation of a term such as "the Pharisees" that has taken on so negative a cast, due to the Gospels' trenchant critique of them. The charge of hypocrisy against this movement (or against some representatives of it) was so shocking precisely because Pharisaism was in its essence something admirable. It was what we would call a lay renewal movement, devoted to working out in concrete terms the meaning of covenantal faithfulness for daily life. Not only the Temple but the home, the marketplace, and every aspect of life were to be arenas of holiness.

If an element of rigidity or self-righteousness had set in, such is the case with many religious movements after the first flush of creativity has passed.

In the difficult time after the destruction of the Temple, Judaism owed its survival to the Pharisaic movement. The Zealots had been defeated, the temple priesthood and the civil authorities were no more, and experiments such as the Qumran community had also been crushed. What remained was prayer, Torah study, and the call to faithfulness—in other words, the program of the Pharisees. In this sense, the Pharisees were the direct ancestors of what came to be called rabbinic Judaism, the rich heritage of which Jews are still enjoying to this day.[16]

FURTHER TOOLS FOR INTERPRETATION

A pastor or any reader of the Bible who wants to consider points such as those made above may wonder how to keep up with all the pertinent scholarship. Fortunately, there are some excellent new tools available for this purpose.

The New Interpreter's Study Bible shows the results of a diligent effort to be sensitive to the question of the image of the Jews and Judaism in the New Testament. This is not surprising when one notes that Walter J. Harrelson of Vanderbilt University, a veteran of Christian-Jewish dialogue, served as general editor of the project. This massive volume (2,300 pages) provides a multitude of insights about the meaning of texts relating to this concern, as well as warnings against common misinterpretations. The numerous special notes and excurses on particular topics provide useful supplements to the verse-by-verse commentary.[17]

Ronald J. Allen and Clark M. Williamson of Christian Theological Seminary in Indianapolis have also produced a highly valuable tool in their book *Preaching the Gospel without Blaming the Jews: A Lectionary Commentary.*[18] This very useful volume provides brief commentaries on all the Gospel lessons in the ecumenical three-year lectionary. The authors' stated aims, with regard to each of these some 150 texts, are the following:

a. to alert the reader to anti-Jewish ways of misreading the text (and thereby, they believe, misinterpreting the Christian faith);
b. to surface themes and echoes from the Hebrew Scriptures and other Jewish literature that enrich one's understanding of the text;
c. to heighten the reader's awareness of the social, economic, and political realities underlying the text; and
d. to clarify the nature of the various Jewish groups at that time (scribes, Pharisees, and so forth) and Jesus' relation to them.

Allen and Williamson have brought to this task a wealth of learning and a great sensitivity to what is at stake for Christian-Jewish relations.

A similar work that sheds light on many pertinent passages is Gerard S. Sloyan's *Preaching the Lectionary: An Exegetical Commentary with CD ROM* (Sloyan is also well acquainted with the Christian-Jewish dialogue and can be counted on to offer frank, even acerbic, comments on passages that he feels have contributed to Christian anti-Judaism). Also worth consulting is Sloyan's extensive study of the nature, causes, and interpretations of Jesus' death in his *The Crucifixion of Jesus: History, Myth, Faith*, also published in an abbreviated version as *Why Jesus Died.*[19]

Finally, the many recent studies of "the Jewishness of Jesus" can be helpful in evoking in Christians a sense of identification with Jews and Judaism, rather than antipathy toward them. Especially valuable are studies of Jesus done by Jewish scholars, who are able to place this material in the context of Jewish history and practice. Geza Vermes, Professor of Jewish Studies at the University of Oxford and an expert on the Dead Sea Scrolls, is particularly noteworthy for having produced three volumes on the subject: *Jesus the Jew: A Historian's Reading of the Gospels* (1973), *Jesus and the World of Judaism* (1983), and *The Religion of Jesus the Jew* (1993).[20] To this he has added yet another volume entitled *The Changing Faces of Jesus* (2001).[21] And a rich array of other Jewish scholars are making distinguished contributions to the study of Christian origins and of the "parting of the ways" between these two sibling faiths.[22]

SUGGESTIONS FOR PREACHING

While all Christians need to learn to read the New Testament in such a way as to avoid anti-Jewish stereotypes and generalizations, a special burden falls on those who have the weekly task of preaching on the appointed lessons, including those we have dubbed "difficult texts."[23] It may be helpful to offer, in conclusion, some summary suggestions for those who bear this particular responsibility:

1. Ask what a text meant *then* (a matter largely of scholarship), and what it means *now* (a matter of faithful and creative interpretation)—realizing that these might not be the same.
2. Emphasize the Jewishness of Jesus and his indebtedness to the finest traditions of his people. Understand his criticism of them as prophetic "speaking the truth in love."
3. Be aware of where the text stands in the historical development of the New Testament, and how it may reflect particular conflicts at the time of its composition.

4. Use a translation that provides sensitive renderings of passages referring to Jews, or else add these interpretations yourself (for instance,
"the Jewish leaders" rather than "the Jews").

5. Offer explanatory comments on difficult texts, either before reading
them or in the course of preaching on them.

6. Be willing to read a text "forwards" as well as "backwards;" that is,
to consider its historical consequences (for good or ill) as well as its
antecedents.

7. Avoid stereotypes such as "legalism" or "works righteousness" in
describing Judaism. Appreciate Jewish efforts to remain faithful to the
covenant, understood as God's gracious gift and guidance.

8. Provide opportunities for people to experience the living reality of
Judaism today through synagogue visits, common service projects, or
living-room dialogue groups.

9. Take special care during Lent and Holy Week to set forth the story of
the Passion without implying guilt for Jesus' death on the part of the
Jewish people collectively.

10. If possible, be part of a clergy group that includes rabbis as well as
priests and ministers, and share your joys and difficulties in the ministry of preaching.

Response

Sarah Henrich

*In this essay Franklin Sherman offers a thoughtful historical critique of New Testament
language hostile to Jews and their faith. Sherman recognizes that such language, and the
preaching and teaching that flow from it, has shaped Christian sensibilities about the Jews for
nearly two millennia, often with disastrous results.*

*His essay raises several interpretive difficulties for Christian Bible readers. He states
one significant problem, namely that New Testament language emerges from a time when
Christian believers were a very small minority group, struggling to sustain communities and
develop an identity in the religious marketplace of the ancient world. After having become a
governmentally approved religious group and a majority in most of Europe and, later, North
America, Christians were able to implement the anger of that early language. I heartily agree
with Sherman that such behavior is wrong for theological as well as humanitarian reasons.*

The real difficulty that Sherman implies in his essay concerns our overall understanding of the Bible as an ancient document with continuing power for Christians. How do we hear and embody the Word when it comes to us from a distant historical context? How can we not hear the negative words against "Jews" or "Pharisees" as pertinent to present day Jews and yet continue to hear ourselves addressed through the text? What kind of historical work of the sort Sherman so ably presents in this essay, must be done before the Bible can function as a guide for ethical, godly behavior?

In this fine and useful essay Sherman seeks to find constructive ways to engage these ancient texts. His own careful, extensive, and excellent work suggests the need for such attention to the biblical text at all times. How language teaches us to "love our neighbors" is always at issue for contemporary believers.

6

◆

Jewish Concern for the Land of Israel

Part I

"Go from Your Country..."

Understanding Jewish Devotion to the Land

Karla Suomala

It is often difficult for Christians to understand the strong Jewish commitment to Israel—the land that Christians have historically referred to as the Holy Land or the Promised Land, and that Jews have referred to simply as *Ha-aretz* (the Land) or *Eretz-yisrael* (the Land of Israel).[1] Yet, understanding Jewish concern for the Land is central to understanding who Jews are—even what Judaism is—and essential to entering into meaningful dialogue. This first part of chapter 6 will explore the nature of Jewish attachment to the Land of Israel by surveying its role and meaning in some of the classical sources of Judaism—including the Hebrew Bible, rabbinic literature, and trends in medieval Jewish thought. These documents demonstrate the significance of the Land of Israel for the Jewish people at different times and places in history, both in terms of their relationship to God and their vocation as a people. They also help us to understand better the critical role that the State of Israel plays in the identity of many Jews today—those living in the Land, as well as those in the diaspora—by showing how, in the earliest layers of Scripture, the people of Israel and the Land of Israel emerged simultaneously, woven together in God's ancient promise.

LAND IN THE BIBLE

The Hebrew Scriptures demonstrate the importance of the Land in a number of ways, some of the most significant being: (1) Land as central to covenant; (2) Land as connected to covenant legislation; (3) Land as having unique qualities; and (4) Land as locus of eschatological hope.[2] The first three aspects are concentrated in the Pentateuch as part of the narrative and legislation that detail the origins of the Jewish people. The last aspect, Land as locus of eschatological hope, is especially prevalent in the prophets of the Babylonian exile.

Land as central to covenant. The first mention of what will eventually become known as the Land of Israel can be found in Gen 12:1-4, where God tells Abram (later Abraham):

> "Go from your country and your kindred and your father's house to the land that I will show you. I will make of you a great nation, and I will bless you, and make your name great, so that you will be a blessing. I will bless those who bless you, and the one who curses you I will curse; and in you all the families of the earth shall be blessed."

It is here that God selects a particular people (Abraham, Sarah, and their descendants), assigns to them a particular land (Canaan), and where all three—God, people, land—are inextricably bound in a covenantal relationship. The only requirement on the part of Abraham in this early form of the covenant is to pick up his belongings and to depart with his family for this, as yet, unidentified land. Over time, God renews this covenant many times; in the course of these reiterations of the promise, the Land is progressively delineated, moving from "this land" in Gen 12:7 to Gen 15:18 where the Land extends "from the river of Egypt to the great river, the river Euphrates."[3]

When God renews the covenant with Jacob in Gen 32:24-28, both the Land and the people finally come to be identified by a new name. It is only with great effort that Jacob is able to walk away, limping, with the name Israel:

> Jacob was left alone; and a man wrestled with him until daybreak. When the man saw that he did not prevail against Jacob, he struck him on the hip socket; and Jacob's hip was put out of joint as he wrestled with him. Then he said, "Let me go, for the day is breaking." But Jacob said, "I will not let you go, unless you bless me." So he said to him, "What is your name?" And he said, "Jacob." Then the man said, "You shall no longer be called Jacob, but Israel, for you have striven with God and with humans, and have prevailed."

By this point, the patriarchs have learned that a land promised is not the same thing as a land possessed; it is up to them to take up permanent residence in the

Land. The Genesis narrative highlights the path the patriarchs take on their way from promise to possession.

Land as connected to covenant legislation. Possession, as the Israelites also discover, is not necessarily permanent. What began as a temporary sojourn in Egypt to survive famine in the Land turns into more than four hundred years of slavery for the Israelites. When memory of the promised Land has nearly faded, God liberates the slaves and renews the covenant at Sinai. This time, however, God adds a set of obligations to the covenant, which are to be met by the Israelites. What becomes known as Torah, the legislation outlined in Exodus, Leviticus, Numbers, and Deuteronomy, was primarily for the society that would be established when the Israelites took possession of the Land once more. On the brink of reentering the Land, Moses exhorts the people: "Now this is the commandment—the statutes and the ordinances—that the Lord your God charged me to teach you to observe in the land that you are about to cross into and occupy, so that you and your children and your children's children may fear the Lord your God all the days of your life, and keep all his decrees and his commandments that I am commanding you, so that your days may be long." (Deut 6:1-2). The legislation includes many commandments and rituals that can only be observed in the Land (such as the laws of the sabbatical and jubilee years, the tithes and offerings to the priests, and the laws of the harvest that guaranteed that shares be left over for the poor), and makes clear that God's presence can only be found in the Land. These features of the covenant further connect both the people and the Land to God.

The idea underlying all of this legislation is that the Land belongs to God as God's unique possession. God allows the people of Israel to live in the Land only so long as they obey the covenant. It is within this context that the greatest rewards for obeying the covenant—peace and prosperity in the Land—and the most severe punishments for violating it—loss of the Land, exile, drought, epidemic, locust, even invasion by and loss of sovereignty to a more powerful nation—are also connected to the Land.[4] At the end of Deuteronomy, the people are reminded once again of the obligations that come with the Land, as Moses declares:

> I call heaven and earth to witness against you today that I have set before you life and death, blessings and curses. Choose life so that you and your descendants may live, loving the LORD your God, obeying him, and holding fast to him; for that means life to you and length of days, so that you may live in the land that the LORD swore to give to your ancestors, to Abraham, to Isaac, and to Jacob. (Deut 30:19-20)

Land as having unique qualities. Throughout the text there is the sense that the Land which God has promised to the Israelites is no ordinary land; it is a land with special attributes. As the unique possession of God, the Land is described as an "exceedingly good land . . . a land that flows with milk and honey" (Num 14:7-8). Later on, Moses tells the Israelites:

> The LORD your God is bringing you into a good land, a land with flowing streams, with springs and underground waters welling up in valleys and hills, a land of wheat and barley, of vines and fig trees and pomegranates, a land of olive trees and honey, a land where you may eat bread without scarcity, where you will lack nothing, a land whose stones are iron and from whose hills you may mine copper. (Deut 8:7-9)

In addition, it is a land, unlike other lands, "that the LORD . . . looks after . . . from the beginning of the year to the end of the year" (Deut 11:12). Finally, the Israelites perceived of the Land itself as being holy, containing "a soil that in and of itself could not tolerate moral pollution . . ."[5] This holiness is "derived immediately and directly from the holiness of God," and the Israelites themselves were responsible for helping to maintain the holy quality of the Land by meeting the demands of the covenant.[6]

Land as locus of eschatological hope. The covenant with its promise of the Land came nearest fulfillment in the time of King David and his son, Solomon, when the borders of Israel approached those God had earlier indicated to Abraham. This golden era was short-lived, however, because upon Solomon's death, the united Kingdom of Israel divided in two. While prophets urged reunification and a return to covenant observance, many were pessimistic about the immediate future of the Israelites in the Land. Despite the warnings of the prophets, the Northern Kingdom of Israel was no match for the Assyrians—it was conquered and dismantled—leaving only the Southern Kingdom.

Later, when the Southern Kingdom was threatened by the Babylonians, Ezekiel in his prophecy emphasized the failure of the People to live up to the Torah legislation as the reason for their imminent destruction and exile from the Land, and goes so far as to suggest that it is God who is responsible for the coming catastrophe:

> Thus says the LORD God: This is Jerusalem; I have set her in the center of the nations, with countries all around her. But she has rebelled against my ordinances and my statutes, becoming more wicked than the nations and the countries all around her, rejecting my ordinances and not following my statutes.

... therefore ... I, I myself, am coming against you; I will execute judgments
among you in the sight of the nations. (Ezek 5:5-8)

But Ezekiel, along with others, also expressed hope for the future. The
prophets understood the covenant as eternal, and believed that God would
return Israel to wholeness in their Land, once the Israelites had taken up the
covenant obligations again. God tells Isaiah, for example: "Speak tenderly to
Jerusalem, and cry to her that she has served her term, that her penalty is paid,
that she has received from the Lord's hand double for all her sins" (Isa 40:2);
and that "I am the LORD, who made all things . . . who says of Jerusalem, 'It
shall be inhabited,' and of the cities of Judah, 'They shall be rebuilt, and I will
raise up their ruins'" (Isa 44:24-26).

In fact, for prophets like Isaiah, the covenant took on more universal
dimensions than it had had before, so that when the exiles returned to Jerusalem, they were to be "as a light to the nations, that my salvation may reach
to the end of the earth." (Isa 49:6). God made it clear that the purpose of the
return of the exiles to the promised Land was not simply to take up where they
had left off, but that the covenant would be renewed on a much bigger scale: "I
will guard and protect you and through you make a covenant with all peoples. I
will let you settle once again in your land that is now laid waste" (Isa 49:8).[7]

LAND IN RABBINIC THOUGHT

By the time that the Temple in Jerusalem was destroyed by the Romans in 70
C.E., Israel as both Land and people had changed significantly from the biblical
picture. Increasingly, Jews were living outside the Land in places such as Syria,
Egypt, and Babylonia, while non-Jews made up a significant part of the population in the Land. During this period, the rabbis worked to reconcile the tension
between the biblical understanding of the Land as the place where the Jewish
people lived and the contemporary reality of the growing diaspora.

On the one hand, the rabbis emphasized the covenantal triad of God-people-
land, pointing especially to the important connection between living in the Land
and fulfilling covenant obligations. This is demonstrated by the fact that the
Land played a significant role in the liturgical practice of the synagogue, in
the legal material of the Mishnah (an early rabbinic legal code) and both Talmuds (Jerusalem and Babylonian), and in the biblical commentary of the rabbinic *midrashim*. For example, fully one third of the material in the Mishnah is
devoted to agricultural commands that can only be performed in the Land,
and a significant portion deals with matters of cultic purity that can only fully
be applied in the Land.[8] Even as fewer and fewer Jews lived in the Land, the
rabbis of the Babylonian Talmud (the most expansive legal code of the period)
maintained that: "One should always live in the Land of Israel, even in a city

with a population that is primarily non-Jewish, rather than in a city outside of the Land in which there is a majority of Jews. Whoever lives outside the Land of Israel is as one who does not have God" (*Ketubot* 110b). This last statement was to cause considerable consternation among diaspora Jews who tried to construe it in such a way that would allow them to remain the people of Israel outside the Land.

The rabbis, like the biblical authors, also maintained that the "The Land of Israel is Holier than all other lands," (*Mishnah Kelim* 1), and as such, study, prayer, and burial are all connected to the Land:

> [The] sanctity of the Land enriches all aspects of life, such as Torah study: "There is no Torah like the Torah of the Land of Israel" (*Sifrei Parshat Ekev*). Even death and burial is elevated in Israel: One who is buried there is forgiven of all sins, as if he or she were "buried under the altar of the Temple itself" *(Ketubot* 111a). This holiness is such that even one who is outside of Israel must "direct his heart to the Land of Israel" during prayer (*Tosefta Berakhot).*[9]

In the *Shemoneh Esreh Prayer* (18 Blessings), Jews showed further connection to the Land as they asked God up to three times daily to be mindful of the Land:

> Be merciful, O Lord our God, in Thy great mercy, towards Israel Thy people, and towards Jerusalem Thy city, and towards Zion the abiding place of Thy glory . . .
>
> Accept [us] O Lord our God, and dwell in Zion; and may Thy servants serve Thee in Jerusalem.
>
> Bestow Thy peace upon Israel Thy people and upon Thy city and upon Thine inheritance, and bless us, all of us together.[10]

On the other hand, the rabbis, to allow those living outside the Land to maintain their identity as observant Jews, expanded the idea of the sanctity of the Land to include any land in which the people of Israel lived. This willingness to reinterpret the role of the Land was certainly influenced by the fact that the Temple in Jerusalem no longer stood, and as a result it was impossible to observe many of the commands outlined either in the Bible or in rabbinic legal material. It is not so surprising, then, that Rabbi Akiva, one of the most innovative sages of the early rabbinic period, conceived of multiple origins of holiness. For him, as for most Jews who followed, "The entire world potentially is sacred space,"[11] and this potential could be made actual through Torah study and observance of the covenant stipulations. The rabbis at the same time made clear, however, that while the relationship between God and the Jewish people could be maintained outside the Land, the covenant could be observed "fully

and perfectly only in the Land of Israel where additional, Land-bound commandments obtain, as Scripture ordains."[12] In this, according to the Babylonian
Talmud, *Sotah* 14a, they looked to Moses as their model:

> Rabbi Simlai said: Why did Moses, Our Rabbi, yearn to enter the Land of
> Israel? Did he want to eat of its fruit or satisfy himself from its bounty? . . .
> [T]hus spoke Moses, "Many commandments were commanded to Israel which
> can be fulfilled only in the Land of Israel. I wish to enter the Land so they may
> all be fulfilled by me."

At any rate, this extension of the sanctity of the Land to other lands "exercised a profound effect on rabbinic Judaism, making 'holiness' portable. Jews
could bring their laws, or at least most of them, wherever they went. . . . Jews
would make any land in which they lived holy."[13]

Land in Medieval Thought

By the medieval period, most Jews in the world had neither seen nor lived in
the Land of Israel. Yet despite this seeming disengagement, there was always a
Jewish presence in the Land—a remnant never left, and others came through
pilgrimage or migration. Even for Jews who did not come into contact with the
Land physically, it was still important symbolically, as demonstrated by its role
in Jewish sacred texts, liturgy, and imagination. As a result, Jewish leaders and
scholars found themselves in the difficult position of having to:

> Walk a treacherous tightrope, balancing diverse and sometimes conflicting
> goals. . . . They had to maintain the importance . . . of the Land of Israel . . . with-
> out undermining the possibility of continued and creative life in the Diaspora.
> They had to instill the consciousness that Jewish religious life was somehow
> incomplete without Land and Temple, yet make certain it would remain full
> and rich enough to merit the loyalties of adherents . . .[14]

Accordingly, the debate about the meaning of the Land, where it surfaced,
reflected both sides of the tightrope. Some insisted the Land was one among
many, and was perhaps a means to a greater messianic future, while others
maintained that the Land was unique and essential to authentic Jewish life and
observance.[15]

Questioning the belief that the Land had intrinsic value and was necessary for Jews to be most authentically Jews, Moses Maimonides argued for a
more instrumental understanding of the Land of Israel in which the Land is
essential to the goal of the "renewal of the messianic kingdom of the Davidic
dynasty."[16] Within this schema, the Land was a means to a long anticipated
end, and was not actually so different from other lands. Perhaps in the interest

of maintaining a consistent view, Maimonides did not believe that settling the Land was one of the 613 commandments. Taking the instrumentalist stance even further, the Karaite Anan ben David held that the Land is not the Land of Israel unless it is inhabited by the People Israel. It is not, in this view, sacred at all times, but only under certain conditions.[17]

Nahmanides, among others, severely criticized Maimonides for his stance. According to him, settling in the Land was a commandment—one that he himself took seriously by migrating to the Land of Israel. In addition, Nahmanides went even further, arguing that the commandments in the Torah were intended for the exclusive performance of those residing in the Land, and that diaspora Jews should observe the commandments only as a means of preparing for a return to the Land. Thus Nahmanides viewed the commandments as instrumental, and the Land as ultimate. He further claimed that Jews must live in their own Land even if this aim can only be achieved through war. Nahmanides considered the battle to live in the Land as one of the daily religious obligations incumbent upon every Jew and not a matter to be postponed until the messianic era.[18]

Other scholars who held the position that the Land itself was significant in and of itself pointed to its unique qualities, building upon both biblical and rabbinic formulations of this idea. Many medieval Jews believed that the Land had a "climate and air quality uniquely conducive to intellectual activity" and that those who lived in the Land were likely to reach a higher intellectual level than those outside, thereby drawing more of God's providential attention to the Land.[19] Another way of defending the significance of the Land depended on the rabbinic formulation that other lands were under the jurisdiction of princes while the Land of Israel was governed directly by God. In the medieval expansion on this concept, events "occurring outside the Land of Israel were part of the ordinary pattern of nature, the end result of a long chain of intermediate causes in which the stars were generally considered to have a dominant role."[20] In the Land of Israel, however, all events were caused by God's direct action, not through intermediate forces.

CONCLUSION

The material above briefly demonstrates the deep commitment of the Jewish people to the Land of Israel throughout history, even in times when there was very little contact between the people and the Land. The nature of the attachment was often tempered by the particular historical circumstances of the community. In times of persecution or unrest, Jews tended to turn their attention toward the Land, and to center their hopes on an immanent return. At other points, when a return to the Land was clearly impossible, Rabbis emphasized the expanded definition of the Land—Jews could still be Jews, even if they did not live in the Land of Israel. At still other points, when the image of the Land seemed to be fading in the minds of Jews, Rabbis worked to remind the people of their connection to the Land, a location essential to proper and complete Jewish observance of the covenant. These varied portrayals of the Land were never mutually exclusive; it was often more a matter of degree of emphasis in which one aspect received more attention than others at a given time. In our time, the role of the Land in Jewish thought and practice has been further complicated by the Holocaust as well as the 1948 establishment of the State of Israel. For many Jews today, Israel is both home and hope, reality and symbol.

Part II

"Above My Highest Joy"

Understanding Jewish Devotion to Israel

John Stendahl
in Conversation with Eugene Korn

If I forget you, O Jerusalem,
  let my right hand wither!
Let my tongue cleave to the roof of my mouth,
  if I do not remember you,
if I do not set Jerusalem
  above my highest joy.
—Psalm 137:5, 6

When the ELCA Consultative Panel on Lutheran-Jewish Relations was at work on the Talking Points for Christian understanding of Jews and Judaism,[21] we found ourselves agonizing more over the section on Zionism than over any other. The discussions did not so much reflect differences over our stance or what we wanted to convey as our self-conscious concern, as about how to say it right, how not to be misunderstood, and how neither to overstate nor under-state each point made. When we sought from Jewish and Lutheran colleagues their reactions to the initial drafts, our sense of being on particularly difficult ground was confirmed: convictions about what the document should say about the State of Israel in both past and current conflicts were deep and passionate.

Some critiques desired a stronger statement of support for Israel while others wanted greater criticism of Israeli policies and actions in relation to the Palestinians. The ELCA's relationship and solidarity with fellow Lutherans on the West Bank and in Jerusalem seemed pitted against its relationship with Jewish friends and with the Jewish people; critical views on both the efficacy and morality of Israeli policies seemed in an excruciating tension with the task of communicating positively the concern for communal and personal security, indeed survival, involved in that policy. Despite intentions of balance and clarity within the limits of what we were trying to say, strongly affirming Israel seemed thrown into a zero-sum relation to the rights and concerns of Palestinians.

The Panel's purpose was not to formulate an ELCA statement on Israel but to explain to a Christian audience, and to reflect on, "Jewish Concern for the State of Israel." Offering such reflections to the Christian community was motivated by the larger goals of interreligious understanding and cooperation that we sought to foster. This more limited task—not a comprehensive statement but a fostering of particular human understanding—we believed to be importantly pertinent to the endeavor for peace in the Middle East.

The summary of *Talking Point* #6 reads simply: "The state of Israel holds a special place in the life and thought of the Jewish people. The need for Christians to understand the depth of Jewish concern for Israel is especially urgent as we seek to participate faithfully in the quest for peace and justice for all peoples in the Middle East." That rather bare statement may not appear as much of a platform, but, given its context among the other points made about Jewish-Christian relations, it has at least two significant implications: (1) Christians need to understand the "special-ness" of the state of Israel for Jews, a sacred particularity which is theirs, not ours, to define, and (2) such an understanding is a sensitivity urgently needed for the working of Christian convictions and attempts to contribute to the particular *tikkun olam* (healing of the world) believers yearn to see in the Middle East.

What follows is a brief attempt to foster the understanding for which we are contending.

DEVOTION TO ISRAEL AND A MULTIPLICITY OF ZIONISMS

The term *Zionism* means devotion to and concern for the state of Israel, or support for the creation and survival of a homeland and nation-state specifically for Jews.[22] Its human history is much richer and warmer than is suggested by that abstracting suffix *-ism*, which denotes an intellectual ideology or a unified political commitment. Many accounts of Zionism's history focus on the publication of Theodor Herzl's book, *Der Judenstaat* (*The Jewish State*) and his subsequent convening of the First Zionist World Congress in 1897. Herzl was responding to the virulent antisemitism that had bared its fangs in the Dreyfus Affair, not only in France but throughout Europe. Himself a secular and significantly assimilated Jew, Herzl had become convinced that without the refuge and status of a national home Jews would everywhere be at the mercy of their "adopted" countries, subject to contempt, persecution, and murder. The anti-Jewish hysteria found in much of the European press, not least in many Catholic and Protestant publications, during that period is a reality that many Christians today have forgotten. Not only hate-filled words but countless nasty cartoons caricatured Jews as monsters and arch-villains, parasites upon the body of our civilization.[23]

Herzl's Zionism, of course, met with strong opposition from both sides of religious Judaism. The Reform movement was more sanguine about Western civilization and Judaism's place in it, embracing the possibility of Jewish life in a cosmopolitan variety of nations and in neighborly relations with the Gentile majority, while the Orthodox viewed the restoration of a Jewish state as the prerogative of the Messiah yet to come. Despite these dual sources of hostility, however, it would be a serious mistake to characterize the development of Zionism as *exclusively* the unfolding of a secular strategy for the survival and dignity of Jews. The yearning for Zion was after all also resonant in both Scripture and liturgy, in the ancient narratives and songs of exile and persecution, homecoming and delight in the Land, and in the repeated hope that ended each Passover *seder* through centuries of dispersion: "Next year in Jerusalem!" Through centuries Jews who ate and lived by the harvests of European soil had continued to offer prayers for good weather on the fields of Galilee. Not only secular, often antireligious Zionists but also religious Jews emigrated to the Holy Land, joining a number of observant Jews already settled there. Seeing the ranks of Jews in the Holy Land further increase as the terrible events of the twentieth century unfolded reflected a very realistic sense that living in potentially stateless diaspora entailed a deadly vulnerability.

This history has a variety of powerful emotional dynamics. For some it represented a turning point in Jewish history when Jews shed the role and image imposed on them by the diaspora. For many, the imagery of pale, often bespectacled and frail, scholars treated as pariahs and victims in the Gentile world now gave way to exhilarating and heroic visions of tanned and strong pioneers building a new land, vigorous farmers making the deserts bloom and warriors defending their young country, or the hope of it, from its enemies.[24] For some, especially after the Shoah, the Holocaust perpetrated by the Nazis, here was the new experience of exodus, the rescue of a persecuted people, their miraculous survival and inspiring journey to claim a place of refuge and belonging. This was for many a Passover story, perhaps the only story that could be told in order to make the Holocaust part of a paschal pattern rather than just sheer obscene horror. For many that story was closely tied to a utopian socialism, often not only secular but atheistic, building a new society of equality and justice on the land; for many others it remained a religious narrative and entailed religious identity and observance.

Some would say also that here was the God-given opportunity at last for Jews to live out their calling in creation and history, to be again a nation among other nations but *also* showing forth the ethical and spiritual heritage entrusted to them, a "light to the Gentiles." The covenant of God with Abraham, the covenant that first established Jewish identity, had after all also been a calling to partnership with God in the work of creation and blessing. Now as then, this particular precious Land had been given as the place for that work. Possession of the Land meant that the sacred obligations and calling of the children of Abraham were once again tied to the building and maintenance of a concrete historical nation, working its soil and shaping a society in faithfulness. For some, that society might be defined in the terms of a pluralistic democracy and for others the principles of faithful monotheism may be paramount, but the quality of sacred calling is felt in each case.

Christians, perhaps most of all American ones, may recognize in this sense of a special and consecrated nationhood something familiar. We may ourselves affirm the notion that we have a calling to live up to, to be, in Jesus' words, "a city on a hill" and to prove a blessing to others. Before we assume that such thought about Israel permeates also all of Zionism, however, we should note that not all Jews would embrace the imagery of special moral calling. Some would instead regard the welcome "normality" of nationhood to mean a shaking off of any such notion: to be simply one of the nations, without any imposition of "higher standards" or "divine destiny." Jews had suffered enough, many would say, from the expectations of some special identity imposed on them by others, whether by Christians or Muslims or by some cruel or inscrutable God. Zionism meant the emancipation of Israel from such tyranny of expectation, the freedom to live in history by no different standards than anyone else, playing by the same rules as her neighbors.

At the same time there were yet other Zionists for whom the religious meaning of the reestablishment of a Jewish nation in Israel seemed a clear affirmation of the ancient Scriptures. The covenant with Abraham, some argued, deeded this Land to his rightful heirs, and no one else could have any legitimate claim to it. After the military victory over Arab nations in the 1967 Six-Day War— an apparent David vs. Goliath triumph that seemed in its quality as an astounding miracle and a proof of God's favor—that sense of literal "deeded-ness" took on a new scope and vigor. The State of Israel suddenly had physical possession not of a mere portion of the ancient Land but of nearly all

of it. It was not hard for some to imagine that God now intended the reunification of the whole of Judea and Samaria, all the land of what began to be called
"Greater Israel." A more extreme portion of such a fundamentalist reading of
God's will fuels the fervor of many of the Israeli settlers in the West Bank. A
particularly frightening proposal from the most radical adherents of this type
of Zionism is the destruction of the Muslim holy places in Jerusalem and the
rebuilding of the Temple. The political and ethical consequences of such an
act are of course terrifying to contemplate; yet there are those who regard it as
simple faithfulness to the word of God.[25]

At the risk of a slight deviation from our main task here, we may note in
regard to this more extreme biblicistic Zionism that there are many fundamentalist Christians who have also identified themselves as Zionists on the basis
of such readings of Scripture. Such Christians have joined the gift and covenant of the Land in the Torah to their elaborate yet naïve interpretations of
prophecy and apocalyptic passages in Scripture, but it appears that they are also
drawn to support of militant Israeli policies by the combination of their attrac-
tion to military assertiveness and their deep hostility to Islam. This "Christian
Zionism," scripturally wrongheaded and perverse though it often appears, is a
political force to be reckoned with in the United States and far from peripheral
to the practical contentions involved in the quest for coexistence in the Holy
Land.[26]

Then again there remain among ultra-Orthodox Jews some who may be
termed fundamentalist in their reading of Scripture and who are passionate for
life in *Eretz Israel* (the Land of Israel), but who also regard the *State* of Israel
as an illegitimate secular abrogation of the messianic kingdom. Sects holding
this position are part of the life of Israel even though they refuse allegiance to
much of that life. They are at once "anti-Zionists" *and* part of the devotion to
Israel as place and people that we are discussing here.

In even this partial enumeration of elements in the devotion of Israel,
there is an additional emotional force that should not be overlooked: simply the
love of the Land. We need also imagine what it is to experience the beauty of it,
to taste and see, to hear and feel, and then to know this, in some deeply rooted
way, as home. Many Christians have had some intimation of that experience in
other settings, returning to places of childhood or heritage, and many of us,
being people of scriptural formation, have also had a sense of it when visiting
Israel and Palestine, but the significance of the Land's beauties and delights—
and the heart-rooted solidarity of her sorrows and sufferings—will clearly be
particularly intense for the many Jews, whether visitors or immigrants, who see
there a homeland.

Even if we have never seen it, such imagining of Israel's beauty, its amazing
landscape, its vistas and wonders, seems a vital exercise for us as Christians who

have other geographic loves and commitments. But then may our thoughts go also to what it might be like to come there as a Jew who arrives, maybe as a refugee from a place of persecution or maybe as just a visitor from some country such as the United States, and finds a country where to be Jewish is no longer to be somehow an outsider or part of a minority but normal. This is not to say that there cannot be alienation and tension in a Jew's experience of Israel, but it is to recognize that, even without the history of oppression, or even without a sense of personal danger in one's own part of the diaspora, to have a place where one's own identity is "normal" is a powerful experience.

All these and still other themes and thoughts coexisted somewhat incoherently in the Zionism that created and that has sustained the State of Israel through repeated crises. There are competing impulses and convictions there, deep strains that produce fault lines in Israeli political life and society. These Zionisms can compete, just as Jews from vastly different backgrounds and cultures jostle and clash with one another. The questions are often obvious, the answers elusive. To what degree is being Israeli being Jewish, and to what extent is being Jewish defined by religious Judaism, and religious Judaism of a certain definition? If, as indeed the country intends and understands, Israel is a democracy as well as a Jewish state, what is the status of the many non-Jews—the Christians, Muslims, and Druze—who are her citizens? What are the compromises and risks necessary to make for peace, or what are the compromises of principle necessary to get security? The questions abound, and all those who struggle with them, or who opt passionately for one side or the other, may still call themselves Zionists.[27]

Thus it should be understood that in this straining incoherence there is not one but rather plural Zionisms. That point is important, for it is so easy for people, not least in passionate debate, to talk past each other, assuming that they know the meaning of an "ism," or of some other important identification, and that therefore they understand what the other intends and feels. The attempt by enemies of Israel in the United Nations General Assembly to label Zionism as a form of racism comes to mind in this regard. It should not be denied that it *is* possible to formulate a racist Zionism, and indeed such a Zionism exists along with fringe groups and parties to represent it. (It is also sadly true that there are Zionists whose devotion to Israel as a Jewish state is not *itself* a racist construction but whose attitude toward Arabs in particular is.) But Zionism has included also strains of deep sensitivity to the mandate of respect for the other and of awareness that a state with a Jewish ethnicity, culture, and values at its core can only be true to that identity if it practices justice toward others. There is a built-in tension between the Jewishness of the State of Israel and its democratic inclusion of non-Jews, but that very tension may be seen as present already within the thought and values of Zionism as a complex movement, and of Judaism as a whole, and is not first due to confrontation with some new non-Zionist, or anti-Zionist principle.

As important and helpful as it is to recognize the multiple and sometimes contradictory forms of Zionist passion, however, it would be a mistake to paint a picture only of vast incoherence and division. First of all, there is an existential urgency about the survival of the Jewish state that unites nearly all Jews across and beyond all these divisions. Concern for Israel is not just ideology and theology, or politics and ethics; it is a matter of life or death, of survival or extermination, of love. Even Jews sharply critical of the actions of the State of Israel can share in that community of concern. Long experience with the hostility of Gentiles, moreover, can make it hard for Jews to credit distinctions made by opponents of Israel identifying themselves as anti-Zionist but not antisemitic. As is true with the distinction Christians have often made between religious anti-Judaism and racist antisemitism, such terms often come down to the same thing in the end, an end that has usually meant death for Jews. The urgency in this concern is such that it gives Zionism a unifying dynamic despite its deep divisions and disputes.

This unifying force, especially in the face of hostility—real or imputed—from Gentiles, is itself an important aspect of Zionism. As religious Judaism is dramatically divided into divergent branches around questions of interpretation and practice, and as the larger Jewish ethnic community is still further splintered, commitment to Israel has been one item that nearly all groups could affirm. So many other enactments of communal identity, such as keeping kosher or wearing distinctive clothing, entailed disputes and disunity, but in devotion to Israel appeared one common cause in which Jews could be united. It was and is a connection made practical and palpable.

Let it be noted, especially if it has not been noticed already, that this description of various Zionisms has to do not just with *Israeli* Jews, those native to the Land and those who have chosen to make *Aliyah* (the biblically resonant term for emigration to Israel). The thoughts and emotions outlined here pertain as much, and sometimes perhaps even more, to those American Jews who have not chosen to live in Israel. Retaining the identity and lifestyle established here, they may nonetheless feel strongly the moral and spiritual claim of a Jewish homeland. Not living in Israel and not sharing directly in the risks and challenges of life there, they may experience a heightened moral duty to support Israel. At the same time, there can be a chastening consciousness that non-Israeli Jews should not presume to lecture or meddle in the hard political world of those Jews who are actually living there, actually in the line of fire or facing the daily anxieties of sudden terror. Thus it is understandable if American Jews are often generous in support for Israel and outspoken in her defense, yet uncritical and accepting of whatever policy her government chooses. Such is of course not always the case, but when it is the reasons for it can be understood and respected.

PROBLEMS AND OPPORTUNITIES

This chapter began with words from Psalm 137. That beautiful elegy of longing for a lost homeland begins:

> By the waters of Babylon—
> > there we sat down and there we wept
> > when we remembered Zion.
> On the willows there
> > we hung up our harps.
> For there our captors
> > asked us for songs,
> and our tormentors asked for mirth, saying,
> > "Sing us one of the songs of Zion!"
> How could we sing the LORD's song
> > in a foreign land? (Ps 137:1-4)

The psalmist's words resonate with centuries of experience. The exile of Babylon evoked the slavery in Egypt before it and prefigured the long history of Israel in diaspora and homelessness. For countless readers of Scripture, moreover, these lines have also evoked other communal narratives or, also, a more individual sense of yearning for a lost place and time and of alienation from the world as it has become. It is a beautiful and haunting song.

But such music exists in time and is historical instance rather than eternal abstraction. In this psalm the loveliness does not last to the end. The song about longing for Zion takes a sharp turn, and suddenly we are confronted with righteous rage and yearning for vengeance. The Edomites and Babylonians who conspired in the destruction of Jerusalem should pay for what they did, their evil requited them with violence. The psalm that began so beautifully ends, "O daughter Babylon, you devastator! Happy shall he be who requites you with what you have done to us! Happy shall he be who takes your little ones and dashes them against the rock!" (RSV).

The murderous words are ugly, but one reason I am glad that this psalm has not been bowdlerized or excised from Scripture is that we *need* to hear and be reminded that even our noblest selves may be overtaken with evil, that oppression and loss can very naturally give rise to murderous rage, and that fantasies of revenge often help to sustain the wretched in the times of their powerlessness. These are human facts, and they are too often papered over with our prettier pieties and best intentions. May God grant that we resist the evil here, that we are able to hear and understand the rage of others, and that, when we have power, we do not execute the righteously vengeful fantasies we harbored in our hearts when we were the victims of our persecutors.

Seen in its entirety, then, Psalm 137 does more than evoke the longing for Zion. It also gives a glimpse of the darker side of history, a darkness in which peoples have suffered and brought suffering to others. For all the good in it, the history of Israel, ancient and modern, is of course not exempt from the tragic workings of such history. Both when in power and when in subjection to others, Jews have known about that.

What often emerges when there is dialogue between Israeli Jews and Palestinians is that a common and intertwined history is told and remembered with very different narratives.[28] This divergence is hardly unique to the Middle East, but the ubiquity of this problem among the world's peoples does not obviate the need to grapple with it. The great Passover and exodus narrative of modern Israel, the rescue of survivors from the Shoah and their coming home at last to the promised Land, a place of rescue and new life, becomes for another people the story of the great Catastrophe, *al Nakba*, the account of expropriations and expulsions, of the Land taken away. Each people has the story of cruelties and atrocities by the other; each tends to deny, minimize, or extenuate those accounts charged by the other; each lives with its own memories of what happened, its own sense of what's happening; and for each there is self-evident, existential truth to which the other seems blind. There have been acts of terror committed on both sides,[29] from long before the foundation of the State of Israel down to the present, and the misery continues. Both peoples have a strong sense and memory of victimhood. Both feel horribly vulnerable to the other.[30]

Anyone who seeks to come to terms with the narratives and emotions of both Jews and Palestinians soon discovers how far apart not only the analyses and arguments but also the memories and experiences are. There are competing presentations of facts, contradictory claims and arguments. Only recently have the two sides been able to give formal recognition to each other's reality as more than an imposed legal fiction, and despite the good pragmatic talk of a "Two-State Solution," genuine respect for the peoplehood and rights of the other remains politically tenuous. Even speaking about the issue of reciprocal violence becomes problematic as partisans of Israel understandably object that there is no moral equivalence between the act of a suicide bomber and a targeted assassination in retaliation, even if such assassination should carry with it collateral damage. From the other side, voices would argue that, evil as such bombing is, it is in line with the historic tactics of liberation movements (including elements of the Zionist struggle against the British Mandate) and a classic way that a weaker and oppressed people have made their resolve known. The greater moral burden, according to such a view, falls more on Israel as the oppressor and aggressor. That characterization, in turn, many on the Israeli side would reject. Thus the argument spins on. To get in the middle of that dispute with a view or an analysis of one's own seems daunting enough, but it is even more so when one feels vulnerable to potential attacks both for being immorally neutral or being prejudicially committed.

This is not to say that interfaith dialogue around the issues of the Holy Land is impossible or fruitless. On the contrary, such conversation will finally be vital in order to have any lasting peace and coexistence. But it is hard work, and at this point in the history of the conflict it may be seen by many as work that has been put aside by political necessity. The violence of the Second Intifada and the failure of the Palestinian Authority to rein in terrorist actions may be blamed in some part on the policies of Israel itself but, whatever the analysis, the trauma and despair experienced by the Israeli public has produced widespread support for the combination of a wall, or "security barrier," and a unilateral disengagement from Gaza and portions of the West Bank. Many Israelis are tired and eager, as much as possible, to stop having to deal with the Palestinians. The security barrier is credited with having reduced the number of terrorist incidents and disengagement holds the promise of fewer, less exposed, and more militarily defensible settlements in the West Bank. At the same time, the election of Hamas as the majority party on the Palestinian side, while understandable in multiple ways, would seem to lower the possibilities of negotiation and an intentional peace process yet further.

While disengagement may be appealing for many outside of the settler movement and apart from those religiously committed to a biblically defined Jewish Land from the River to the Sea, there are humanitarian issues that need still to be pressed. The security barrier is built brutally into Palestinian land, dividing families, cutting off access to fields or jobs, impeding travel to jobs and schools, medical care and hospitals. The barrier is credited with having saved Jewish lives, and any criticism of it needs to recognize that preservation of any human life is a sacred duty. Likewise any defense of it must also reckon with the massive costs to the Palestinians whose lives and livelihood have been affected. It continues a long story of expropriation and disrespect, worsens the desperate poverty and economic suffering of the Palestinian people, and fosters greater bitterness in those it seeks to exclude. The disengagement as currently envisioned still leaves injustices unaddressed and festering wounds untended. That damage cannot be long ignored if Israel is to have real and honorable peace.

In the work of attending to such issues, it may be that American Christians and Jews can play a helpful role. After all, Jews, and some Christians, in this land are significant sources of support for Israel, and, to a far lesser extent, for the rights and aspirations of Palestinians. But often the same kinds of deadlock and noncommunication across the lines of solidarity occur here as in Israel and Palestine. Christians concerned for Palestinians on either side of the Green Line need to assure our Jewish colleagues, friends, and neighbors, not only by honest speech but also by careful listening, of our interest in and understanding of their concerns and passions. American Christians say, almost universally, that we are strong in our support for Israel, but we may learn or need to be reminded why our words are not fully trusted. Christians need to make clear, and be willing to express publicly, our own horror at violence inflicted against Jews and at antisemitic propaganda being poured out in so many parts of the world.

Christians need to do that, and actively seek opportunity to do it, because if it is true it is also right. Christians need to do it because we have committed ourselves (and believe that God has committed us) to dialogue and cooperation. But Christians also need to do it because we are called and committed to other tasks as well. We bring to the table our own consciences and understandings. We bring our relationship with Palestinian Christians, joined to us by that curious sacramental identification we call the Body of Christ, and we bear responsibility to speak for them and of them when they cannot represent themselves. We bring our grief over the spiritual as well as the physical ravages of the conflict on the Palestinian side as well as on the Jewish community, and our sad knowledge about rage and violence. We bring our own concern for Israel in times when we believe her policies do not serve her security but are themselves potentially suicidal. We as Christians are not all of one mind on this, but neither, despite the emotional unity of Zionism, are our Jewish friends. We do ask to be trusted and heard, however, and we hope that out of that trust and conversation more might come, overflowing into the conversations and negotiations of the Middle East. We would hope to lower the level of fear and suspicion, the sad symmetries of victimhood and reprisal.

But we must know that in order for that to happen we as Christians need to win that trust. If it sounds as if our outrage at the taking of innocent lives is only a rhetorical ploy in order to get on to our criticism of Israeli policy, or if our clear perception of terrible reciprocities—"vicious cycles"—in the Israeli-Palestinians relationship is allowed to operate as a dismissive and excusing calculus of moral equivalence, then our dialogue will not be helpful. To get beyond such perceptions may take more work than we anticipated.

Christians may also be put off from the task of helping dialogue by our own self-consciousness and fear. Can we speak what is on our minds without sounding antisemitic? If, for example, we speak of concern about the power of an increasingly right-wing pro-Israel lobby, are we falling into an old antisemitic stereotype of hidden Jewish wealth and influence? If we point out that the increasing tendency to speak of Muslims as unwelcome and culturally danger-ous aliens in the "Judeo-Christian" West mirrors what was once the theme about Jews in Christian Europe, would such an observation be taken amiss as no more than a debating point? We as Christians face issues of trust as we go into dialogue, and it takes courage and hope to proceed. Yet, as the ELCA Talking Point affirmed, what is at stake is not just our relationship with our Jewish neighbors, precious as that is, but "the quest for peace and justice for all peoples."[31]

"A SACRED OBLIGATION"—A COUNSEL TO CHRISTIANS

In 2002 the Christian Scholars Group on Christian-Jewish Relations issued an excellent statement entitled "A Sacred Obligation: Rethinking Christian Faith in Relation to Judaism and the Jewish People." Often I have been drawn back to that phrase, "a sacred obligation," and it seems to me in this context that many of us as Christians are indeed multiply bound in holy duty in regard to Israel and the Holy Land. As a Lutheran, my own ties with the Evangelical Lutheran Church in Jordan and the Holy Land (ELCJHL) bind me to a sacred obligation of standing in their behalf. When Palestinians are stereotyped as terrorists, it is my sisters and brothers who are being held in contempt. I am called to witness to what I have seen with our own eyes and what I have heard from my partners in faith. When a barrier is described as making safe the people of Israel, I am obliged to describe the way much of it is also a wall that claims Palestinian land and separates people from their fields, their jobs, their hospitals, and their families.

I am, of course, called to advocacy for the oppressed *regardless* of their faith, but here is a *particular* responsibility to those whom I know and who ask for my help. Largely invisible in much of our American conversations, they have no strong lobby and few to speak for them. It falls to us. This advocacy is not optional; it is my duty.

But of course I have other obligations to neighbors and strangers, obliga-tions no less sacred, not only to known truth but to hearing the experience of others, obligations not only to righteousness but to peacemaking. And we are responsible, as I once heard my father say, not only for what we say but for what we are heard to say. Without care, advocacy for Palestinians is too easily heard in ways that make commitment to Israel more bitter and defensive. We may assume our support for Israel's survival is a trusted given when it is not. We may also forget that, for all Israel's military power, many see her as immensely vulnerable, despised by much of the world, attacked with racial hatred, threat-ened with annihilation.

Thus we Christians need first to be explicit in support for Israel's survival. We further need to back up any criticisms of Israeli policy (or U.S. complicity in injustice) with the authority derived from our concrete obligations. We are not playing ideological games. For example, one concrete obligation is our Lutheran concern for Augusta Victoria, our hospital on the Mount of Olives, hampered and threatened by Israeli government actions. Solidarity with real people is, after all, part of Jewish engagement with this issue, as well. The specific and personal is what we can witness to.

But note that we are morally obliged to join such concerns to an understanding of Israeli and Jewish fears. Legitimate criticism of Israel's security barrier, for example, must acknowledge the lives saved by that measure. Let it not be thought—or construed—that Israeli lives have no value for us. We have a duty to be clear that our protest is not to the right of self-protection but with the particular placement of the wall on Palestinian soil. It is also important to reject rhetoric that compares Israeli actions to Nazi Germany or racist South Africa. Whatever legitimate points might be intended in such analogies can be made without argument that enrages and shuts down communication. Further isolation and polarization are all that is achieved by our identifying a Jewish homeland and refuge with such regimes of pure evil.

Still, let us not be swayed from the obligation of witness. And let not the passionate voices of disagreement and attack discourage us from speaking what we are obligated to say. We may be increasingly accused of selling out to Islamist zealots on the Arab side, or of condoning antisemitism, or failing to care about Muslim oppression of non-Muslims. A coordinated campaign seeking to discredit church leaders in these terms is currently being waged.[32] In the face of such attacks we need to remain respectfully clear in our responsible protest against policies of occupation and expropriation.

If we are careless in these obligations, choosing either faithless neutrality or arrogant righteousness, we shall have furthered the dynamics of war and hatred even while we mouthed slogans of peace and justice.

ISRAEL AND DEEPENED CHRISTIAN REFLECTION

Let it finally be noted, currently just a bit outside the scope of this brief piece, that there is also a wealth of theological learning and growth waiting for us if we Christians let ourselves be drawn more deeply into conversation around the existence of the modern state of Israel. Christians would be forced, I think, to think more actively about the function of land and place, space and memory, in *our own* religious experience.[33] We would be drawn also to explore the important question of God's meaning and message for us in the survival of the Jews and their coming into the land. The distinction and the connection of nationhood and peoplehood, a vital concept in both the ancient Scriptures and the New Testament, might engage us more fully, and we would have to think, I believe, in fresh ways about what constitutes being "a Gentile" in its several senses and what it entails to become part of the *people* of God.

It is a great irony that, while Christian Gentiles long despised and attacked Jews for being a people without a nation, a cosmopolitan "other" in a world of landed belonging, the early writings of the church excitedly endorsed precisely such an alienation. Believers are strangers and exiles in this world, with no abiding city. Such reflection will further force us to ponder issues of power and powerlessness in both Scripture and ethics. We would need to consider the hermeneutical significance of the way that, through most of our synchronous history, Jews needed to apply texts born in a nation's life in a new context of exile and landlessness, while Christians were taking the texts of a powerless minority and applying them with force in the settled nations of dominant Christendom.

The historical incarnation of covenant, both traditions know, is a messy and challenging business. Now that a Jewish state has been added to the terms of Jewish identity, complete with all the difficulties and tragic dilemmas involved in the exercise of power, what do we as Christians have to learn? And what do we have to share out of our long, and terribly flawed, experience of exercising power as nations ourselves? May it be of use.

Response

Eugene Korn

This essay is sensitive and balanced. I would like to expand some of its points.

Because of the wonderful equality in America and Jewish success there, it is easy to miss how much Israel is a profoundly existential issue for most Jews. Israel is no mere political interest, but something American Jews feel in deep in our being. The pogroms that our grandparents endured and the Holocaust that murdered half of all European Jews are very much with us. Jews number only fourteen million worldwide amidst 1.5 billion Christians and 1.2 billion Muslims. History has taught us that we are enormously vulnerable, and only sovereignty with the means to defend ourselves can substantively increase our security. Given the tragedies of Jews in the twentieth century, Israel is the only real basis for Jews believing that the future can be better. Our vulnerability is sharpened today when most Arabs refuse Israel recognition and peace and Iran publicly threatens her with extinction. So when people unfairly criticize Israel, espouse anti-Zionist rhetoric, or perpetrate terror against Israelis, Jews in America feel personally threatened. This powerful historical and geopolitical awareness is always present for Jews in discussions regarding Israel.

Jews do have many positions about Israel, yet the overwhelming majority (80 to 85 percent) are Zionist, moderate, and pragmatic. Only a fringe on the right is against territorial concessions and Palestinian statehood, and a fringe on the left rejects Jewish statehood. Even the majority of Orthodox Jews—who believe that God promised the Land of Israel to the Jewish people—are pragmatists and willing to compromise because they understand that peace is possible only when Palestinians, too, have their own state. Importantly, absolutist fringe groups never determined Israeli or American Jewish policy. The Israeli government fought incidents of Jewish terrorism in the 1940s and '80s, jailing the terrorists. There is no symmetry between isolated Jewish extremism and Palestinian terrorism, which has long been the strategic policy of mainstream Fatah and Hamas. Nor is there similarity between the Jewish fringe rejection of Palestinian statehood and the principled Arab rejection of Israel. Since the 1947 UN Partition Plan until today, Israel and the Jewish people have agreed to an Arab state—but will not agree to commit suicide to accommodate it. This means that Lutherans and other Christians will find most Jews ready partners to discuss fair and pragmatic solutions to the Middle East that can ensure peace and justice for both Israelis and Palestinians. We dare not view the conflict as a zero-sum game. Both Israelis and Palestinians can win, if each side is willing to compromise.

Religious Jews also see Israel as an essential part of their divine covenant and religious history. The Jewish return to our biblical homeland is an exception in history. Moreover, Christianity traditionally taught that its truth vitiated the Jewish covenant and metaphorized the biblical category of Land, so it is difficult for many Christians to appreciate how Jews interpret Israel as a deeply religious phenomenon. Jews are a people—in both the spiritual and physical dimensions—who are committed to living the covenant in human history by building a society that mirrors the biblical values of justice and mercy. As a people we can only do this in our own land, where we have the opportunity to shape society according to our values. In this way, Israel represents the possibility of Jewish self-determination. Jews and Christians need to understand the profound differences between our theologies around land, peoplehood, and religious history.

Finally, Jews know well that Israel falls short of the prophetic ideal of a society ensuring peace, justice, and security for all, and that Israel makes mistakes. Fair criticism is entirely legitimate and makes honest interfaith discussion possible about Israel. But unfair criticism, one-sided views, and intolerable double standards undermine understanding and communication. If we avoid these traps, Jews and Christians can reflect constructively about Israel, deepening our understanding of each other. This is our sacred task.

7

•

Healing the World and Mending the Soul
Understanding *Tikkun Olam*

Karla Suomala
in Conversation with Richard Sarason

TO BE A BLESSING

In Genesis 12, God promised Abraham three things: land, descendants, and to be a blessing to the nations of the world. The first two promises are fairly straightforward, while the third is less clear: What does it mean to be a blessing? At issue here is the function or purpose of a particular community in the larger world. How should the descendants of Abraham, the Jewish community, relate to those around them? Jews, and later on Christians, struggled with this promise, trying to make sense of what it has meant to them in different historical situations. According to one Jewish legal scholar, "This rather opaque phrase"—namely, to be a blessing—"was explained in ancient and medieval times in several ways: Abraham was to serve as the model by which other men would bless their sons; he was to bestow the blessing of prosperity on all people, or all peoples were to share in the blessing which would come to the world for his sake; the nations of the world would fuse with the Jewish people, children of Abraham."[1] Being a blessing, then, might involve gaining converts, setting a moral example, or social action in the material realm.

The ideas wrapped up in "being a blessing" are for many of today's Jews connected to the ancient Hebrew phrase *tikkun olam*, which entails repairing, healing, or perfecting the world. The Hebrew word *tikkun* appears only in the book of Ecclesiastes (1:5, 7:13, 12:9), where it means "setting straight" or "putting in order." The phrase *tikkun olam*, however, is first found in the *aleinu* prayer, a prayer still used in worship but which was composed by rabbis as early as the fourth century. There *le-takken olam* means "to establish the world in the kingdom of the Almighty" or "to bring about God's rule on earth," and refers entirely to God's action rather than any human effort. It shows up again among the writings of medieval kabbalists with a more mystical bent, and it has been reframed in the last century to refer to "the betterment of the world, including the relief of human suffering, the achievement of peace and mutual respect among peoples, and the protection of the planet itself from destruction."[2]

Biblical Texts. The search for answers for this age-old issue of the relationship between the Jew and larger society has been informed by other biblical texts as well. For example, Gen 1:27 states that "God created humankind in his image." What does it mean to be created in God's image? Many sages have seen in this verse a connection between God and humanity in that both have certain spiritual qualities in common, including the intellect, the soul, and the will. Some of these spiritual qualities are grounded in God's many attributes that include both strict judgment and compassion/mercy. These are qualities that humans, albeit imperfectly, share and can act upon.

Other scholars have seen in this verse a charge or command that links us to those around us. In his reading of this verse, Rav Soloveitchik sees a direct link between being created in the image of God and the role of the Jew in the world. "Created in the image of God," he notes, "we are charged with the responsibility for the great confrontation of man with the cosmos"; we are "involved with the rest of mankind" in that confrontation; we "co-ordinate our efforts"; "we stand shoulder to shoulder with mankind . . . for the welfare of all."[3] Others have seen in this verse a description of a "special feature," so to speak, that gives humans the ability to obey the divine will.[4]

Another rationale for Jewish involvement in wider society is found in Isaiah. The prophet Isaiah announces that God, in speaking to the Israelites, has stated, "I have called you in righteousness, I have taken you by the hand and kept you; I have given you as a covenant to the people, a light to the nations" (Isa 42:6). Here again, the same questions are valid: How is Israel to be a light unto the nations? "Some writers suggest that the statement that Jews would serve as a 'light unto the nations' was meant as a prophecy rather than as an obligation and that it applies only when all Jews finally reside in Israel."[5] Others, however, disagree. They have defined Judaism "as a preoccupation with a continual sanctification of God's Name (*kiddush ha-Shem*) and an alignment with the thrust of history and Providence."[6] In other words, being a light requires action in and involvement with the non-Jewish world.

Finally, Jeremiah seems to provide some guidance with respect to the role of the Jew in society when he speaks to the exiles in Babylon, "Seek the *shalom*

[NRSV: 'welfare'] of the city where I have sent you into exile, and pray to the Lord on its behalf, for in its *shalom* [NRSV: 'welfare'] you will find your *shalom* [NRSV: 'welfare']" (Jer 29:7). This verse seems to offer "a religious justification for civic involvement without prescribing precisely how that should be done." Stern points out that it would be "a distortion of Jewish tradition to ignore that injunction . . ."[7]

SOCIAL ACTION IN CONTEXT

Traditional Jewish Literature. Interestingly, neither the phrase *tikkun olam* nor references to activity aimed at improving or perfecting the world are widespread in traditional Jewish literature. In large part, this has to do with the historical realities that Jews throughout most of the world faced. "Life in the diaspora over two millennia did not offer frequent opportunities for Jews to expend their energies on disinterested political activity aimed at universal social and communal betterment."[8] In fact, most countries excluded Jews from fully participating in the political life of the community. This does not mean that Jews were completely indifferent to community concerns but rather that whatever "political influence Jews had in pre-Enlightenment times and places was generally directed toward physical survival and eliminating the most oppressive features of inferior political status."[9] In effect, Jews were not been in a position to play active, visible roles in the wider community, and this would certainly limit possibilities for considering the welfare of the non-Jewish neighbor or non-Jewish state.

From the point at which the Second Temple was destroyed in 70 C.E. until 1948 with the founding of the nation of Israel, Jews have lived primarily in the Diaspora—outside of the promised land—with limited rights and very little power. Many rabbinic authorities throughout this time, in fact, "viewed non-Jewish society with suspicion, if not with contempt. This yielded a fairly parochial view of the world, in which there was little obligation on the part of Jews to come to the aid of non-Jews."[10] Given that situation, the Talmudic use of *tikkun olam* primarily referred to legislation within Jewish society, providing extra protection to those who were potentially at a disadvantage in the legal realm by dictating justice in the writing of divorce decrees or in the freeing of slaves. In general, the rabbis worked from the understanding that "God is responsible for universal reform while the Jew is responsible for his own society."[11] This idea is contained in Jewish liturgy, most notably in the second paragraph of the *aleinu* prayer, where "*tikkun olam* is connected to the messianic era in which all the world will know and serve God."[12] Hope for renewal is expressed in prayer, "but it is God who is expected and urged to bring it about."[13]

Other rabbis, however, insisted that the religious obligations of compassion applied equally to Jews and non-Jews. Rabbi Chanina, for example, charges the Jewish community to "pray for the welfare of government, for were it not for the fear of it, people would swallow each other alive," (*M. Avot* 3:2). The rabbis were also aware that there were times for prayer and times for more direct action. Regarding the exchange between Moses and God as the Jews were standing before the Sea of Reeds with the Egyptians right behind them: "The Holy one, Blessed be He, chastised Moses for praying at great length rather than instructing the Jews to travel."[14]

Some texts go even further, urging direct action toward those in need without distinguishing between Jew and Gentile, as in a rabbinic commentary of Gen 3:21, "And the LORD God made garments of skins for the man and for his wife, and clothed them," which states "Just as God clothed the naked . . . so you too ought to clothe the naked" (*Sotah* 14a). In a move that more clearly moves Jewish responsibility into the political realm, another rabbinic commentary on Gen 33:18 talks about how the patriarch Jacob came to the city of Shechem and "was gracious to the city." In trying to understand how Jacob was "gracious" to the city, Rav speculates that Jacob "instituted coinage for them"; Samuel suggests that Jacob "instituted markets for them"; and R. Jonathan claims that, "He instituted [public] baths for them" (*b. Shabbat* 33b). Regardless of the circumstances, there always seems to be a sense of the neighbor, whether inside or outside of the Jewish community.

The great medieval thinker Maimonides saw Jewish responsibility to wider society particularly in the realm of morality. He asserts that "Moses commanded [the Jews] to compel all human beings to accept the commandments enjoined on the descendants of Noah." In other words, Maimonides encouraged Jewish responsibility for Gentile morality, through both teaching and persuasion.[15] Maimonides, however, does not ignore the social realm, and makes a comment that suggests a more material approach to Jewish participation in society, saying that Jews are to bury the Gentiles "with the dead of Israel and [support] their poor among the poor of Israel."[16] He cites as proof the verse, "The LORD is good to all, and his compassion is over all that he has made" (Ps 145:9), and since humans are created in the image of God, they should have mercy on their fellow human beings.

Jewish Mystical Texts. In medieval mystical material, rabbis emphasized acts of *tikkun* (repair) in a cosmic sense.[17] Rabbi Isaac Luria developed the doctrine of the restoration of the flawed universe to its original design to explain the origins of evil. He believed that shortly after God created light, the vessels of the universe proved unable to contain it and shattered, scattering the light through the physical world. The shattering of these vessels was the "symbolic

mean that six million Jews were dead, a third of the world Jewish population? Could Judaism itself survive? Was there any reason for it to survive?

THE NEW *TIKKUN*

Thinkers such as Irving Greenberg assert that the relationship between God and the Jews fundamentally changed as a result of the Holocaust. The authority of the covenant was broken, "but the Jewish people, released from its obligations, chose voluntarily to take it on again."[29] In the face of the greatest assault in their history and in the absence of any visible response from God, Jews came together and "rebuilt the old and established new communities throughout the world."[30] The idea of working as partners with God, or cocreators, became even more firmly established for many Jews in the post-Holocaust era. The celebrated twentieth-century thinker and theologian Abraham Heschel, for example, affirmed that while the "universe is done. The greater masterpiece still undone, still in the process of being created, is history. For accomplishing this grand design, God needs the help of man. Man is and has the instrument of God, which he may or may not use in consonance with the grand design."[31]

Emil Fackenheim, another leading twentieth-century Jewish philosopher and theologian, also saw in the Holocaust something new and unprecedented in Jewish history, an event that fundamentally changed Jews and Judaism. The Holocaust, for Fackenheim, was essentially a rupture in Jewish faith and life, as well as all things considered human. He wondered, in the face of such a rupture, if one could still affirm an authentic *tikkun olam* or "mending of the world."[32] Fackenheim goes on to suggest a post-Holocaust *tikkun*, a radically different sort of mending, which began in the midst of the Holocaust itself in resistance to Nazi horrors. The fact that some did not succumb to destruction is remarkable, claims Fackenheim, and the seed for today's new *tikkun* is located in their witness and survival.

In 1948, just three years after the Holocaust, the State of Israel was founded. From the lowest point in their history, many Jews saw promise fulfilled in this new state. "If the Holocaust showed the Jewish people in its most abject powerlessness, then the reestablishment of the State of Israel signified the Jewish people's return to power and their reentry into history as a whole nation."[33] Fackenheim's new *tikkun* becomes embodied in the existence of the State of Israel, concrete evidence of and hope for *tikkun olam* in a world that has undergone total rupture.

Within a decade of the founding of Israel, the phrase *tikkun olam* came to be associated with social action work in North America. The first usage of the expression *tikkun olam* in the United States was by Shlomo Bardin, the founder of the Brandeis Camp Institute of California, as early as the 1950s.[34]

By the late 1970s, New Jewish Agenda, an organization devoted to progressive religious social values, employed the expression *tikkun olam* to capture the spirit of its ideology. For them *tikkun olam* has come to be associated with Jewish responsibility "not only for their own moral, spiritual, and material welfare, but for the moral, spiritual, and material welfare of society at large.[35] According to a leading Reform rabbi, "Our conviction [is] that somehow it is necessary for the public sector of society to intervene compassionately and protectively on behalf of the disadvantaged, the sick, the poor, those in whom the spark of divinity burns too dimly and who need the breath of compassion to fan that spark into full light."[36]

In the 1999 statement made in Pittsburgh, just over one hundred years after the very first Reform platform was adopted, Reform Judaism reaffirmed and even strengthened the role of social justice through *tikkun olam*:

> Partners with God in עוֹלָם תִּקּוּן (*tikkun olam*), repairing the world, we are called to help bring nearer the messianic age. We seek dialogue and joint action with people of other faiths in the hope that together we can bring peace, freedom and justice to our world.
>
> We are obligated to pursue צֶדֶק (*tzedek*), justice and righteousness, and to narrow the gap between the affluent and the poor, to act against discrimination and oppression, to pursue peace, to welcome the stranger, to protect the earth's biodiversity and natural resources, and to redeem those in physical, economic and spiritual bondage. In so doing, we reaffirm social action and social justice as a central prophetic focus of traditional Reform Jewish belief and practice.[37]

A brief survey of synagogue mission statements and programming reflects the importance placed on *tikkun olam* in current Reform identity and activity. At the Temple Israel in Minneapolis, for example, Rabbi Jeffrey Wildstein affirms that

> Reform [Judaism] makes *tikkun olam* (repair of the world) a priority. It recognizes our obligation to feed the hungry, improve the lives of those in distress, and help those less fortunate than we. Reform meets the challenges of the world; it does not run from problems or lose itself in self-centeredness. Reform seeks out those who believe differently, looking for partners among other peoples and religions to make our world a better place.[38]

Brooklyn Heights Reform Synagogue states simply in its mission statement: "Work to improve the world is an essential part of our spirituality. Since 1983 BHS has housed a homeless shelter with volunteer cooks and staff. We have an active social justice program aimed at the larger Jewish and non-Jewish communities with activities ranging from helping recent Russian immigrants learn English and adjust to life in the U.S. to holding a holiday toy, book, and coat drive for the December holiday season."[39]

Reform Judaism is certainly not alone in championing *tikkun olam*—most other Jewish denominations including Orthodox, Conservative, Reconstructionist, and Renewal have all made use of the phrase in connection with social action in recent decades. Adat Shalom Reconstructionist Congregation in Bethesda, Maryland, states that "the mitzvah of *tikkun olam*, 'obliges us to help alleviate hunger, homelessness, disease, ignorance, abuse, and political oppression among all people. In addition, we have a responsibility to preserve the health of the global ecosystem upon which all life depends.'" Adat Shalom, in its mission statement, also reflects on the challenges of pursuing *tikkun olam* in today's world. There has historically, and continues to be today, tension between focusing on exclusively Jewish concerns, and those concerns that affect a wider segment of society. The congregation notes that it "seeks to maintain a balance between its particular concerns to be active on behalf of the Jewish people and its universal commitments to help bring about world repair."[40]

THE DREAM OF JUDAISM

Central to Jewish literature and tradition, and made explicit in the modern usage of the expression *tikkun olam* is that the world can be perfected. It can be whole. According to Greenberg, the first chapter of Genesis "records a dream, a vision of the world in its perfect state, an Eden of order and beauty in which life emerges from the divine ground of existence . . ."[41] According to this account, the "world originally was and is still meant to be a paradise. But only when there is peace, with abundant resources, and an untrammeled right to live, will the world be structured to sustain the infinite value of the human being. This," claims Greenberg," is the heart of Judaism, the dream."[42]

In Hebrew, the notion of perfection, *shelemut*, is intricately bound to the word for peace, *shalom*, which denotes wholeness or completeness.[43] In Jewish tradition and literature, *shalom* is a concept that extends to every aspect of human life—a state of personal well-being, comfort, prosperity, safety from harm or danger, ease, harmony between individuals or nations, the work of justice, and the voice of truth. It is a word that has content—it does not merely refer to the absence of war and enmity" or "to the absence of quarrel and strife." *Shalom*, in fact, "ranges over several spheres and can refer in different contexts to bounteous physical conditions, to a moral value, and, ultimately, to a cosmic principle and divine attribute."[44] In fact, "notions of wholeness, health, and completeness inform all variants of the word."[45]

Shalom is central to Scripture. The word appears in 210 passages in the Hebrew Bible, notes Christian biblical scholar Claus Westermann, in virtually every book, "and in all the literary and preliterary layers known to us."[46] The value of *shalom* is demonstrated both by its frequent use as well as the connection made between God and *shalom*. In Judges 6, Gideon erects an altar to God and calls it "Yahweh *shalom*," or God is peace. The phrase is more complicated than it sounds in that can mean, and probably does, both that God is *shalom* and that God makes *shalom*.[47] This linking of God and *shalom* is found elsewhere, especially in the Psalms, where biblical writers indicate that God "delights in the *shalom* [NRSV: 'welfare'] of his servant" (Ps 35:27), and that God "makes *shalom* [NRSV: 'grants peace'] within your borders; he fills you with the finest of wheat" (Ps 147:14).

In rabbinic texts, *shalom* also "signifies a value, an ethical category—it denotes the overcoming of strife, quarrel, and social tension, the prevention of enmity and war."[48] While most texts focus on the internal peace of the Jews, there are texts that go beyond, for example: "He who establishes *shalom* between man and his fellow, between husband and wife, between two cities, two nations, two families or two governments . . . no harm should come to him" (*Mekh. Bachodesh* 12). Sometimes peace is paralleled with other values such as truth and justice. According to Rabban Shimon, "The world stands on three things: on truth, on judgment, and on peace; as it is stated [in Scripture]: 'Execute the judgment of truth and peace in your gates'" (*M. Avot* 1:18). Another rabbi claims that "By three things the world is preserved, by justice, by truth, and by peace, and these three are one; if justice has been accomplished, so has truth, and so has peace" (*JT Ta'an.* 4:2). For the rabbis, there is no higher value or goal than *shalom*, and they point out that *Shalom* is one of God's names, as well as the name of the Messiah.

Shalom is not simply an abstract idea within Jewish tradition, it is part of Jewish practice as well. The Jewish Sabbath forms a bridge between the poles of harsh reality and abstract wholeness. The Sabbath, or *Shabbat* in Hebrew, literally means "to rest," "to pause," or "to cease from activity." This pause or rest is commanded by God, and serves to identify the covenant between God and the Israelites. At its best, the Sabbath carves out a time in which our expectations of the world, and the world's expectations of us, are actually met and provides "a picture of perfect happiness," in the face of our culture that markets unhappiness.[49]

In the Sabbath evening prayer, Jews ask God to "Embrace us with a tent of Thy peace,"[50] or more literally "to envelope us in Your *shalom*." Traditionally in Jewish communities "it was understood that the whole community was responsible for ensuring that all families had the food, wine, shelter, and companionship to celebrate *Shabbat* with joy rather than pain. Through this practice,

Shabbat became a time to affirm and act out—for only a moment, and therefore imperfectly—the social equality of all Jews."[51] In effect the Sabbath allows Jews actually to practice living in a perfect world—to learn how to enjoy it, appreciate it, and be at ease in it. It brings together both worlds—this world and the world to come—and it is an example of both worlds. According to Heschel, "the Sabbath is joy, holiness, and rest; joy is part of this world; holiness and rest are something of the world to come."[52] It also provides a powerful and tangible sense of what perfection is like, so that the week with its calling to work has focus and meaning.

Greenberg notes that "as human involvement in work deepens, the labor itself can become a form of slavery. The test of stopping short of servitude is the ability to stop working, to assert mastery over the work instead of the succumbing to its lures and demands. This is the central function of *Shabbat*."[53] The rest that the Sabbath calls for has purpose in that it extends to every aspect of existence; it is "the armistice in man's cruel struggle for existence, a truce in all conflicts, personal and social, peace between man and man, man and nature, peace within man."[54] In pausing from work, the "*Shabbat* rest teaches us that change is completed by peace and action is enriched by contemplation."[55] The Sabbath tells us: "The world was meant to be perfect. . . . Experience that perfection. Now go and make it happen."[56]

TIKKUN OLAM AS VOCATION

Norman Beck, a professor of theology at Texas Lutheran University, asserts that the Lutheran concept of vocation is being enhanced by our exposure to the Jewish concept and practice of *tikkun olam*. He goes on to point out that "the most significant roots of our Lutheran Christian concept of vocation penetrate the same soil as the Jewish *tikkun olam* concept," especially in the call stories of Abraham, Moses, Elijah, Amos, and others in the Hebrew Bible.[57] Unfortunately, the Lutheran understanding of vocation has often been reduced to the view that one's calling or vocation is tied to one's job or occupation. This is partially true, but it does not get at the whole idea of vocation as Luther understood it or as biblical texts demonstrate. In addition, the limited understanding of vocation as distinction in one's occupation limits its connection to the goals of justice, service to neighbor, and partnership with God that are all part of both a Christian view of one's role in the world and the Jewish understanding of *tikkun olam*. In fact, according to Lutheran scholar Marc Kolden, "defining vocation as occupation allows us to restrict it largely to self-serving actions" and even justify our "modern irresponsible conformity."[58] He goes on to note that Luther's understanding of vocation was controversial in his time, and represented the antithesis of the official Christian and societal positions.

In reading Luther more carefully, it turns out that Luther's highest criterion for vocation was the neighbor in need, even the neighbor with the greatest need. Such a criterion, notes Kolden, was "not a means of protection for one-self and one's own group."[59] As Luther himself says, "A man does not live for himself alone . . . but he lives also for all men on earth; rather, he lives only for others and not for himself. To this end he brings his body into subjection that he may the more sincerely and freely serve others."[60] This understanding of service as central to vocation emerged in part from Luther's study of Galatians, where Paul writes, "For you were called to freedom, brothers and sisters; only do not use your freedom for self-indulgence, but through love become slaves to one another. For the whole law is summed up in a single commandment, 'You shall love your neighbor as yourself'" (Gal 5:13-14). In Lutheran tradition and biblical interpretation, the center of Christian living is found in this complex reality of Christian freedom where one is both Lord of all and servant of all at the same time. Freedom is not about escaping from something, but rather it is freedom for something. Luther did not look at calling or vocation as a burden or a punishment, but rather as a part of living out one's life in Christian free-dom. Noted Luther scholar Timothy Lull in his discussion of Luther's work underscores this point:

> Our vocation is a primary channel for the use of our freedom. Vocation is a personal calling, not simply an occupation. Luther closely linked freedom to vocation—his biblical conviction that all God's people are called to meaning-ful work in the world. God works through our diverse callings to serve the world's needs.[61]

Lull goes on to say that the full realization of freedom can only come about in the willing and voluntary service toward one's neighbor.

Luther's commentary on Genesis provides further clues to his view of vocation and service to the other. In looking at the creation of humans in Genesis 1 in a way that resonates with rabbinic interpretation, Luther noted that "the world is God's good creation, not only in terms of its original coming into being but especially in terms of God's ongoing creative work in upholding and directing all that is and in constantly doing new things."[62] In this framework of creation, men and women were created in the image of God, and therefore represent God within creation as faithful stewards of all that God made. Again, like the rabbis, Luther goes further to show that active partnership with God in service to the world was what God actually intended:

> . . . God could rule the church through the Holy Spirit without the ministry, but He does not want to do this directly. Therefore he says to Peter: 'Feed My sheep (John 21:16). Go, preach, baptize, absolve.' In the state He says to

the magistrate: 'Watch, defend, use the sword, etc.' Therefore Paul calls the apostles 'fellow workmen with God' (1 Cor 3:9). To be sure He alone works. But He does so through us.[63]

In yet other contexts, Luther emphasizes the universality of being called. Every human being, as a good creature of God, has a vocation. Luther asks, facetiously, at one point, "How is it possible that you are not called?" He then goes on to point out that each and every person has at least one role—a wife, a husband, a boy, a girl. Each person also has more than enough of what he or she needs in faith to live and thrive, and has, in fact, a surplus such that "we should devote all our works to the welfare of others."[64] Vocation, in this view, refers to far more than dedication to one's occupation. It refers "above all to the whole theater of personal, communal, and historical relationships in which one lives."[65]

In looking at Luther's framing of vocation there are striking similarities between his ideas and the Jewish understanding of one's role in the world in relation to the other. Lutherans and Jews have both viewed vocation not only as a necessary part of life, but a form of service to the world, to the rest of humanity, and to God.[66] Unfortunately, for most of Christian history, Jews and Christians have not been able share these stories in community, being completely cut off from each other. As Christians and Jews have come into more serious dialogue, especially in the last half-century, there is much that they can learn from each other, and contribute to the world together.

In learning about the concept of *tikkun olam*, Christians might consider the following:

- Judaism has generally maintained a very positive expectation of what the world can and should be, and has maintained that a perfected world is possible "in history."
- In their understanding of *tikkun olam*, Judaism has the sense that the ability and desire to improve the world is part of our very make-up as humans.
- The relationship between God and human beings has the potential to be very rich within the framework of *tikkun olam*. We can be instruments of, partners with, or even cocreators. Great hope and expectation is placed on human potential.
- The work of *tikkun olam* demands attention to the balance in our communities between internal and external concerns, from self to other.
- The work of *tikkun olam* is also flexible—it adapts to the very specific realities of history, perhaps in order that those realities might be changed.

◆ Finally, the work of *tikkun olam* is universal in its invitation—everyone is called to be part of the work of *tikkun olam*.

In conclusion, one Jewish community states that their "commitment to *tikkun olam* is a calling, a vocation, and it is unlikely that the Jews could survive, and it would be unseemly if they did, except as a community organized around values and committed to *tikkun olam*."[67] Is this statement transferable to other communities? To our church? To me or to you? After all, Rabbi Tarfon says that "It is not incumbent on us to finish the task, but neither are we free to desist from it altogether." It is in the process of healing or repairing the world, that we experience healing within ourselves.

Response

Richard Sarason

The use of the phrase tikkun olam *as the Hebrew equivalent of "social justice" ("mending the world," in Fackenheim's felicitous turn of phrase) is very recent, passing into common parlance only in the mid- to late 1970s or early 1980s. It is of North American origin; some maintain, as Suomala notes, that Shlomo Bardin used this coinage in the 1950s at what is now the Brandeis-Bardin Institute in southern California. The usage has virtually no support in traditional rabbinic parlance. The phrase in the* aleinu *prayer,* letakken olam bemalkhut shaddai, *does not refer to human action, but to divine action at the end of days: "Therefore we hope soon to behold Your majestic glory, when idols shall be removed from the earth and false gods destroyed, when the world shall be perfected under the rule of the Almighty, and all mankind will call upon your name." It is God who brings this about, not human beings.*

The phrase mipnei tikkun ha'olam *occurs in Mishnah Gittin, chapters 4 and 5, and related literature, where it refers to a precautionary ruling instituted "in order to maintain the proper order of the world = social relations / for the sake of the general good." The expression is also juxtaposed there with another,* mipnei darkhei shalom, *"for the sake of peace / in the interest of peace," dealing with relations among neighbors (including Jews and Gentiles: "Greetings may be offered to gentiles in the interest of peace" [!].*

The word tikkun *in Lurianic kabbalah refers to an act of cosmic "mending" or "repair" or "restoration" that is effected every time a Jew performs a commandment with proper intent, and so forth. Both the divine and human realms are in need of "repair" after the divine/cosmic catastrophe that occurs in the process of creation, which the kabbalists call* shevirat hakelim, *"the breaking of the vessels." The morphology here is Gnostic, as Scholem and other scholars have pointed out. The creation myth seeks to explain the cosmic origin of evil and disarray.*

Essentially, tikkun olam *is not a traditional Jewish term as it used today; that usage is modern. But the notion of social concern and social justice obviously does exist in Jewish tradition in a major way. This is a concern not only of the biblical prophets, but also of the legal literature, both biblical and rabbinic. The ideal of a just society, in which the poor, sick, widowed, and orphaned must be cared for by all, is understood to be divinely mandated: as God takes note of the socially disadvantaged and hears their cries, so must we all.* Tzedek tzedek tirdof! *That is a native articulation of the value; so is* mitsvot shebein adam lahavero, *obligations that obtain between one person and his fellow. Jacob Neusner, in his various studies of Mishnah Seder Nezikin, has demonstrated that mishnaic legislation materially aims to reduce social and economic inequalities: both extremes of wealth and poverty are to be avoided through legislation and adjudication.*

It is important to stress for Christian audiences who have been brought up on the dichotomy of "law and gospel" that that is a caricature—that the "spiritual" in Judaism is to be enacted through, and to pervade, that which is socially concrete: specific human actions.

On exploring the connection between vocation and tikkun olam, *the traditional Jewish vocabulary would be something more like* mitsvot shebein adam lehavero *(obligations that pertain between one human being and another, contrasted with those that pertain between the individual and God)—because vocation or calling is also related to the notion of obligation. In Jewish tradition, socially responsible behavior toward other human beings is not simply an ideal, but it is also a divinely ordained obligation or duty—it is a* mitzvah. *Here is a difference in the morphology and rhetoric of the two religious traditions. What is* imitatio Christi *in Christianity is both* imitatio Dei *and a divinely ordained commandment in Judaism that is further adumbrated in rabbinic social legislation.*

So the real issue that Suomala phrases (and this, too, sadly has a polemical background in Jewish-Christian relations) is the extent to which Jews and Jewish religion historically and today are concerned about the betterment of humanity as a whole and social justice beyond the confines of the in-group (since within the group this has always been a paramount concern addressed both through moral exhortation and legislation—but, since Jews are real people with real human flaws like everyone else, not everyone at all times has lived up to these ideals!). It is certainly the case that medieval Jews, particularly in the ambit of Christendom, were often quite parochial in their social dealings (but so were Christians in their attitudes toward Jews!). But it is also certainly the case that Jews tended to see themselves as a model for the rest of humanity—kiddush haShem, the sanctification of God's name (= reputation) in public, before the Gentiles also was supposed to dictate Jewish behavior with and toward non-Jews. God's reputation was always on the line in such behavior!

8

◆

Christians and Jews in the Context of World Religions

Darrell Jodock
in Conversation with Mark N. Swanson and Rabbi Barry Cytron[1]

AMERICA AND PLURALISM

Throughout most of American history, Christians have had to come to terms with denominational diversity. The framers of the U.S. Constitution recognized that no single denomination had sufficient adherents to become a national church.[2] They opted for a separation of church and state. Congregationalists, Baptists, Episcopalians, Presbyterians, Lutherans, and many others all had to recognize that theirs was but one denomination among others. Until the 1950s Roman Catholics were often treated as "outsiders," but eventually they, too, gained acceptance and became one of America's denominations.[3]

Only a relatively small percentage of immigrants belonged to non-Christian religions. There were some Buddhists on the West Coast, but elsewhere the non-Christians were mostly Jews from western Europe, who arrived in relatively small numbers during the first half of the nineteenth century and quickly gained entry into the middle class. After 1881, however, considerably larger numbers of Jews left Russia, Poland, and eastern Europe and settled mostly in the Northeast. "Old World" in appearance, gathered in urban enclaves, they were far more noticeable. Soon restrictions began to be imposed. Many businesses, large and small, would not employ Jews. Jews were prohibited from country clubs, resorts, and beaches. Jewish doctors could not treat patients in non-Jewish hospitals. Even top-flight colleges and universities had admissions quotas that kept the number of Jewish students below a certain percentage.

And Jewish families were not allowed to purchase houses in many urban neighborhoods. Overtly anti-Jewish sentiments reached their high point in the early 1940s and then began to decline.[4] In a city such as Minneapolis, Minnesota, discrimination against Jews in employment and housing was not prohibited until 1947.

Following World War II many factors caused overt antisemitism to decrease. As the story of the Holocaust became known, it became clear that Jews had been the victims of our World War II enemy, Nazi Germany. Many Americans from outside the Northeast had, for the first time, come to know individual Jews as a result of service in the military and/or service in a war-related industry. As a new generation of Jewish Americans moved up the educational and social ladder, they joined non-Jews in a migration to the suburbs, thereby emptying ethnic enclaves and mixing together hitherto separate groups of Americans. Politicians began to speak of America's "Judeo-Christian" heritage. Although the precise meaning of that phrase was seldom clear, it did signal an expansion from *denominational* diversity toward *religious* diversity. The inclusion of Jews into American society provided a tentative step in the direction of *religious* pluralism.

As the second half of the twentieth century continued to unfold, most ordinary Americans began to experience this new diversity. That is, they became aware of the presence in their own neighborhoods and communities of people from religions other than Christianity. Typically the circle of their acquaintance included one or more Muslims, Buddhists, Hindus, or Jews. As a result, American citizens have had to face and accommodate the social and political consequences of religious *pluralism*—that is, the acceptance into the body politic of more than one religion. *Denominational* diversity permitted the continuance of the social arrangement known as "Christendom"—where Christian values were given a privileged place in society. *Religious* pluralism has meant a gradual end to certain practices associated with Christendom. The transition can be seen, for example, in public schools, which now endeavor to explain Jewish and Muslim and other holidays or have renamed an Easter recess as "spring break" or a Christmas program as a "holiday concert." Public ceremonies that once included an invocation by a Protestant pastor are now likely to feature representatives from more than one religion. Many of these changes have, of course, been—and continue to be—controversial. In addition to accommodating the social and political consequences of religious pluralism, Christians in America have faced a theological problem: how to understand the relationship between Christianity and the other religions of the world.

At first, many assumed that all non-Christians were "pagans." Their primary image of "pagans" included uneducated adherents of tribal religions, usually in Africa, whom they considered to be superstitious "savages." Often the term had as much to do with cultural differences (being "uncivilized") as with religious differences. But, here in the United States in the second half of the twentieth century, their new neighbors did not fit this image. Often they were educated; typically they were "civilized"; more often than not, their traditions exhibited high moral standards. What were Christians to think of them?

When the issue was *denominational* pluralism, public figures and many Americans borrowed ideas from Deism to build a conceptual framework within which to accommodate the diversity. Deism claimed that all denominations were basically the same. The churches all believed in God; they all taught morality; and they all expected life after death. Yes, there were disagreements, but these, the Deists said, were about peripheral matters, which went beyond the rational core of religion. Various churches, they claimed, all believed basically the same thing, so other denominations should be accepted as "American" and as "Christian."[5] One response to *religious* pluralism was to employ the same framework and to say that "all religions are basically the same." The eighteenth-century Deists had already regarded Islam and Judaism in this way. But they knew little about other world religions. As knowledge of the latter grew, the Deist framework became inadequate. Clearly the major religions of the world are not all the same, whether in basic beliefs or in expected behaviors. To say that the Hindu belief in many gods is the same as the Christian (or Jewish or Muslim) belief in one God and one God only seemed, at best, implausible.

Others took the opposite position, and asserted that other religions had nothing in common with Christianity. Such a position is reflected in statements, still heard today, that Jews or Muslims pray to a different God than do Christians. Whereas the Deist framework had broken down because Hindus and Buddhists understand God differently from Christians, this second option broke down because Jews and Muslims do acknowledge the same God as do Christians—that is, the God of Abraham, Isaac, and Jacob.[6]

As Christians thought about religious pluralism, it became clear that more careful delineations were necessary. One could say neither that all religions are the same nor that all religions are fundamentally or completely different. One needed to be more precise about their specific similarities and their specific differences. In addition to describing other religions accurately, it also became important to understand them theologically. How was a Christian to regard other religions? As adherents became neighbors, this question became all the more urgent.

Before exploring the issue in more detail, it may be well to pause for several general observations:

◆ Whenever two religions are compared, it is important to compare "best" to "best." That is, one should compare the best of Buddhism to the best of Christianity and not the worst of Buddhism to the best of Christianity. It is as easy to find examples of bad behavior among Christians as among the adherents of any other religion in the world.

- Whenever two religions are compared, it is important to interpret each religion in such a way that an informed adherent of that religion would agree with the description.

- Whenever a member of one religion enters into dialogue with a member of another religion, he or she should be ready to learn something new, to see the world differently. This learning may not prompt a person to join the other religion, but one must be prepared for a genuine learning and a resulting change in the way one looks at religion and/or the world.

- Whenever a member of one religion endeavors to understand another religion, he or she should be careful not to interpret the ideas of the other religion as if they fit into the overall framework or outlook of one's own. For example, "being saved" and "original sin" are peculiarly Christian ideas. There may be nothing equivalent in the other religion. Trying to use these categories to interpret its teachings can lead to misunderstandings. Speaking as a Jew to fellow Jews, Rabbi Irving (Yitz) Greenberg offered this reminder: "In light of the Holocaust, Jews must develop a theology of non-Jewish religions that will articulate their full spiritual dignity. One cannot simply treat them as pale reflections of Judaism."[7] His advice applies to Christians as well. Christians should not view and interpret other religions as if they were but pale reflections of Christianity.

With these reminders, let us turn to the main topic of this chapter.

Two interrelated questions will occupy our attention: (1) How should Christians understand the relationship between Christianity and Judaism? And (2) to what degree can Jewish-Christian relations function as a case study for understanding the relationship between Christianity and the other major religions of the world?

CHRISTIANITY AND JUDAISM

Let us observe first that the relationship between Judaism and Christianity is in many ways unique—that is, it is unlike the relationship between Christianity and other religions.

- For example, Christians and Jews share a common Scripture—the TaNaK or the Old Testament or the Hebrew Scriptures—and to quite a large extent agree about its general interpretation. By "general interpretation," I mean that Jewish scholars and Christians scholars can agree about the meaning of many passages and find in the Hebrew Scriptures the same general themes. Christians may give greater weight to some sections and Jews to others, and occasionally they disagree about passages that for Christians seem to anticipate Jesus, but for the most part there is little more disagreement about the Hebrew Scriptures between Jews and Christians than there is disagreement among Christian scholars or among Jewish scholars. Islam affirms that God sent the Torah to Moses and the psalms to David, but Muslims have paid far less attention to the texts of the Hebrew Scriptures than have Christians. For Muslims, the Hebrew Scriptures have been superseded by the Qur'an. "Islam has re-imagined the Scriptures of Israel and of the Christian community as in a sequence that culminates in the Qur'an . . . and Muslims have managed very well without the texts,"[8] while Christianity has reimagined Israel *without* discarding the texts themselves. And here (that is, with Judaism and, to a lesser extent, with Islam) the similarity ends, because no other world religion acknowledges the authority of the Hebrew Scriptures.

♦ *Christians and Jews worship the same God and understand that God in very similar ways.* God is the creator and sustainer of all that is. God is the ruler of the world. God loves humans and shows mercy to them as well as expecting them to "do justice, and to love kindness, and to walk humbly with [their] God" (Mic. 6:8b). In fact, contemporary Christian discussions of "God and suffering," for example, are full of references to Jewish thinkers on that same topic, and vice versa. The witness of the New Testament is so thoroughly steeped in Old Testament thinking that, while it reenvisions the kingdom, it has little new to say specifically about the identity of God. In both communities the basis for thinking about God is the Old Testament (or TaNaK).

♦ *Both Christianity and Judaism employ the concept of "covenant" to interpret their relationship with God.* "The covenant is nothing less than God's promise that the goal [the triumph of life] is worthy and will be realized, that humans will be accompanied all the way, and that God will provide an ongoing model of how to be human."[9] Both Judaism and Christianity consider themselves to have been chosen or elected by God. And Christianity's own sense of covenant is dependent on and in some very important ways an extension of God's covenant with Israel.

♦ *Both look forward in hope to a messianic age—an age of righteousness and peace.* Christians regard this age to have dawned with the resurrection of Jesus, but it is not fully present. They thus expect a "second coming."

For both Jews and Christians the messianic age is not fully present. Its arrival is a guiding hope.[10]

+ *For both, religious community is important.* There are two dimensions here. One is that neither religion leads to a solitary expression; fellowship is important, not only because humans are inherently social but also because the ethical discernment and the moral courage needed to carry out God's will in the world are nurtured in community. The other is that the community has a role to play in healing the world. To use different words: for both, history matters. Faith does not lead to a withdrawal from human affairs but to an engagement with them, because God is understood to be engaged similarly.

+ *Judaism and Christianity have lived in proximity throughout the past two millennia.* The identity of each has been shaped by that proximity. Christianity has often borrowed from Judaism and then also defined itself over against Judaism. Likewise, Judaism has often borrowed from Christianity[11] and often defined itself over against Christianity.

The first five of the points listed above lead to such a high degree of similarity as to support the conclusion that Christianity has more in common with Judaism than with any other world religion.

In order to fill out the portrait, it may be helpful also to mention some dissimilarities.

+ *Christians regard Jesus to be the Messiah, the initiator of the messianic era.* In Greenberg's words, "From this perspective, one difference between the two religions can be stated thus: whereas Jewish tradition affirms that the final goals can be attained under the leadership of a human avant-garde, Christianity adds the claim that God became the human model that leads humans into the final state."[12] As both the Messiah and the suffering servant described in Isaiah, Jesus for Christians reveals God more clearly than God can be seen elsewhere and provides the assistance humans need in order to be right with God. For Jews the Torah is the best revealer of God. In this view, Jesus was a fine Jewish teacher, but he was not the Messiah, because an era of righteousness and peace was not yet fully present during the years that followed his life. Neither, in Jewish eyes, was Jesus a new authority who could, as Christians claim, challenge the traditional understanding of Torah.

+ *Christians consider humans to be in a condition of sin, alienated from God, and needing special assistance to be right with God.* Traditionally called "original sin," this condition has in more recent times often been called "corporate sin" in order to signal its universality. The Jewish perception of human nature is less dire. Humans are highly conflicted, pulled by competing forces of good and evil, but they are not incapable of acting rightly. One is tempted to think that the difference comes because Jews are thinking of humans already in covenant with God, but the disagreement goes beyond that, because on their view some non-Jews can also be "righteous."

♦ *Christians put greater emphasis on beliefs.* In order to safeguard against erroneous beliefs and to ensure some degree of agreement, they have formulated creeds. They use beliefs as a marker for locating the boundaries of the community. Those who profess the creeds and accept those beliefs are "in." Those who do not are outsiders. Judaism has no formulated creeds. Religious beliefs may be part of the community's outlook, but they are not boundary markers, and there is room for considerable disagreement about them.[13] The boundary is instead membership in the community (through birth or conversion) and identification with that community.

Let us reserve judgment about the consequences of the similarities observed above and focus on Christianity's understanding of its relationship with Judaism.

SUPERSESSIONISM

One way Christians have understood their relationship to Judaism is supersessionism (a concept that has already been discussed in other chapters of this book). Supersessionism teaches that Christianity has replaced Judaism. There is only one enduring covenant—namely, God's covenant with the Christians. After the coming of Jesus, supersessionism believes, Jews are no longer in covenant with God, so if Jews are to be right with God, they need to convert to Christianity. There is thus no reason for Judaism to continue to exist. It is a "fossil" of the past, and its adherents are "stiff-necked" in their refusal to recognize the messiahship of Jesus. The corollary of supersessionism is thus anti-Judaism—the view that Judaism is of no value and/or that it misleads people.[14]

There are two major problems with supersessionism. In the first place, it does not enjoy the support of Scripture. The Scriptures again and again witness to the amazing faithfulness of God. God remains true to his covenant with the Israelites even when they disregard or abandon him. They may go, as the prophet Hosea charged, a-whoring after other gods, and they may grieve God deeply; but God's steadfast love will not allow God to give up on them. Passages in both the Old Testament and the New Testament accuse God's people of abandoning the covenant, but the consistent message of the Bible is that *God* has not abandoned his covenant with the descendants of Abraham.

A great deal is at stake here for Christians, because they rely so directly and fully on the fidelity of God. To believe is to trust God and to trust God's promises. If God is not in fact trustworthy and does not exhibit steadfast love, there is little hope for Christians. Given all that Christian believers down through the centuries have done to undermine the purposes of God, the only positive future for Christians is if God's steadfast love keeps God true to God's covenant even when people disobey and abandon it. In the words of Paul van Buren, "If God is not faithful to His people, if He does not stand by His covenant with Israel, why should we think that He will be any more faithful to His Gentile church?"[15]

The first problem with supersessionism is therefore theological. It asserts that God has abandoned God's covenant with the Jews, an assertion that lacks scriptural and theological support.

The second problem to which supersessionism has led and continues to lead to a denigration of Jews. If Judaism has no value, then its adherents wind up being portrayed as deluded, stubborn, irrational, and so forth. Centuries of such portrayals (anti-Judaism) made it easy for Nazi racial antisemitism to take root. The former made the latter seem plausible. For Nazism, all Jews were subhuman. They were the internal enemy, a kind of cancer that needed to be removed. For Germany to flourish, the Jews needed to be expelled, and when historical circumstances made expulsion appear no longer possible, the Jews needed to be annihilated. That a continent as heavily influenced by Christianity as Europe could countenance the extermination of two-thirds of its Jews indicates all too graphically the dangerous consequences of supersessionism and anti-Judaism. As painful as it is to admit, such genocide also indicates the moral failure of Christianity.

In other words, in addition to a theological problem, there is also a moral problem. One way to state this problem is to point out that the denigration of another is a violation of Jesus' instructions to love one's neighbor as oneself. The sad irony is that anti-Judaism denigrates the very group of people to whom Jesus and the apostles belonged. A second way to state the problem is to ask— once one has acknowledged that the goal of the Christian community is to transform humans into peacemakers who courageously challenge evil for the sake of the world God loves, and once one has acknowledged that Christians stood by while Jews and the Roma people (popularly called Gypsies) and other "subhumans" were being deliberately, systematically, and needlessly killed— how can the Christian community, with moral integrity, say to Jews, "Come join us, because we have the better way"? If the Christian community cannot make this claim with moral integrity, and I believe we cannot, then the claims of supersessionism are morally untenable.

ALTERNATIVE TO SUPERSESSIONISM

The second way to understand Christianity's relationship to Judaism has many variations, which will not concern us here, but in general it affirms the ongoing validity of God's covenant with the Jews. Either God has established one covenant with two variations (Judaism and Christianity), or God has established two covenants, one with the Jews and the other with the Christians. In what follows, instead of repeating these options at every juncture, let us, for the sake of simplicity, speak as if there are two covenants.[16] On this view, then, the second covenant was an expansion of God's election. The descendants of Abraham were already included in the first covenant. The second covenant opened the door for others, for the Gentiles. For those not in the first covenant, Jesus is "the way" (John 14:6) into covenant with God.

When assessing biblical support for this nonsupersessionist view, one of the most important passages is Romans 9–11. It is helpful to recall that Paul is writing during a kind of "in-between time," somewhere in the 50s C.E. By "in between," I mean that the Gentiles who believed in Jesus as Lord were being accepted into the synagogues, but the Temple still stood. Judaism remained diverse enough to include the followers of Jesus. There may have been tensions, but the split between Judaism and Christianity had not yet occurred. If one asked Paul, he would have considered himself a Jew, not a member of a separate religion. So in Romans 9–11 Paul is not really discussing the relationship between Christianity and Judaism as separate religions but instead the relationship between those who are faithful to the covenant, including Gentile believers, and those who are not. With regard to the Jews, his words are straightforward: "I ask, then, has God rejected his people? By no means! I myself am an Israelite, a descendant of Abraham, a member of the tribe of Benjamin. God has not rejected his people whom he foreknew" (Rom 11:1-2). He continues, "So I ask, have they stumbled so as to fall? By no means!" (Rom 11:11). "And so all Israel will be saved. . . . As regards the gospel they are enemies of God for your sake; but as regards *election* they are *beloved*, for the sake of their ancestors; for *the gifts and the calling of God are irrevocable*" (Rom 11:26, 11:28-29, emphasis added).

Of special importance are the opening affirmation, "God has not rejected his people," and the closing affirmation, "the gifts and the calling of God are irrevocable." Such statements lend support to the second way Christians can understand Judaism. God's covenant with the Jews remains valid. Christianity is a "new covenant" alongside the covenant with Abraham or a new manifestation of that same covenant.

To repeat, this does not make Judaism and Christianity the same. As Greenberg points out, Christianity emphasizes aspects of the covenant relationship that Judaism does not, and Judaism emphasizes other aspects that Christianity does not.[17] He goes on to argue that neither apprehends fully the entire richness of God's covenant; hence it is possible for Jews and Christians to benefit from mutual critique as well as from the cooperation that accompanies mutual recognition. To borrow an image from van Buren, "Faith is not primarily a matter of thinking, but of walking in a certain Way."[18] (We should note that, according to the book of Acts, the earliest believers were called followers of "the Way," and rabbinic Judaism worked out a code of behavior, called a "way of walking" = *halaka*.) According to van Buren, Jews and Christians may not be on the same path, but they walk on parallel and adjacent paths, and it is possible for each to encourage the other.

What, then, if someone asks, "Are Jews saved?" If "saved" means "in covenant with God," this second approach would answer, "Yes." But "saved" has other meanings. It could mean something more akin to "individually right with God and destined for eternal life." In that case, the most appropriate answer, I would say, is "I don't know." Why is this strange answer appropriate?

- ♦ It is appropriate because Christians see themselves as recipients of unmerited grace. God saves even the unworthy. "God proves his love for us in that while we still were sinners, Christ died for us" (Rom 5:8). Without requiring anything beforehand, God restores the relationship. Faith acknowledges what God has done, is doing, and will do, but faith is not itself a prerequisite for God's adoption. That this is so can be seen in infant baptism, for there, most Christians teach, God adopts a child into God's kingdom without any prior commitment or profession of faith on the part of the infant. The implication is this: if God's grace is unmerited, then no one can determine the limits of that grace.[19] If one is not saved on the basis of one's morality, then one cannot say that immoral people are excluded. If one is not saved on the basis of a correct theology, then one cannot say that those with the wrong theology are excluded. A recipient of God's undeserved mercy has no basis upon which to say, "because of so and so, it is available to person x but not available to person y." If asked whether some other individual has been "saved," the answer should be, "I don't know." Such caution is all the more appropriate when the person under discussion is someone who is in covenant with God.

- "I don't know" is appropriate because it seems to be in accord with Paul's conclusion at the end of Romans 11, where he throws up his hands and declares "O the depth of the riches and wisdom and knowledge of God! How unsearchable are his judgments and how inscrutable are his ways!" (Rom 11:33). In Romans 9–11 Paul states clearly that everything depends on the mercy of God, but he does not answer every possible question about the consequences of that mercy. So it is today; those who affirm the mercy of God do not have answers to every question they may have about the implications of their affirmation. In the context of what precedes it, Paul's doxology, "For from him and through him and to him are all things. To him be the glory forever. Amen" (Rom 11:36), is roughly equivalent to affirming that Paul does not know all the ins and outs of God's mercy.

- This "I don't know" response is appropriate because it contradicts Christian arrogance. It advances the kind of humility that acknowledges human limits.[20] We can know only what has been revealed to us, and among those things not revealed is the standing of other individual persons before God.

The point here is that one cannot say about Jews in general that they are or are not "saved," and one cannot say about a specific Jew with whom one has not spoken that he or she is or is not "saved." The qualification is important. One *can* know something (even if not everything) about the other person's relationship with God *if* one actually talks with that person. But generalizations about groups of people are excluded. What is important is to talk with a person and listen to what that person has to say about the character and purposes of God and about the shape of one's calling. One may discover congruence and rejoice together, or discover differences and explore them. The first job of a Christian should be to encourage a Jew to explore fully the best and deepest religious insights of Judaism before encouraging them to consider adopting Christianity. If, after serious dialogue and conversation, someone decides to convert, whether to Judaism or to Christianity, that is an expression of freedom to which no objection should be made, but Christians have to be especially careful not to "target" Jews and especially sensitive to the well-remembered, centuries-old pattern of intimidation and coercion. As van Buren says,

> Any proselytizing from either side must therefore satisfy two requirements: First, it must not be undertaken in such a way as to encourage anyone to deny the reality of God's continuing concern and love for His people and His church. The special circumstances of particular individuals must not blind us to the larger historical fact of God's dealing with His creation up to this point.

He has provided two ways for walking in His Way, one for the Jews and one for the Gentiles. Second, due to the loss of one-third of God's people in the Holocaust, special care must be exercised by the church for the foreseeable future not to weaken the Jewish people. In sum, all care should be exercised by the church—and we can also hope by the Jewish people—to make ours a cooperative competition in the more faithful service of God's purpose for His whole creation.[21]

Adolf Hitler wanted Europe to be "Jew-free." Christians need to be careful lest vigorous, targeted proselytizing becomes an alternative way to make the world "Jew-free" and thereby to give Hitler a "posthumous victory."[22] God promised Abraham that his descendants would be a blessing to the world. Christians should not deny the world that blessing. Yes, Christians can claim that they are part of the fulfillment of the promise, but the richness of having two covenanted communities suggests that Christians should not arrogate to themselves the sole and complete fulfillment of that covenant-forming promise. There is no Judaism without Jews. Ridding the world of Jews (by making them all Christians) is not an appropriate goal for Christians, since the advantages of having two covenanted communities would then be lost.

What then are the benefits of closer relations between Christians and Jews? Let us mention two.

One benefit is finding allies. Both Christians and Jews are called to transform the world—that is, to create justice, to uphold human dignity, and to work for peace. If "evil" is the name for those social forces that work against justice, human dignity, and peace, then the forces of evil are powerful enough so that any group that pursues an alternative path needs allies.

An analogy can be drawn between ecumenical and interfaith relations. We begin with the ecumenical: within Christianity, World War II precipitated the formation of the World Council of Churches. To be sure, the ecumenical movement had begun prior to World War II, but with that war came the recognition that, when faced with a totalitarian government hostile to Christian values, various Christian communities needed to work together. Otherwise the government would simply "divide and conquer." And then, to complete the analogy, we turn to interfaith relations: within today's religiously pluralistic society, interfaith cooperation has the same urgency as did ecumenical cooperation earlier in the twentieth century. If Jews and Christians (along with Muslims and others) together advocate for the homeless, the hungry, and those without medical care, they can be a more effective political voice than if any one group tries to do it alone.

Not only can Jews and Christians be spokespersons for others, but either may become targets of prejudice. Under those circumstances they also need each other. When Christian churches are bombed or burned, or when synagogues are defaced and Jews attacked, a common witness is helpful. Indeed, Christians speaking out in behalf of Jews, or Jews speaking out in behalf of Christians, can be more effective than either speaking out on their own behalf.

A second benefit is an enriched appreciation for one's own tradition. A Christian's understanding of his or her own religious tradition is always incomplete. Because of the specifics of one's upbringing or religious education, or because of incomplete study or limited experience, some aspects of Christianity are overlooked or underestimated. Given how much Jews and Christians share, a serious encounter with Judaism can often prompt Christians to discover in their own tradition something important that they have overlooked or underestimated. Some examples:

- *A corporate sense of redemption.* For Jews, individuals cannot be redeemed in isolation. If redemption is to occur, if an era of peace and justice is to come into existence, it must include the whole community. When a contemporary American Christian encounters such an emphasis, it may at first seem strange, but soon one begins to notice how corporate are the references in the New Testament to the kingdom of God. Out of interfaith understanding comes an appreciation for a Christian idea that is all too easily obscured by the individualism of American "God-and-me" versions of the faith.

- *A deeper appreciation of deliberation.* For rabbinic Judaism, religious and ethical questions are adjudicated through debate and deliberation. Yes, the Torah functions as an authoritative document, but its application to contemporary life is seldom self-evident. Such matters are to be decided through deliberation. Christians in the United States are often uncomfortable with debate within the church. They often expect an already-worked-out set of beliefs. Many want the Bible to provide "answers" to their religious and moral questions. And they just as often expect harmony. This discomfort is heightened by societal developments that prompt many Americans to expect little from deliberation. When American media describe ideas in a polarized way (as if there are only two possible positions), and when these positions are articulated by highly partisan spokespersons, citizens often see little hope of finding common ground. Moreover, deliberation can be slow and time-consuming. Healthy debate requires that people become informed and participate. When complex issues are under discussion, deliberation can be messy and confusing. Contact with Judaism can help an American Christian recover a sense of the importance of deliberation. I say "recover," because it is present in the tradition. The book of Acts records instances where the apostles came together to deliberate, and the Christian creeds were worked out through a process of deliberation. Luther's participation in debates extended and enriched his theological insights. Christian ethics has always been formulated through the give and take of deliberation. Dialogue with Jews can help Christians recover an appreciation for the importance of thoughtful deliberation that runs deep within their own tradition. And this recovery can prepare them to understand more fully the importance of deliberation in their lives as citizens. If we are to avoid ever-escalating culture wars, the search for common ground is important.[23]

• *A deeper appreciation of human participation in healing the world.* One stream of Jewish thought has regarded humans to be "cocreators," in the sense of sharing with God responsibility for the care of the world. This tradition is rooted in passages such as the second chapter of Genesis where Adam is put in the garden "to till it and keep it" (2:15) and participates in naming the animals, passages such as Genesis 18 where Abraham intercedes for Sodom, and passages such as Exodus 32 where Moses intercedes for the people in the wilderness. Christians have correctly emphasized that one's relationship with God is restored via a free gift and that God alone can do this restoring. They have also been drawn to the different image of God found in Genesis 1 where God speaks and it is done, where God's emperor-like power is evident. But, unless balanced by the down-to-earth, hands-on image of God in Genesis 2, such an emphasis can create passivity—a tendency to "just let God take care of it." Dialogue with Jews can help Christians recover their calling to be cocreators, coresponsible along with God for the well-being of the world, not in the sense of controlling it, but in the sense of tending it or "husbanding" it or serving it. One implication of the incarnation is that God has chosen to work through human beings. Just as Jesus opposed the forces of evil, even when it was personally costly, so believers are called to stand up for justice, human dignity, and peace. They are empowered to act. Forgiveness is not a substitute for action, but is concomitant with action. Such action is risky both because it challenges the status quo and because it is inevitably based on only partial and incomplete knowledge of the human condition. If God works through humans, then humans need to act; for believers passivity is not an option. For example, if ecological disaster is going to be averted, it will have to come through the participation of human beings who care enough about God's creation to challenge their own and their society's destructive habits of consumerism. There are some things God can do alone, but healing the earth is not one of them.

♦ *For several centuries Jews have lived as a minority in Western society.* They have learned ways to exercise their calling. Christians in Western society have gotten used to being in a privileged position, which we have called Christendom. The advent of religious pluralism is requiring that Christians in the United States adapt to a post-Christendom society. On the world's stage only about one quarter of the people are Christians. Globalization also requires that Christians adjust to a minority rather than majority status. Christians can learn from Jews an alternative outlook, one that allows them to serve creatively without dominating or controlling. It may give them a new appreciation of early Christianity, lived as it was in a pluralistic society prior to the advent of Christendom.

This list could be extended, but perhaps these examples are sufficient to suggest that the self-understanding of Christians can be enriched by closer contact with Jews and Judaism. Christians who have participated in Jewish-Christian dialogue can attest to this from their own personal experience. Rather than diluting or diminishing their commitment to their own tradition, the experience of interfaith dialogue has deepened and enhanced it.

CHRISTIANITY AND OTHER RELIGIONS

Given what we have been saying about Christianity and Judaism, to what degree can Jewish-Christian relations function as a case study for understanding the relationship between Christianity and the other major religions of the world?

If one is thinking about the content, the belief systems, of various religions, the answer is that it cannot, because Judaism is different from all the other religions and because no other religion shares as many teachings in common with Christianity as does Judaism. Moreover, it is unclear from the biblical witness (where Buddhism, Islam, and Hinduism are not discussed) whether religions outside of Judaism and Christianity are in covenant with God and whether being in covenant is even an appropriate standard for assessing those other religions.

If one is thinking about an outlook, however, then the answer is, yes, Christianity's approach to and understanding of Judaism can function as a case study for the relationship between Christianity and the other religions.

First, when a Christian thinks about persons in other religions and wonders about their personal relationship with God (in the sense of being "saved"), the same response is appropriate—namely, "I don't know." One doesn't know because no human can know the limits of God's mercy, because the answer has not been revealed, and because a Christian affirms that all humans are created by God. What are the implications of the doctrine of creation? What sort of relationship does it establish between God and other human beings? Exactly what does it mean that all human beings are made in the image of God? A Christian needs to think carefully about these questions, especially since the Scriptures provide no clear answers regarding God's relationship to the adherents of the world's major religions. Exactly what does it mean that God made a promise to Noah (the ancestor not just of the Israelites but of all humans) and established a sign of that promise (Gen 8:20—9:17)? Could it be that all people are in some sense already in covenant with God? Again, no clear answers. Exactly what does it mean that in Isaiah's prophecy and in Micah's prophecy all the nations stream to Zion and recognize God? Since "all the people walk, each in the name of its god" (Mic 4:5), could this mean a recognition of the divine that is not, strictly speaking, a conversion? The Scriptures provide us with images and hopes, but (on this question) no clear answers.

"I don't know" is not a cop-out. It yields a major benefit. If a person claims to know the answer in advance, there is no reason to talk. But if one does not know, then one engages in conversation in order to discover what the other has to say about God, about God's mercy, and about the human response to divine grace. "I don't know" requires that a person relate to real people rather than deal with abstractions such as "Buddhism" or "Hinduism" or "Islam."

But does this "I don't know" mean that Christians have nothing to offer? By no means. They can share the good news of what God has done, is doing, and will do. Such good news is a gift they have to offer. They can also share the instruction (the Torah) that they receive through the Scriptures, because in the end, when properly understood, it too turns out to be "good news," for it leads to a fuller, richer life. These gifts are just that—gifts to offer—and therefore not the basis for anything coercive or manipulative and not the basis for a new triumphalism or a new Christendom.

Do Christians then have any incentive to evangelize? If "evangelizing" means sharing the good news, then yes. The incentive is a mixture of their own joy and their own responsibility to love the neighbor. Any person who experiences something joyous immediately tells others about it—usually one's family and friends. But if every living person is my neighbor, as the parable of the Good Samaritan seems to say, and if I am to love my neighbor as myself, then there are no limits on the circle of people with whom the good news is to be shared. Joy and love of neighbor are incentives enough to take a person across social boundaries and into the "uttermost parts of the world."

Second, recognizing the integrity of Judaism can be a model for recognizing the integrity of other world religions. As we have argued, there is no way to know whether everyone in those religions is or is not "saved," but this does not prevent Christians from acknowledging the reality of their experience of the sacred. If the essence of any religion is wonder, awe, and gratitude, then the other major religions of the world are clearly religions. They are expressions of an encounter with the sacred—of wonder, awe, and gratitude.

Third, just as Christians do not need to stop being Christians in order to acknowledge the religious value of Judaism, so Christians do not need to minimize their loyalty to Christianity in order to acknowledge the integrity of other world religions. When a Christian believer acknowledges with John that Jesus is "the way, the truth, and the life" and "no one comes to the Father except through me," the believer affirms that "if you know me, you will know my Father also" (John 14:6-7). In other words, a Christian sees a congruence between Jesus and God. They have the same purpose, the same character, and so on. To engage in dialogue is to listen and learn; it is to be open to mutual learning. But at some point the Christian will need to assess for oneself the results of the conversation. If the Christian remains committed to Christianity, the inescapable basis of assessment is whether God is being perceived in a way that is consistent with what one sees in Jesus. In that sense Jesus is the touchstone for Christians as they assess what they learn and relate it to their own convictions and priorities. Jesus is for them *"the* way."[24]

The techniques worked out in intra-Christian ecumenical dialogue helped prepare Christians for interfaith dialogue and cooperation with Jews. Similarly, the questions and issues confronted in Jewish-Christian dialogue can prepare Christians for conversation with members of other world religions.

When engaged in dialogue with someone from another religion one often discovers that, at some deep level of apprehension, the divine is being understood similarly. Such experiences are not reason enough to declare that the religions are the same, but they are reason enough to expect that dialogue is worthwhile and that interfaith understanding can be an agent of peace in the world.

Both Judaism and Christianity affirm that God's purpose is *shalom.* If respectful interfaith dialogue can serve that goal, if it can offer an antidote to all those forces that create conflict and bloodshed, then is it not in some sense serving the will of God? I, for one, would say yes.

Response

Mark N. Swanson

I am grateful for Darrell Jodock's essay, which I believe succeeds in showing how Christian-Jewish dialogue can function as a case study for Christians' conversations with people of yet other faiths. His list of rules for fair comparison of religions is helpful, as is his stance of hopeful agnosticism with regard to the eternal destiny of those who do not come to explicit Christian confession in this life. He gives excellent examples of how Jews can help Christians to see their own faith afresh, in all its strangeness, with its weaknesses and its need to recall elements that may have been ignored or suppressed. While his list is specific to the Christian-Jewish encounter, one can expect parallel lists to emerge from the encounter of Christianity with Islam, Buddhism, and so on.

Jodock is striving for simplicity, but I wonder whether some of his formulations are a little too easy. Can one really say that the New Testament "has little new to say specifically about the identity of God"? Surely when the New Testament claims that it is at the name of Jesus that every knee shall bow (Phil 2:9-11), and so forth, something new is being said about God's identity—even while the language of Isaiah 45 is being used to say it. This observation serves Jodock's larger point, however. If Christian-Jewish conversations about the identity of the one God are complex, all the more do they become a model for Christian conversations with Muslims (in particular), as well as for yet more difficult interreligious interrogations of divinity.

At the end of the essay I found myself hoping for Jodock to say just a little bit more about the possibilities of interfaith dialogue. While dialogue certainly will involve making comparisons and assessments and seeking similarities ("at some deep level of apprehension"), the hope of dialogue goes beyond this: that in the encounter of real difference, *new language that allows for genuine conversation and new apprehension of reality will somehow be enabled. To the degree that Christians and Jews experience this as a real possibility in their encounters, the groundwork is laid for their engagement with people of yet other faiths. This fits with the main contention of Jodock's essay—with which I am very much in agreement.*

CASE STUDY

•

The Arab-Israeli-Palestinian Conflict

Peter A. Pettit in conversation with John Stendahl

This is not the place to begin reading this book.

It may be tempting to start here; I will say more about why that is so. But the strong temptation makes it all the more important to explain why this is not the place to begin reading this book.

The arguments made here—the suggestions proposed, the perspectives advanced—all are grounded in the work of theology, history, and ethics that the writers of the preceding eight chapters have done. That work reflects and grounds the insights which framed the Talking Points, inviting the church into conversation about our relationship with the Jewish people today. Without exploring the evidence and discussion that underlie those insights, the reader may well find that the present chapter seems arbitrary and tendentious in its handling of a complex topic fraught with ambiguity and tension. Without the background of the preceding chapters (or at least of several of them), this effort may not get the hearing it deserves.

Moreover, by reading this chapter first, all that goes before may not get the hearing it deserves. How any given theological or historical or ethical insight might bear on the Arab-Israeli-Palestinian conflict cannot be the sole criterion for evaluating its value. There is much at stake in that conflict and in the church's engagement with it, and many readers will care deeply one way or another about the directions in which this chapter points. The value of a new relationship with the Jewish community, with its many implications for our life as a church, cannot stand or fall simply on its usefulness in addressing this one moral challenge. Apart from how I have used their work, the authors of the foregoing chapters deserve to have their efforts examined in their own right and for their intrinsic value.

This chapter stands in continuity with the rest of the book in an important way. Each of the foregoing chapters has been written "in conversation with" a colleague, usually Jewish, so that the work is the product of an embodied encounter. So, too, with this chapter. This case study is not a policy statement of the Evangelical Lutheran Church in America, nor does it express a consensus position of the Consultative Panel on Lutheran-Jewish Relations of the ELCA. It is, as the title says, a case study. It is one person's effort to apply the insights of a new relationship with the Jewish community to an issue of pressing concern in that relationship.[1] It is also, however, partially the fruit of conversation between myself and a trusted, valued partner, with whom I have worked closely in writing the Talking Points and have enjoyed hours of discussion over the past decade of our mutual service on the Consultative Panel.

Sharing, as we do in the "community of moral deliberation" that the church strives to be, John Stendahl and I bring our own respective experiences, perspectives, competencies, biases, and limitations to the moral challenge of engaging the Arab-Israeli-Palestinian conflict. Like those who will read this book, we do not share all the same assumptions. Nor do we agree at every point of applying insights that emerge from our common work on Lutheran-Jewish relations. We represent, in our conversation, the kind of discussion that we hope to engender among all members of the church and those with whom we travel together in life, of many faiths and no faith, of varied experience, manifold gifts, and strong convictions. There is no straight line from theology and history and ethics to an unambiguous profile for engagement with life's challenges. We have only the line that runs through our hearts and minds and communities to the best understanding of which we are capable at a given time. I am grateful to John for joining me on this journey and for the many ways in which his partnership has made my understanding better than it began.

It may be tempting to begin reading the book here just because this chapter brings us to engagement with one of contemporary life's most resistant challenges. The images of conflict and suffering, the narratives of triumph and tragedy, and alliances with people who have a direct stake in the outcomes of the Arab-Israeli-Palestinian conflict make this a crucial place where the church's voice registers powerfully with us.

Furthermore, the Christian community interacts most prominently with Jews on the global stage in relationship to the State of Israel. No other country has been the focus of as many United Nations resolutions as Israel (roughly 30 percent of all adopted UN resolutions). No country receives more foreign aid from the United States. No other country's politics and policies figure as prominently as Israel's in the manifestos of governments and movements that do not share a border with it. And no other country's nationalist movement commands the allegiance of foreign Christians, especially American Christians, the way Zionism does.

So it is understandable that readers may be drawn to begin their reading here, where "the rubber hits the road." If doing so helps to engage the imagination and stimulate critical thinking, without judging either a half-century's work on Jewish-Christian relations or the ELCA's engagement in Israel and Palestine on the basis of this exploration, then perhaps this could be a place to start.

Given the limited space available and the modest goals of a case study, I will draw on insights from five of the foregoing chapters to suggest ways in which a new relationship with the Jewish people may shape our approach to Israel's continuing conflict with the Palestinian nationalist movement and with neighboring Arab states. There is certainly much more that a new relationship with Jews and Judaism will offer the church than this; implications for our life as the people of God together with the Jewish people extend to worship, education, devotion, social action, and evangelical witness. We cannot explore all of them here. But in this case study I want to offer an example of the influence that this new thinking can have on every arena of the church's life and work. In that effort, I will work through five insights and the impact they may have on our engagement with the Arab-Israeli-Palestinian conflict.

- *Talking Point #6—Jewish Concern for the State of Israel:* Recognizing the distinctive concern that Jews have for the State of Israel, I suggest that North American Christians engage the conflict with a distinctive voice and contribution to the cause of peace on behalf of all those involved with the conflict.
- *Talking Point #1—Judaism Then and Now:* Because the Jewish people and the church are simultaneously God's people in covenant through what Paul names "a mystery," I suggest that the church cannot turn aside from the Jews' deepest yearnings and anxieties any more than we can from those that live within the church.
- *Talking Point #2—Covenants Old and New:* In light of the central role that the land holds in God's continuing covenant with the Jewish people, I suggest that the church must take up the challenge of articulating theologically the place of the land in our understanding of that covenant today.
- *Talking Point #5—Difficult Texts:* Just as we have begun to use biblical language with much greater care and respect for its literary-historical context, in order not to slander Jews unwittingly, so I suggest that we must take care to render a fair witness to the realities of this conflict in our own language and to be trustworthy interpreters of meaning across cultural divides. Moreoever, as world leaders in uprooting anti-Jewish

and antisemitic images that are the legacy of our past contempt, we will also decry any similarly hateful misrepresentation and slanderous symbolism applied to Arabs, Palestinians, and Muslims.

- *Talking Point #3—Law and Gospel*. Embracing the classic Lutheran insights regarding the dialectical relationship of law and gospel, I will suggest that we avoid oversimplifying issues of peace and justice or splintering those paired biblical virtues into opponents.

DISTINCTIVE PLACES, VOICES AND ROLES

Rufus E. Miles coined Miles' Law, that "where you stand depends on where you sit."[2] It is as true in Jewish-Christian relations and in the Arab-Israeli-Palestinian conflict as it in the public administration arena where Miles developed it. The position that one will hold on an issue—and even the range of positions that one can consider—is constrained by the place one occupies in the situation that is at issue.

We recognized this truism in drafting *Talking Point* #6, "Jewish Concern for the State of Israel." All the other Talking Points approach Christian topics from a theological angle, informed by a new relationship with the Jewish people. In looking at the State of Israel, though, we realized that there is very limited prior work and nothing approaching consensus to support a theological treatment of the issue. In considering our new relationship with Jews, however, it was evident that many Christians could benefit from the effort to describe a Jewish perspective on the State of Israel.

Jews sit in a different place relative to Israel than Christians do. The connection that most Jews throughout the world feel to the State of Israel is unlike any other nationalism or ethnocentrism with which we may be familiar; we must understand it thoroughly in its distinctiveness if we are to gain insight into Jewish identity. Moreover, the State of Israel has not been a focus of theological reflection by many Christians for very long. Christians do not yet fully agree among themselves that Israel must be considered covenantally, as I will suggest below, nor do we have a common set of criteria, priorities, principles, and objectives for doing so. While such commonality also eludes the Jewish community, there are few Jews who have not developed an opinion about Israel. Just by sitting in the world as a Jew, every Jew must take some stand with regard to Israel.

There is a distinctive stand that Palestinians and Arabs have on the conflict with Israel as a result of where they sit as well. Sitting adjacent to a thriving democracy with a strong economy, buttressed by the world's fourth-largest military, and a standing alliance with the world's only remaining superpower, many of the Palestinian people and their leaders take the stand that Israel is their biggest problem and the United States their best hope to influence Israel's policies. Many Israelis, understandably, take a different stand. They see Israel sitting in a hostile Arab neighborhood where the Palestinians are the point of a sword aimed at Israel's heart and the United States is a vital ally in guaranteeing their continuing existence.

The Israeli and Palestinian stands have sustained a conflict that now spans six decades. The two communities' narratives about those decades, as well as their prior history, have been deeply shaped by their stances. The repeated pattern of failed peace talks over the past two decades shows how difficult it is for either one to grant credence to the other's account. From such entrenched positions, both look to the United States and to the global church for advocacy and alliance. Israeli advocates have long lobbied the U.S. government and cultivated their cause among American Jews, while Palestinian Christians have in recent years been particularly active in courting the partnership of the North American churches and others around the world.

Partisans on all sides of the conflict strive relentlessly for media placement and positive spin, devoting energy and money to Internet sites that lament and lampoon those media sources that offend their respective standards for fair coverage. In the view of these partisans, biases and blind spots are the norm in the major media; only constant vigilance by a network of savvy reader/viewers keeps them from becoming a public relations bureau for "the other side." Israelis and Palestinians appear regularly at public rallies and church assemblies, striving by their indigenous credentials to sway people from a "distorted" perspective to see the reality of the situation—from where they sit.

Given the relative ignorance of most Christians regarding the Middle East and the minimal attention that the modern situation has received in Christian circles, our churches are particularly vulnerable to appeals from both sides to add weight to their cause. We are called on to join them in advocacy with the government, the United Nations, and other world powers on behalf of their people and their position. We are invited to be the megaphone that amplifies their voices in the arena of public opinion.

There certainly are times and circumstances when the church must lend its voice to lift up the cry of those who are neglected by worldly powers. The church has often been the only voice that would confront those powers with their responsibility to the marginalized (in biblical terms, "the poor, the orphan, and the widow"; "the stranger"; "the least of these brothers and sisters"). To abdicate that role in the name of "fairness" or "balance" could be a failure of faith, which calls us to proclaim a liberating gospel in the face of every enslaving power.

The danger that we face in a conflict such as the present one is that lending our voice to only one side of the conflict can be just as much a failure. Pragmatically, of course, we may misjudge the forces that are at work in the conflict; we risk lending our aid to a cause that is not entirely just or standing against a power that is not entirely at fault. Such judgments, though, are the stuff of discernment and commitment, so the accompanying risks are necessary ones. More fundamentally though, we may fail to recognize and respond to the extent to which all parties are enslaved by the conflict itself.

This is a point at which the distinctive position of the North American church (and others outside the Middle East arena) can contribute much more than just a megaphone to the situation. We are not directly caught in the daily realities of the conflict and hence can offer a perspective that differs from those who are. We can hear the painful parallels in the rhetoric of the Israeli and the Palestinian, each of whom feels the pain of victimization and vulnerability so deeply. We can hear the mutually delegitimizing characterizations that exaggerate faults and ignore virtues. We can see the mismatches between rhetoric and reality that overstate the virtue and victimhood of one's own community while branding the other with excessive malice and power. Our seat outside the immediate arena of conflict allows us to stand in more prudent assessment of the claims made by the parties, claims that are shaped and misshaped by the demands of the conflict setting.

In such a situation, we are challenged to find paths of accompaniment with the several parties to that which will best contribute to peace.[3] One visible path of accompaniment is the World Council of Churches' "Ecumenical Accompaniment Programme in Israel and Palestine." Participants come from WCC member churches to work with Palestinians, Israeli peace activists, and advocates for Palestinian rights. Their role is to serve as witnesses, monitoring and recording human rights abuses; to join with local activists in nonviolent resistance; to offer protection as a nonviolent presence during confrontation; and to engage in public advocacy. They have witnessed courageously and tirelessly by their accompaniment at West Bank checkpoints and in olive groves and at house demolitions, as well as in demonstrations against abuses by the Israeli military and harsh policy from the Israeli Knesset.

Perhaps because accompaniment is a mission model that serves churches in their relationship to one another, there has been no similar accompaniment by WCC volunteers on Israeli school buses or among young soldiers hitchhiking home for Shabbat, in nightclubs, coffee shops, or wedding halls that can be targeted for attack. Here, too, the witness and intervention of courageous Christians could serve well to deter violence. In those settings, however, just as in the Palestinian settings, the very courage of those who accompany participants in the conflict would bring them into the conflict setting, thus mitigating the distinctiveness of the role their home churches can also play. Those who accompany usually learn quickly to identify with the community in which they live. They now sit among the embattled and so learn to stand where the embattled stand on the issues. It happens as much with American Jewish youth who accompany their Israeli peers for a year or two as it does with WCC youth who accompany Palestinians.

Another dimension of accompaniment could therefore be explored by churches that do not sit in the war zone. That is a dimension that accompanies all the participants in the conflict with both comfort and critique.[4] It takes seriously as gifts the relative disengagement and distance of a North American context and seeks to use them constructively for the well-being of those in the conflict. The church then speaks with its own voice and refuses to serve merely as a megaphone for any one voice in the conflict. We learn from our experience with Jews that they have a distinctive relationship to the State of Israel and that diaspora Jews sit in a different relationship to Israel than do Israelis. We can apply this insight constructively when we engage the conflict from the distinctive position of North American Christians, different from Palestinian Christians and Palestinian Muslims and Israeli Arabs and every other participant.

Otherwise, a crucial opportunity is lost: to address the conflict from the distinctive position of a concerned advocate for peace who is not identified with any side in the conflict.[5] "Where you stand depends on where you sit." The global church, as part of the people of the God of Israel, is gifted to sit both astride and beyond this conflict. We are called to use that gift with all our other gifts, as peacemakers, but we cannot do so when the churches' seat is drawn into the arena of the conflict on one side or the other. As an outsider to the conflict, the credible posture of the global church is standing on its own two feet in its own place, deeply engaged in accompaniment and advocacy from there, but not carried into the fray on the shoulders of our brothers and sisters who live there, whether Palestinian or Israeli.

As we move through other insights of the Talking Points and the implications that I suggest they bear for our engagement with the Arab-Israeli-Palestinian conflict, this first insight will be foundational. The distinctive position in which we sit relative to all the primary participants in the conflict is crucial to our reflection on where we will stand on individual issues. That distinctive position leads us into accompaniment with all the participants in different ways and precludes our fully identifying with any one of them. When we are faithful to the distinctive context God has given us for our ministry, we offer our best gifts on behalf of peacemaking, which itself will be a gift of God that can only be embodied by those who sit now in gravest danger and deepest fear.

ISRAEL: PEOPLE, LAND, AND STATE

When the Talking Points identify the Jewish community as "a powerful partner with the church" (*Talking Points* #1), the Jewish people, known biblically as "Israel," and the State of Israel take on a new significance for the church. Up to this point, I have used "Israel" to refer to the state and have referred to the people as "Jews" or "the Jewish people." To be precise, though, "Israel" names a people, a land, and a nation-state. There is nothing quite like this in Christianity, and any effort to distinguish crisply among the three imposes an unnatural separation on Jewish self-understanding. In the discussion henceforth, I will more precisely refer to land, people, and state where it is most helpful. When I use the more ambiguous term "Israel," I will often mean to make the issue more complicated just because it can refer to all three.

For many centuries Christians claimed that the Jews were condemned by God for having rejected Jesus as the Messiah. God punished them, so it was taught, by driving them out of Jerusalem in the first century C.E. and making them homeless permanently, aliens in every country where they resided ("the wandering Jew"). In such a view, the very legitimacy of a Jewish homeland could be challenged as contrary to God's will and word.[6] The church has largely repudiated this central element in the teaching of contempt, yet its implications continue to reverberate in opposition to Israel both as a state and as a people.

The United Nations voted in November 1947 to partition what remained of the post–World War I British administrative territory of Palestine; the intent was to establish adjacent Jewish and Arab states linked in an economic union. Ever since, neighboring Arab nations have repeatedly rejected Israel's legitimacy as a state. Only Egypt and Jordan have recognized Israel, in treaties signed in 1979 and 1994, respectively; the Palestinian Authority also recognized Israel in the Oslo Accords of 1993. As recently as the summer of 2005, however, the Palestinian faction Hamas responded to Israel's withdrawal of settlements from the Gaza Strip with a renewed call to armed struggle. One stated goal of Hamas is the destruction of Israel, a stance that precluded its participation in the 2007 Annapolis Conference to restart the peace talks. More widely, the continuing use of derogatory, indirect language such as "the Zionist entity" as a substitute for "Israel" indicates that several Palestinian factions would deny Israel any place in the family of nations.[7] When the president of Iran called for Israel to be "wiped out from the map of the world," he was not denounced by the governments and media of the surrounding Arab world.[8]

The sustained history of this rhetoric and periodic accompanying violence has left many Israelis and Jews in doubt about the world's commitment to the State's existence, with implications for the people's continued existence, as well.

In his recent analysis of the Israeli-Palestinian peace process of the 1990s, Kenneth Levin reported:

> Shortly after the start of the Oslo process, the writer David Grossman declared that to see the process to its fruition in peace Israelis must concede to the Arabs not only geographic territories but territories of the soul. . . . They must also give up the belief that the creation of Israel represents a national return for the Jews from a long and too often horrifyingly painful exile. They must even yield their belief in the value of Jewish peoplehood.[9]

It is telling that Grossman voices the fear of delegitimization even in the very peace process that takes as one objective the full recognition of Israel by the Palestinians and neighboring Arab states.

In a similar vein, Anglican Canon Naim Ateek speaks for many Palestinians when he challenges Jewish belief in God's election as narrowly "nationalistic," saying it fails to rise to the "higher concept of God . . . the only worthy concept of God."[10] Their experience of dislocation through multiple wars and of the resulting occupation under the Israeli military is felt as a delegitimization and dehumanization that cannot possibly stem from any source that knows the God of life that they worship. When Lutheran Bishop Munib Younan and others warn against allowing a day to come when there is a Holy Land without the holy people ("the living body of Christ") who began there, he speaks the fear of a people who see their ultimate dislocation and dissolution as an imminent threat.[11]

When faced with such fears of delegitimization, the church has an instinctive alliance with Palestinian Christians that draws on more than a century of development, education, and mission experience working in Arab villages in the region. To be sure, there is a broad slander in many Western venues that we must counteract, a negative stereotype that grossly compounds an Orientalist prejudice against natives, Palestinian Liberation Organization terrorism of the 1970s, and the image of Osama bin Laden since September 11, 2001. The church has a daunting challenge to testify against these delegitimizing images and uproot them. The commitment and energy to undertake that task, though, is rooted in the solidarity we can feel with those who share the gospel and familiar patterns of worship and devotion. There is nothing inherent in the church's heritage that makes us a participant in prejudice against Palestinians.

We are not as fortunate in relation to Jews and the legitimacy of their claim to a sovereign state on the land promised in Scripture. Before we can take up the challenge of confronting and uprooting images and language that delegitimize the State of Israel, we must take account of the role that the church played in engendering those images and language. Since the practice of delegitimizing Israel has roots in Christian teaching, so the church above all now has reason to challenge this unfortunate consequence of its former pedagogy. The reason touches on three essential aspects of Christian belief: our understanding of revelation, our own identity as God's people, and the way the church deals with disappointed expectations about the fulfillment of God's kingdom. We will look at each of these in turn.

First, Christians began teaching that Judaism had lost any legitimate national identity because they found God's revelation in historical acts. The Romans had driven the Jews from Jerusalem and Judea, and early church theologians understood that act as a demonstration of God's will.[12] The church has largely repudiated this understanding of the particular event, but it has not rejected the idea of history as a locus of revelation. The Bible teaches us that God acts in history and that the people of God are called to discern God's hand in historical events. So, while rejecting the old teaching of contempt that the Roman destruction condemned all Jews to eternal wandering, we yet must look for the meaning God would give to the Jews' exile and the further events of Jewish life over the past two thousand years. We must seek their theological significance in light of God's continuing covenant with the Jews.[13]

In reassessing the past twenty centuries of Jewish experience, the church has primarily focused on correcting the teaching of contempt. We have done very little to fashion new self-understandings or articulate new insights about God in light of Jewish endurance. As we begin to do so, though, we must reject anything that invalidates the Jewish people and the Jewish state in their essence. What God reveals to us in the history of the past two thousand years cannot contradict what God has previously revealed about divine commitment to the Jewish people. This is the first part of the reason the church today must stand against any delegitimizing of Israel as people and state.

The second part of the reason touches on Christian identity itself. Our identity was once rooted in the idea that Christianity replaced, or superseded, Israel. Thereafter, Israel had no valid claim to be God's people. But this has now been rejected. The church must learn to articulate its own identity as the people of God in continuity with Israel's peoplehood, not replacing it. Moreover, if we are God's people together in addition to Israel, then together we represent that "holy people" who have their beginnings in the Holy Land. The ongoing dignity, well-being, and thriving of Jews in the Holy Land becomes as important to the church as the dignity, well-being, and thriving of brother and sister Christians in the region. Thus the German theologian Helmut Gollwitzer has observed, "whatever hits Israel must also pierce the very heart of the Church."[14]

There is a third part to the reason that the church will defend Israel's integrity as a state. God promised through the prophets to restore Israel, and these promises have not been withdrawn from Israel. The church understands that some of the prophecies have been fulfilled in Jesus, though not all (see chapter 4 on promise and fulfillment). But Jews, who remain God's people, do not understand the promises in the same way. They have waited long centuries for their restoration. Some Jews see the founding of the State of Israel as a fulfillment, and go on waiting for still more. In a similar way, the church must reckon with Israel's newly restored sovereignty in the context of prophecy and God's work in history.[15]

To be sure, the church will not affirm every historical development as reflecting God's will; but when biblical promise and the prayer of God's people have so consistently looked forward to an event, we cannot dismiss its occurrence—however unexpected its form—without taking account of it theologically. If the establishment of the State of Israel is not the fulfillment of biblical hope and of Jewish expectation as God's people, then Christians as God's people must explain why it is not. And if it is, then we are called to bear witness to God's promised favor poured out on God's people.

Our reason for defending Israel's legitimacy as people and state thus grows out of our identity and theology as Christians. Our experience as Christians also protects us from abandoning our post in this regard. We may at times find it difficult to defend Israel, and we may be tempted to give up on it. After all, Israel as a state and as a people seem to fall short of God's ethical standards with disturbing frequency—probably no more and no less than other nations and the church itself. But Israel's failings and limitations do not in themselves bring God's covenant with Israel to an end, so we cannot give up on them either.

Different dynamics and considerations than these will inform our defense of Palestinian and Arab dignity and legitimacy. Our relationships with Palestinians and Arabs are grounded differently and have different historical trajectories than our relationship with Jews. With the recognition that the Jewish people and the church are simultaneously God's people in covenant through what Paul names "a mystery," I suggest that the church cannot turn aside from the Jews' deepest yearnings and anxieties any more than we can from those that live within the church. Both Palestinians and Israelis feel those deep yearnings and anxieties in relation to the particular land in which they have been fated to live side by side since the late nineteenth century, and our next task will be to bring insight from the Talking Points to the question of that land.

LAND AND COVENANT

What, then, of the particular land where Israel regained statehood in the twentieth century? The United Nations, looking back to the Balfour Declaration of 1917, decided to constitute the Jewish state in a portion of the territory ruled by Israel in biblical times. That territory had not been under autonomous local political control for many centuries leading up to 1948, and the Jewish presence had been scanty, albeit continuous, prior to the several waves of immigration that began in the 1880s. How does the church's acknowledgment of "God's continuing faithfulness to the covenant with the Jewish people" (*Talking Points* #2) affect our assessment of the Israeli presence in this land?

Contrary to some radical Palestinian and Muslim claims that no Jewish Temple ever stood on Mt. Zion, we cannot doubt that Jewish attachment to the land of biblical Israel is both historical and religious. Archeologists have unearthed ample evidence corroborating the literary and historical witness that Jerusalem was the capital of David's kingdom and that the first and second Jewish Temples stood atop Mt. Zion (the present-day Temple Mount or Haram al-Sharif). Three times each day for almost two thousand years, Jews have prayed for the rebuilding of Jerusalem. The concluding word of hope at both Passover and the Day of Atonement is that the observance be held "next year in Jerusalem." Despite consideration of other options—Uganda, most famously—it was Jerusalem and its surrounding region that became the focus of the Zionist movement at the turn of the twentieth century.

For Christians, Jesus' connection to Jerusalem and the land of biblical Israel adds significance to that land. It is to this land that Mary and Joseph return with their child, according to Matthew's fulfillment citation, "Out of Egypt I have called my son" (Matt 2:15). It is in the Jerusalem Temple that Luke portrays the young Jesus teaching the Jewish scribes in his "father's house" (Luke 2:49). John shows Jesus challenging Temple practices at Passover in Jerusalem at the outset of his public life (John 2:13-25). The Synoptic story of Jesus' activity, first set out by Mark, leads inexorably to Jerusalem, where all four Gospels agree that the Roman governor, Pontius Pilate, put Jesus to death with the apparent collaboration of the Jewish high priest. This Jerusalem/Israel pattern in the Gospel accounts reflects the significance of the city and region for Jews of Jesus' time.

It is a significance they learned from their Bible. The written Torah of Judaism—the five books that Moses is said to have brought down from Mt. Sinai—were given their final shape during Israel's exile from the land. Perhaps because they were languishing in Babylon, the priests who did the editing gave prominence to the covenants of God that emphasized the promise of the land (Genesis 15, 17; Exodus 20—Num 10:10; Deuteronomy). In the Prophets, David's dynasty is to rule in the land (2 Samuel 5, 7, 23) and God's new covenant for a renewed community after the exile will be in a Davidic mold with Israel restored to the land (Jer 33:20-25, Ezek 37:24-27, Isa 55:2-3). Among the Writings—the third segment of the Jewish Bible—the psalms focus on Zion and Jerusalem throughout, the people's covenant after the exile is celebrated in and tied to Jerusalem (Nehemiah 8–13), and the book of Lamentations bewails the destruction of the city by the Babylonians. The Scripture in which Jews find God's dealings with ancient Israel point over and over to Jerusalem and the land.

The focus on this particular land goes beyond the need for territory that every nation has. If that were the criterion, then the Ugandan option, or any other land, could serve just as well. Rather, the specificity of the biblical promise of land demands our theological assessment. Only the Christian claim that God's covenant with Israel had been transferred to the church nullified the promise of the land as the place where God promised to restore Israel.[16] Since the church has rejected that supersessionist claim in recent decades, it must do what it has not done for nearly two millennia—consider the place of the land in God's covenantal promises to Israel.

Christian churches today do not yet agree on the significance of the particularity with which the biblical promises name a land as part of the patrimony of God's people, Israel. Nor will we be able in the brief space of this chapter to propose an adequately thorough theology of the promised land. Work on such a theology continues and is a crying need in the church today.

Christian Zionists operate from a biblicist reading of the promise as straightforward and uncomplicated; the restoration of the people Israel to the land of Israel accords with their end-times expectation and therefore is to be supported. In recent years, moreover, the dualistic worldview that characterizes apocalyptic communities has demonized militant Islam and vaunted Israel as the front line in the defense of Western civilization and godliness, even before the West awoke to the danger.[17] This theology is clear enough in its presentation, but it will not be satisfactory for those who do not share its principles of Bible reading, its antagonistic worldview, or its apparent lack of compassion for those who must be deemed expendable in order for the vision to bear fruit.

Neither can the church be satisfied with a calculation that measures only populations and historical trajectories. One such calculation begins with mandatory Palestine following the Treaty of Versailles and builds a case based on its successive partitioning, looking on the one hand to shifting population ratios and on the other to the relative virtue of the political regimes and military campaigns that shaped the land into a particular configuration. Another such calculation looks back to antiquity and notes that both Jews and Arabs have had some continuous presence in the land, thereby establishing the basis for their respective claims to it. Neither of these, nor any other that fails to account for the biblical promise of land to the Jewish people, will serve adequately in a church that affirms that God's covenant promises to Israel remain effective.

Between recognizing the need for such a theology and bringing it to articulation lies a substantial distance to be traversed, for which the experience of the church in the modern world will not offer a ready guide. That experience has largely been one of negotiating the separation of church and state, finding the best role for the church in a political arena that is formed not by divine covenant but by "the consent of the governed." It has not demanded of the church a theology regarding promised land that mediates between the claims of biblical promises and the historical realities that have developed in intervening millennia. Nor have the rising religionist movements of American conservative Christianity and global militant Islam offered promising models for revisiting theocratic polities. In some ways it is quite ironic that the very secularism that has protected Jews in the United States undermines the claims regarding Israel's covenantal relationship to the land.

Yet Israel's unique covenantal relationship to this particular land must be part of our consideration, since the covenant that promises the land remains unbroken. It seems to me the church could no more easily dismiss the particularity of this land than it could dismiss the use of bread and wine in the Eucharist, or the human particularity of Jesus' incarnation, or the Davidic character of his messianic identity. Its covenantal relationship to Israel is not the only factor we consider in weighing competing claims to the land, but it is an indispensable one.

At the same time, the covenantal tie between Israel and the land helps set the terms for assessing Israel's exercise of political power in the land. Just as many in the Jewish community have said, so the church must say: The people Israel, in their national expression through the State of Israel, have a covenantal responsibility to nurture the values of Torah on behalf of all who live there.

From a Christian standpoint, this expectation does not establish a double standard between Israel and other nations; in Paul's words, "there is no authority except from God" (Rom 13:1), so every government is accountable to the same divine constituting power. The State of Israel has come into existence in conjunction with a religious vision. It also debates its public policy in terms drawn from religious sources more explicitly than most nations. Nevertheless, the standard of accountability for political power applies equally to all nations, and Christians are neither justified in applying it more rigorously to Israel than to others, nor theologically justified to exempt Israel from such ethical accountability.

Here I have only been able to suggest that a serious theological assessment of the "landedness" of God's covenant with Israel is necessity in the church. I have suggested the broad outlines of such an assessment and identified some of its boundaries, addressing in part some of the key issues that vex the discussion of land in the Arab-Israeli-Palestinian conflict. I further believe that more, serious work on this theology of the promised land will have to be done before the church can hope to find consensus on our approach to this dimension of the conflict. The perspectives and participation of Christians who live in the land will be crucial elements in the framing of such a theology. This is a Christian task to which we are called by our affirmation of the continuing validity of God's covenant with Israel; it cannot be resolved or defined by Jews, but to accomplish it we must also have an ongoing dialogue with Jews for whom the land is intrinsic to and unalienable from the covenant.

FAIR WITNESS AND THE POWER OF LANGUAGE

One of the evocative biblical quotations printed together with *Talking Point* #5 is the Eighth Commandment: "You shall not bear false witness against your neighbor" (Exod. 20:16). In his Small Catechism, Martin Luther explained this commandment by saying, "We are to fear and love God so that we do not betray, slander, or lie about our neighbor, but defend [our neighbor], speak well of [our neighbor], and explain [our neighbor's] actions in the kindest way." One need not venture far into discussion with advocates on all sides of the Arab-Israeli-Palestinian conflict to find examples enough to document how far from this standard the current debate stands.

In recent years, the church has with difficulty come to understand how our traditional language about Jews dealt carelessly and unfaithfully with the truth. The heart of *Talking Point* #5 is the principle that emerges from studying the "difficult texts" of Christian biblical tradition. That is, "Christians are morally obligated to understand the New Testament's harsh words against Jews and Judaism in their original contexts, without translating those polemics into anti-semitism." This has led us to try to understand Pharisees from their own perspective, not only as contemporary anti-Pharisaic Jews understood them, and to hear Jesus' disputes with scribes as intra-Jewish debate rather than Christian rhetorical victories over Jews.

Yet in some Christian discussion of the present conflict, we can still find examples of New Testament words and images used against Jews and the Jewish state without regard for their original context. Moreover, outside Christian circles there are voices that have taken up Christian anti-Jewish imagery and rhetoric for clearly antisemitic purposes. The church must stand against such misappropriation by others of its heritage—a heritage it has largely repudiated—and must continue to scrutinize its own language to rid it of any remaining or newly emerging examples of false witness. As a partner in peacemaking with the Jewish community, the church must also raise its voice in opposition to false witness about Arabs and Palestinians spoken in the cause of Israel's defense. Only so can we hope to stand as fair witnesses to the complex realities of the conflict, beginning by example with a careful assessment of our own language and materials.

I was a participant in January 2005 when the ELCA held a consultation to map out what became its strategy for engagement with Israel and Palestine.[18] The strategy eventually emerged as the "Peace Not Walls: Stand for Justice in the Middle East" campaign of awareness building, advocacy, and accompaniment. The focal image of the wall—the separation barrier that Israel began to erect in April 2002—pervaded the consultation, which included a screening of the Mennonite Central Committee video, "The Dividing Wall." Eventually, the image was incorporated into the title of the campaign and prominently into the graphics accompanying campaign materials.

The ELCA was not alone in raising up the wall image as an impediment to peace and peacemaking. Within Israel, protests and lawsuits followed the beginning of the erection of the separation barrier in April 2002, with the Israeli Supreme Court eventually ordering the government to reposition some sections to ease its impact on the Palestinian community. The World Court in July 2004 had declared the barrier illegal and called for removal of those portions that lay on the Palestinian side of the 1967 ceasefire line that has been the de facto border between Israel and Palestinian territory. In 2004 and 2005, several North American church bodies, including the Presbyterian Church (USA), the United Church of Christ, and the Episcopal Church considered and/or adopted resolutions calling for removal of the barrier altogether. Similar proposals were adopted at several ELCA synodical assemblies during the same period.

There can be no doubt about the impact of the separation barrier on Palestinian life. Villages have sometimes been cut off from the fields and groves that sustain them. Travel between communities and to vital governmental and health services has been disrupted and rerouted, in some cases multiplying travel times many times over. Economic interchange with the Israeli economy, long a major employer and supplier for Palestinian society, has been all but stopped. Those who live in the West Bank often summarize their experience of the barrier's construction as having been put into prison. It is ugly physically and in its symbolism, particularly where it is a wall. That is one reason the imagery is so powerful in American church settings.

In 2007, the imagery of the wall was removed from the campaign Web site, except in the titles and logos that have characterized the campaign from the beginning. In the narrative portions of the site the consistent terminology for the construction was changed to "separation barrier." In making that change, the church recognized that the "wall" language had become counterproductive, perhaps even inappropriate, as I would argue. There are biblical texts that speak of walls, and the biblical context is important in considering the use of the image. There are also physical and political contexts to the barrier's construction; they too should inform our choice to use the image or not. Let us examine these in more detail.

The key biblical text that has been attached to campaigns against "the wall" is Ephesians 2:14: "For [Christ] is our peace; in his flesh he has made both groups into one and has broken down the dividing wall, that is, the hostility between us."[19] The image of Christ breaking down a wall that divides is most appealing, to be sure, and one cannot know all that is in the minds of those who choose a biblical verse as the epigram for a project. It seems ironic, though, that the author of Ephesians specifies that the dividing wall is "the hostility between us," when this barrier was erected to interdict the hostility of Palestinian attacks in Israeli territory, and in 2004 had reduced suicide attacks within Israel by 90 percent from one year to the next.[20]

In the wider biblical context, too, the image of walls is more complicated. Walls can divide and isolate, but more often in biblical imagery they protect and reassure. Thus the Song of the Vineyard in Isaiah 5 portrays the devastation wrought in God's vineyard when its wall is broken down. Solomon and other kings are commended for building the walls of major cities (1 Kgs 9:15, 11:27; 2 Chron 27:3, 32:5). Ezra confirms that "God has not forsaken" the exiles by saying that God would have them set up a temple and repair its ruins, and that God would give them "a wall in Judea and Jerusalem" (9:9). God promises Jeremiah, when the people attack him, that they shall not prevail because Jeremiah will be "a fortified wall of bronze" against them (Jer 15:20). Those who deal well with Nabal are said to be "a wall to us day and night" (1 Sam 25:16). Even the name of God is "a strong tower" (Prov 18:10), and the heavenly Jerusalem envisioned in Revelation, which has need of neither sun nor moon, still is surrounded and protected by a wall. How often does the psalmist call on God for defense and protection? We Lutherans are not misguided each Reformation Sunday when we sing Luther's paraphrase of Psalm 46, "A Mighty Fortress is Our God." We know that proper walls, preventing the transgression of essential boundaries of social and interpersonal relations, can be gifts of God for our good. At the very least, our biblical heritage would ask us to witness to all the characteristics of a wall that are pertinent in the present case.

In its physical and political contexts, wall language also reduces a complex situation to a simplistic slogan, undermining the witness we might make. We have already noted the positive effect the barrier has had on the number of attacks within Israel. One must also note that the wall segments constitute less than 5 percent of the separation barrier, and that they are, in fact, easier to remove than the segments that include several parallel lines of barrier accompanied by subterranean sensors. Use of the wall image and prison language to describe it emphasizes the sense both of isolation and of permanency that attaches to the barrier. Granting that such a sense is the felt experience of the Palestinian community, the church's witness to the situation should also include Israel's stated position that the barrier can be removed once the threat from

Palestinian terrorists has been removed, and the fact that most of the bar-rier, for most of its length, is not the imposing behemoth portrayed in many campaign photos. Biblical context, physical context, and political context all demand our respect as we identify language adequate to our role as witnesses for peace, as the ELCA's new commitment to "separation barrier" language now affirms.

A similar complexity attaches to the "difficult text" of references to Jesus as the first Palestinian to be persecuted by the leaders of Israel. Here it is not a single text, but the composite narrative of Jesus in his Passion that is cited, as in the "Contemporary Way of the Cross" published by the Sabeel Ecumeni-cal Liberation Theology Center.[21] Christian tradition beginning with Paul has addressed the baptized members of the church as those who "have been united with [Christ] in a death like his," so that we shall also "certainly be united with him in a resurrection like his" (Rom 6:5). Identifying with Jesus' suffering and death during periods of persecution has been a powerful mechanism for sus-taining hope of a metaphorical resurrection in the defeat of the oppressing powers. The Sabeel Via Dolorosa draws on this powerful tradition, as does Sabeel's founder, Canon Naim Ateek, when he portrays today's Palestinians imprisoned in a tomb as Jesus was, shut in by a stone of "occupation" that must be removed before there can be justice and freedom.[22]

At the same time, the use of this heritage in a situation where Jewish authorities are portrayed as the oppressors also draws on another long-standing Christian trope, that of Jews as Christ-killers. This libelous charge was clearly repudiated by the Roman Catholic Church in the Vatican II document, *Nostra Aetate*, and has been broadly rejected by other Christian churches and theo-logians since then. Nevertheless, it continues to enjoy a certain currency in relation to the present conflict, as is evident from two political cartoons. On April 3, 2002, during the standoff between the Israeli Army and Palestinian fighters in the Church of the Nativity in Bethlehem, the Italian newspaper, *La Stampa,* published a Giorgio Forattini cartoon, "Tanks at the Manger," show-ing an Israeli tank with its gun turret trained on a Palestinian in a manger at the Church of the Nativity and the caption, "Surely they don't want to kill me again?!"[23] After Israel assassinated Sheikh Ahmed Yassin with helicopter-based rocket fire in March 2004, Brazilian cartoonist Osmani Simanca showed Yassin crucified in his wheelchair by Israeli missiles.[24]

When cartoons such as these are still found in mainstream publications, the use of crucifixion language and imagery to characterize the experience of Palestinian Christians is at least problematic. It is the perspective of a North American church, learning from the reexamination of the New Testament's "difficult texts," that can offer a vantage point for recognizing the layers of resentment and fear that such imagery would have to penetrate before it could be understood by Israelis and other Jews as anything other than antisemitic. The imagery is authentic, in its way, to both traditions that contemporary Christians inherit; it has been powerfully comforting to persecuted Christians, and it has been terrifyingly threatening to Jews. The choice to use it is best made when we recognize both contexts as real for different communities and take them into account.

It is not only biblical imagery and language that demands our care and attention as it is pressed into service in this conflict. Another category for vigilance deals with the allusive use of language and imagery in circumstances that do not justify the implications of the allusion. In addressing the separation barrier, there is widespread reference to it as a tool of "apartheid," alluding to the racist legislation of South Africa. There, a minority ruling group legally instituted and enforced apartheid in order to oppress a majority citizenry systematically on racial grounds. It forced the relocation of many in the majority population to racially segregated compounds or "homelands." These are essential characteristics that are implied by making reference to apartheid. In the case at hand, Palestinians are not racially categorized, but are dealt with according to whether they hold Israeli citizenship. The Palestinians in the West Bank and the Gaza Strip are not citizens of Israel, and would not constitute a majority if they were. West Bank and Gaza Palestinians have not been forcibly relocated.[25]

The factors that characterize apartheid are not present in Israel's dealing with the Palestinian community, so the adequacy of the language in regard to the conflict must be questioned, as has been done in the strong outcry against former U.S. President Jimmy Carter's book title, *Palestine: Peace Not Apartheid*.[26]

Another example concerns the application of Nazi imagery to Israel in political cartoons and anti-Israeli rhetoric. The National Socialists in Germany in the 1930s sought to expand their *Lebensraum* by unprovoked annexing and attacking of neighboring sovereign states and by systematic genocide. Israel, by contrast, never had a secure, recognized, international border until it gave up territory in the peace treaty with Egypt. Its ongoing territorial conflict concerns land that has had no sovereign indigenous government for more than a century.[27]

Israel is not trying to rid its land of Palestinians by genocide or ethnic cleansing. The implications of the allusion do not stand up, and using Nazi imagery to depict Israel and its leaders will invite a diversion into arguments over its aptness, rather than making an effective argument about some aspect of Israeli rule. Given the freshness of the pain many Israelis and Jews feel in regard to the Holocaust, it will always raise questions about the intentions of the person who brings a Nazi image into play.

The misuses of language are manifold in common daily life, and all the more so in situations of conflict. One of the pioneers of post-war Jewish-Christian

166 COVENANTAL CONVERSATIONS

dialogue, Bishop Krister Stendahl, has rightly said that "we are responsible not only for what we say, but also for what we are heard to say."[28] At the 2005 Chicago meeting of the International Council of Christians and Jews, Rabbi David Rosen reminded us of the Hasidic tale in which a rabbi learns the true meaning of "Love your neighbor as yourself" from a peasant who told his friend, "Ivan, if you don't know what causes me pain, how can you truly love me?"[29] Through years of dialogue, Christians have begun to learn what it is that causes pain to our Jewish brothers and sisters, particularly in the realm of Christian language. As we take responsibility for our language more and more, not only in what we intend but also in how it might reasonably be understood, we will more credibly make our witness for peace.

That witness will also include our challenge to images and language that are derogatory of Arabs and Palestinians. The anti-Israel examples I have cited can be paralleled with equally demeaning sources that misappropriate language and images to prejudice the perception of others in the conflict. Our focus here is on the lessons we have learned about Christian anti-Judaism, so we cannot provide as full a critique of prejudicial language in Israeli and Jewish sources, but a few examples will illustrate that the depth and breadth of such invective stretch as far on this side of the conflict as on any other.

Drawing attention to the etymological connection of "Palestinian" to "Philistine," however accurate, uses an irrelevant fact to bias the portrait of the modern-day people. Branding Palestinian society as a "culture of death" because of the current prominence of suicide bombers—suggesting that the situation will not improve until "they love their children more than they hate Israel"—stereotypes an entire culture and diverse community on the basis of a prominent, vocal minority. Blaming the Palestinians for "still being in the refugee camps" in 1967, when Israel gained control of those camps, both disregards the role of the Arab states in shaping Palestinian life from 1948 to 1967[30] and ignores the humanitarian concerns that became Israel's responsibility after 1967. To speak of "settlements" encourages an image of relatively small, temporary, or tenuous gatherings of pioneers on a frontier, rather than the urban and suburban enclaves, fully serviced with public utilities and accessed by dedicated highways, that now dot the hilltops of the West Bank. How one might define the "natural growth" of such settlements, as allowed for in the Oslo Accords, has also become a point of significant dispute, given the broad application of the term that Israel has allowed.

In each of these cases, regardless of their source or target, we can apply what we have learned from reexamining the difficult texts of the New Testament. When we use language that has established connotative meaning in common discourse, we must accept the responsibility of being heard to mean what the language says, not only what we might choose to mean. When we would characterize a group of people with powerful rhetoric taken from another set-ting, we must give due consideration to the literary and historical context of the rhetorical source, understood as fully and broadly as possible. We in the church should be able to understand the dire consequences of a failure to do so, since it is our habits in reading the New Testament that have contributed so much fuel to the fires of anti-Jewish and antisemitic animus.

The rhetoric of the Arab-Israeli-Palestinian conflict is an arena rife with examples of powerful language deployed to gain advantage in the court of world opinion. Some of it distorts the truth, some of it obscures the truth, some of it brands the truth as damning evidence of another's immorality. In recent years, the church has with difficulty come to understand how our own traditional language about Jews dealt similarly with the truth. It may be the case that "in war, truth is the first casualty,"[31] but the Christian community can use its hard-won sensitivity in order to be vigilant in protecting from harm that precious, vulnerable asset for peace, which ultimately benefits all the parties in the conflict.

LAW AND GOSPEL, JUSTICE AND PEACE

If truth is difficult to discern and even more necessary to protect, there is no point at which this is more telling than in setting the priorities of justice and peace in seeking a resolution to the Arab-Israeli-Palestinian conflict. "With-out justice, there is no peace" is a familiar slogan, as are several variants: "No justice, no peace—know justice, know peace"; "If you seek peace, work for justice." Alternatively, the argument can be made that justice must sometimes be compromised when peaceful relations do not yet exist, or that justice is only possible among members of a society who live at peace with one another. Both positions have their strengths and attract widespread support. We enter on dangerous ground when we lose the sense of dialectical relationship that peace and justice enjoy, so that they are turned into competing values rather than complementary aspects of God's vision for the whole creation. Here the central Lutheran theological insight into the relationship of law and gospel can be helpful in strengthening our witness and avoiding error.

The discussion of peace and justice can be complicated by a simple but erroneous alignment of Judaism with law and Christianity with gospel. Justice can be defined as the effective application of law to life, so one might surmise that Jews would settle for a narrow legal justification for Israel's actions. On the other hand, the gospel is proclaimed through the Prince of Peace, so we might look for Christians to press for peace even at the expense of justice. But the slogans giving priority to justice are more often voiced by Christians, and the argument deferring justice for the sake of peace is more often heard from Jews.

Such are the complexity and irony that this conflict can raise for both communities. It makes clear the fact that Judaism does not equate to law and that the Christian gospel is only God's word as it is proclaimed in tandem with the law.

What insight can we gain, then, from the comparatively recent realizations expressed in *Talking Points* #3: that the Torah (Jewish law) "is a powerful mentor more than a legalistic taskmaster," and that Jesus and early Christians, Jewish and non-Jewish alike and fully committed to the gospel, sought like Pharisees "to discern how God's will applied to the details of daily life"? How will careful attention to the dialectical relationship of law and gospel aid us in negotiating the troubled waters of peace and justice for Israel, the Palestinians, and Israel's Arab neighbors?

It will help to recall that the law serves multiple functions in Christian theology, particularly as articulated by Martin Luther. In traditional language, it has several "uses." The first use is civil and conventional—the law operates to give shape to virtue in everyday society, while restraining evil and punishing wrongdoing. It is wielded by Christians and non-Christians alike in this regard, and can be put to good use as effectively by one as by the other. In its second use, the theological use, the law speaks God's righteous demand to live fully in accordance with the divine will. Since no human can do so, the law in this regard always accuses us. Only Jesus' atonement on the cross can reconcile us to God for such an affront to our creator. In its third use, the law serves as a guide to conscience in living out the Christian life.[32]

This Christian distinction among the uses of the law bears on the issue of justice in two ways. At the outset, the Christian—especially Protestant—preoccupation with the second use is quite alien to Jewish thought. Judaism does recognize the extreme challenge—perhaps even the impossibility—of perfect human obedience to God's will. But in Jewish thought this is a characteristic of creation, not a rupture in it; it is a fact of life, not a fall from grace. Thus Judaism counsels a more pragmatic approach to justice. Given time and an effective negotiation process, Judaism posits that a reasonable approximation of justice is achievable. While Christian doctrine points with caution to the sinful ramifications of any attempt to implement justice, Judaism aims at a workable *modus vivendi* between neighbors who are never likely to love one another.

The difference between Jewish and Christian approaches to law goes further than defining objectives; it also sets up misunderstanding and unnecessary conflict. Christians see sin in everything, even the church, so we speak fairly easily about its presence and its effects. In recent decades we have become especially adept at identifying "systemic sin" in political and corporate arrangements. We can speak of Israel's "sin" in this way; we mean that its actions have a negative component that cannot be avoided without fundamentally changing who Israel is. All systems and structures have such inherent sin. We are only being descriptive.

To Jewish ears, however, it can sound accusatory and threatening. Because Judaism does not see sin as inevitable, even if it is ubiquitous, sin is a specific breach of reasonable standards; therefore, depicting something as sinful accuses the person or system as bad. Moreover, calling for "systemic change" sounds too much like "regime change," a particularly charged term in Middle East politics in the early twenty-first century. If only to facilitate our ongoing communication, we must take account of the very different meaning that Judaism and Christianity put on the word *sinful,* growing out of our very different perceptions of "law."

The second way in which the Christian distinction among uses of the law affects our approach to justice goes more to the heart of the matter. The Christian's first and third uses of the law parallel the Jewish image of the Torah as a "powerful mentor." This is God's guidance for human life day by day. Justice is a fundamental aspect of it. So strongly does justice figure in God's design for creation, in fact, that the Bible depicts Abraham challenging God: "Shall not the Judge of all the earth do what is just?" (Gen 18:25). As Theodore Parker said, the arc of the moral universe is long, but it bends toward justice.[33]

This long arc of justice can trip us up, however. Many in the Christian church analyze the Arab-Israeli-Palestinian conflict using a model drawn from liberation theology, with a particular understanding of justice taking a prominent place. It is not an understanding that finds an easy counterpart in Jewish thought, however.

As liberationist theologians understand the Bible, God has a "preferential option for the poor" that defines justice primarily as redistributing society's benefits more fairly. Starting from the exodus story, liberation theology discerns that God stands consistently throughout Scripture on the side of the poor, the dispossessed, the oppressed, and the marginalized. This is as true for God in Christ, who eats with sinners and defends the socially outcast, as it is for the God of Israel, who rescued Israel from Egypt and sent Jonah to preach repentance to the people of Nineveh. In this reading, once an underdog is identified, it is clear where God's weight will be felt in the argument for justice.

This stands in some contrast to a Jewish emphasis, which one rabbinic colleague has summarized as "rendering judgment fairly to all with compassion."[34] Such impartiality is derived from the command in Lev 19:15, "you shall not be partial to the poor or defer to the great: with justice you shall judge your neighbor." As Hayim Halevy Donin has put it, "just as it is wrong to pervert justice in favor of the rich or the privileged, so it is wrong to do so out of a sense of compassion, in favor of the poor or the underprivileged. While the tradition required justice to be tempered with mercy, the delicate balance between the two must not be so upset as to cause injustice to others."[35] How can one maintain the "delicate balance" of impartiality when *imitatio Dei* calls on us to show a preference for the poor? The language of Christian theology simply sounds contradictory to what Israel has known as the standards of justice for millennia.

But more is at stake than simply adjusting our terminology to avoid miscommunication. On this point the real question remains: Does God regard the poor preferentially in relation to the rich? And, in spite of the call for impartiality in Leviticus, should we also show a preference for the poor? Liberationist justice is sought by imitating God's preferential option for the poor. Will it in fact contribute to peace, or will it breed resentment that increases hostility, as the rabbis warned?

It would be hard to dismiss the evidence that liberation theologians have brought to support their point. Notwithstanding isolated counterexamples, the Bible pervasively advances the theme of God's involvement in human affairs on behalf of the underdog. From the Genesis pattern of advancing the younger sibling over the older, through the paradigmatic tale of the exodus, to the Deuteronomic refrain enjoining care of the alien, the orphan, and the widow, and on to Jesus' reputation for associating with "publicans and sinners," his parable of the Good Samaritan and the early church's considerable success among the lower classes of Roman society—the consistency of the theme cannot be refuted.

In applying this insight to daily life, however, it is not so easy to discern who is among "the poor." The distinction between "poor" and "rich" is made difficult for Christians by two factors. First, because sin is pervasive, we never fully escape its sway in the present age. In Luther's terms, we are *simul iustus et peccator*—at one and the same time we are freed from condemnation by the justification that Christ affords, and we remain sinners. Life is lived in the dialectical, paradoxical, challenging intersection of both realities.

Recall one of the insights of *Talking Point* #3, that Jesus and the early church, just like the Pharisees, sought "to discern how God's will applied to the details of daily life." They addressed daily life, not an idealized situation. They addressed people who were a mixed bag of justification and sinfulness, shifting from moment to moment, even presenting both faces at the same moment, in their identity before God. They addressed people like us, like present-day Israelis and Palestinians, who cannot be simply categorized as poor or rich, oppressor or oppressed. Indeed, not even one person among them can be so simply categorized, let alone either group as a whole. So a distinction is complicated by the complex nature of the people we are trying to classify.

Second, "poor" and "rich" refer not only to economic circumstances, but to the broader conditions of life. The circumstances of Israelis and Palestinians are such that their relative power, and perhaps more importantly their felt relationship of power, is complex and ever changing. As noted in *Talking Point #6*, "both Israelis and Palestinians can at various times be especially vulnerable, eliciting appropriate Christian concern, advocacy, and action." No one escapes the ups and downs of human emotion, of social interaction, especially in a region as volatile as the one shared by these two communities.

When our life feels like it is going poorly, then we are the poor of the world, and the gospel promise is that God will never forsake us—indeed, that God takes special note of our poverty and intervenes to raise us up. But just as quickly as we hear it, our sense of ourselves can swing to arrogance, where we are so full of ourselves, so rich in our self-esteem, that we become the rich for whom it is more difficult to enter the kingdom of heaven than it is for a camel to pass through the eye of a needle. Hence the varying dimensions of poverty and wealth that affect all people also complicates such a distinction.

Inasmuch as poverty and wealth are economic realities that position us in a social sphere, the Jewish view retains its validity: Neither the rich nor the poor get special treatment. Inasmuch as poverty and wealth are conditions of the human spirit, the Christian theme of God's preferential option for the poor retains its power as a word of comfort, promise, and hope for those on the margins of life. Yet one cannot generalize about the spiritual condition of an individual from one moment to the next, let alone of a whole society. Thus Jewish evenhandedness is once again a prudent summary of the way in which we should approach all people.

Here is the powerful contribution of the law/gospel dialectic to the topic, for the greatest temptation of the church has been its readiness either to separate or to confuse these two parts of the one word of God. When we simplistically identify Palestinians as the poor and Israel as the oppressor, we separate law and gospel—addressing comfort without an awareness of guilt to the one, while condemning the other and setting out conditions of approval that must be met. In a similar separation, the church for long centuries condemned the Jewish people for clinging to the law, while making the gospel into a club with which to beat them. But when we understand that the two cannot be separated, but must always be "rightly divided" in our proclamation of God's word, we realize as Luther did that the gospel was known in Israel even before the time of Christ and that the law retains a certain proper effectiveness in the church. So, in the present situation, rightly dividing law and gospel will lead us to recognize that Israelis may also need to hear a gospel word of assurance and Palestinians may face accountability before God and the just demand of a lawful society.

God's preferential option for the poor is indeed a theme of the gospel message throughout Scripture. On that point the liberation theologians are correct. But that message is not the whole of God's word for anyone. Rather, we must "rightly divide" law and gospel, discerning in the moment those poor for whom the gospel message will come as true comfort. Depending on the circumstances, that comfort may be brought by an emphasis on either peace or justice; neither can claim the upper hand. In the complicated reality of action and emotion that characterizes the Arab-Israeli-Palestinian conflict, we may find at any given time that both the Israelis and the Palestinians are God's "poor." And when all of those poor have good news preached to them, we will know that the Prince of Peace is at hand.

CONCLUSION

This case study has emphasized many themes that will resonate with Israelis and their supporters around the world, since the intent was to show ways in which the rethinking of our relationship with the Jews affects our approach to the Arab-Israeli-Palestinian conflict. There is much that could and must be said about the circumstances and perspectives of Palestinians, both Christian and Muslim, of internal Palestinian dynamics, and of the role of neighboring Arab states and other world powers, including the United States, if a complete analysis and strategy for the church's involvement were to be developed.

Any involvement we would seek, though, must be informed by the new relationship of the church to the Jewish people and the new realities it poses for the church's identity. These matters are not important only because they are of concern to the Jewish people. They are important because the character and identity of the church are bound up in them, as they have been from the earliest days when a pattern of Christian self-definition over against the Jews established itself. That adversus Ioudaeos pattern can no longer serve as it did, and relinquishing it—indeed, eradicating it—has ramifications in every element of the church's life. Here I have sought to articulate some of the ramifications for our engagement with the Arab-Israeli-Palestinian conflict.

In sum, I have drawn five assertions in relation to five of the Talking Points. They do not amount to a policy for the church regarding the Middle East, nor do they even establish clear positions on particular points in the conflict. Rather, they tend to reframe the questions and realign the foundations on which we address them. The difficult ethical task of choosing a course of action remains for the Christian community in its interaction with all those who are affected. No essay or case study could hope to set out such a course with any lasting value, particularly in a situation as volatile as this one. But we do affirm certain principles that will inform our ethical task in new ways because they seriously seek to incorporate the insights of our new relationship with the Jewish people.

First, the distinctiveness of Jewish concern for the State of Israel reminds us of the distinctive voice that we have to contribute to the search for peace. Working together with our Palestinian Christian brothers and sisters, as well as with their Arab and Muslim neighbors and with Israelis and Jews from around the world, we will make our own witness, capitalize on our own strengths, and offer our own particular gifts to the cause of peace.

Second, because Israel the people retains its vitality as God's people and has come to political expression as the State of Israel, the church will oppose every effort to delegitimize Israel's peoplehood and will seek to discern the theological significance of Israel's national restoration.

Third, because God's covenant with Israel remains in effect, the particular land that is so central to the promises of the covenant takes on a covenantal significance for Christians. Without forfeiting the universal perspective that the gospel has nurtured among us, we must articulate that significance of the land in Christian terms that are compatible with a Jewish understanding (though it is unlikely they will be identical).

Fourth, just as we realize that difficult texts in the New Testament have had loathsome consequences because they were wielded out of context and without careful understanding, so we will be vigilant in our own use of provocative language and imagery. We will lead the way in repudiating the appropriation of anti-Jewish themes for anti-Israeli and antisemitic purposes, as well as challenging similar misuse of imagery and language to denigrate Arabs and Palestinians or to obscure Israeli offenses.

Finally, the law/gospel dialectic, properly understood, cautions us against any simplistic identification of oppressor and oppressed in the context of the conflict and against a counterproductive opposition of peace and justice as competing values. Moreover, recognizing that Jews and Christians understand the character of sin differently will help us to avoid miscommunication in discussing the conflict.

As a church, we have a profound responsibility and a high calling as witnesses for peace in the Arab-Israeli-Palestinian conflict. With the distinctive position that we enjoy in the United States, ours should be a distinctive voice addressed to the powers of our own land as well as to the participants in the conflict and others who influence it. In living out our calling, we receive gifts from many who journey with us on this difficult road. We learn much from our brothers and sisters in the Palestinian Christian churches. We also have learned much over the past half-century from our experience in Jewish-Christian encounter, enough to speak of a new relationship between Jews and Christians in this twenty-first century that continues to inform our life as the people of God. As we are able to use all the gifts of God in their proper time and place, we will make our distinctive contribution to the peacemaking that is so urgently needed and for which we yearn and pray.

Response

John Stendahl

Not unlike his sainted namesake, my friend Peter has stepped out on troublous waters, taking up the challenge of applying the principles we put forward in the Talking Points to the particular case of Arab-Israeli-Palestinian conflict. Before we move beyond the title, we are reminded how complicated and problematic this undertaking can prove: his assertion that this conflict is tripartite and involves non-Palestinian Arabs is a sophistication of the analysis that will be deemed helpful by some, a distraction by others, and still not complex enough by yet other observers, and he has only stepped forward as far as a heading.

I appreciate much of what Peter has written here and find it consonant with the concerns and counsel I offer in chapter 6. Especially important is his recognition of the "distinctive contribution" that we in our church can make to the cause of peace because of our relationships and commitments on different sides of the conflict. Actually making such a contribution, however, will require a kind of balance and fairness that identifies with, but can also be critically distinct from, each side in the conflict. The matters that trouble me as I read these pages are not disagreements in precisely locating the fulcrum for such balance or in defining just where the lines of fairness lie; like almost all observers and participants we shall have disputes of that sort. Without room here to engage all such issues of historical fact or contemporary interpretation I shall simply commend further reading and study. As a member of the Consultative Panel, however, I ask to put the following thematic topics on the table for that further conversation toward understanding, which the Talking Points intend to inspire and advance:

* Theology and Covenant: *I argue in chapter 6 for both respectful understanding of the importance of Israel for Jews and for the theological value of conversation around the existence of the modern state of Israel. Such understanding and respect, however, do not require that as Christians we take a particular side in the lively intra-Jewish debate over Israel's identity or that we adopt the way of applying covenantal categories we see here. The Talking Points do not require it of us, and even many who rejoice in the existence of Israel can be cautious or even agnostic as*

to just exactly how God's will played out in either 70 or 1948 C.E. (Nonetheless, covenantal responsibility for justice and mercy in the land—our nation as well as Israel—does seem to be a strong paradigmatic theme in our use of these Scriptures apart from claims to divinely certified ownership. The urgency of such a reading of texts seems to me deeply compelling even as I have serious hermeneutical misgivings about Peter's application of covenantal theology.)

◆ Liberation and Justice: *Peter's interesting argument about the use of "preferential option" thinking in Christian advocacy seems to me in need of some further sophistication. Advocacy for Palestinian rights can certainly be "liberationist," but also draws on appeals to justice of the sort he rightly sees as a Jewish value. Moreover, popular support for the State of Israel frequently appeals to the theme of vindication for a people long oppressed and despised, an appeal resonant with liberation theology. Indeed, I have heard the concern raised by Jewish Israelis that their nation has suffered from too great a self-definition on the basis of Passover's rescue and liberation motifs and not enough appropriation of Shavuot—that is, of the call from Sinai to shape a communal life of law and justice.*

◆ Legitimacy and Annihilation: *I worry about two major dangers that lurk in the focus here on delegitimization in critiques of Israel. The first is the inference—not drawn by Peter but all too easily assumed—that insistence on the legitimacy of Palestinian experience constitutes a denial of the legitimacy of Israel's existence. The narratives conflict, but we in our "distinctive role" are not obligated to choose one in a zero sum negation to the other. We must ourselves not fall into the trap of delegitimating one side because its adherents have failed to legitimate the other. How else can we help them out of that trap?*

The further problem is that insistence upon "legitimation" (like that upon a "theologized" Israel) leaves us in an unhelpful impasse. Certainly there are those who now refuse to recognize Israel or deal constructively with her. But there are others—in fact, many—who are willing and able to recognize Israel and deal with her even though they cannot from their own experience and conscience call the events of 1948 "legitimate" or God's sacred will. I may personally celebrate the creation of Israel, but I also know that it is possible to accept and defend the security rights and sovereignty of a nation without declaring its historical origin divine or sacred. That is in fact rather normal. (One may defend the sovereignty of Iraq and still see that nation as an accident of British neocolonialism.) And it is after all precisely with such nonlovers of the State of Israel—those who can nonetheless accept its reality and live with it—that Israel will have to make her peace. It is they who will be her partners in peace. While it is of course not Peter's intent, the peril against which I would warn in the "delegitimization" argument is that it can tar all such people with the same brush as exterminationist antisemites. Support for Israel must not put all non-Zionists beyond the pale.

- ◆ Rhetoric and Reality: *We are stewards of powerful words that seek to affect hearts and effect responses. This volume has recognized the way prophetic language becomes very different when spoken from outside and against a people rather than in passionate love from within, and different also when spoken by the powerful to the weak. This ethical insight is key for our reading of Scripture but also relates to arguments about Israel today. Words intended to open eyes, challenge, console, or inspire can be heard with other ears and in other contexts to judge unfairly, to attack the legitimate, to condone violence, to speak contempt. Moreover, conflicting narratives of victimization reciprocally inform the speech and hearing of both Jews and Palestinians. I, too, would argue that our explicit understanding is needed as to how insensitive and unfair language about a wall or a tomb can sound to those who think rather about the lives of children protected from terrorists or who recall the baleful old connection between passion stories and pogroms. But I am moved to underline, as I believe that Peter agrees, that such needed sensitivity must not cover up the realities behind the rhetoric: experiences of expulsion, expropriation, humiliation, and yet defiant hope. The language is not mere cynical propaganda; it speaks in a natural Christian idiom and out of genuine human experience.*

    There are valid distinctions to be made between the separation policies and security measures of South Africa's old regime and those of Israel's government today—and yet more between the best ideals and principles of those states—but the care that we should take in handling the rhetoric linking the two must also be a care not to allow our distinctions to discount or dismiss the experienced reality of terrible similarities. Such truths also we are obligated to midwife into hearing, to make them bearable, to seek to bring them forth into more fully covenantal conversation.

APPENDIX

•

Talking Points
Topics in Christian-Jewish Relations

USER'S GUIDE

"Talking Points" is a set of eight leaflets issued by the Office of Ecumenical and Inter-Religious Relations of the Evangelical Lutheran Church in America to set forth propositions for discussion and debate on theological issues in Christian-Jewish relations. They are intended to stimulate reflection and response on certain key issues as part of an ongoing study process within the church.

In each leaflet, the basic point or proposition is printed in a box at the top of the first page, followed by several paragraphs of explanation and commentary, and concluding with suggested questions for discussion. These propositions have deliberately been formulated in such a way as to push and test ideas that might otherwise go unexamined.

Most of the topics dealt with are pertinent to Christians generally. Some, such as "Law and Gospel," deal with issues that have been more prominent in the Lutheran tradition. For the most part, the points are intended for discussion among Christians, as part of their "homework" for interfaith encounter, but having a Jewish guest or guests when discussing some of the topics would be likely to add special interest and insight.

These Points have a historical background, both in Christian-Jewish relations generally and more specifically in the work of the ELCA. The past forty or fifty years have seen a transformation in the stance of many Christians and many church bodies toward Jews and Judaism. Various factors have influenced this development, including the Holocaust, the establishment of the State of Israel, and the continued experience of living together peacefully and productively in a pluralistic American society. Theological developments have also played a major role, including a new recognition of the Jewishness of Jesus and the Jewish roots of Christian worship.

All of this has led to the most substantive reevaluation of Christian attitudes and behaviors toward the Jews and Judaism since church and synagogue parted ways. Repentance for past injustices and injuries, repudiation of anti-Jewish and antisemitic expressions, and overtures to a new relationship have marked these recent decades.

Within the ELCA, two documents exemplify this remarkable change. The "Declaration to the Jewish Community" of 1994 decisively repudiated Luther's anti-Jewish views, expressed remorse for the harm they have done, and pledged "to live out our faith in Jesus Christ with love and respect for the Jewish people." The 1998 "Guidelines for Lutheran-Jewish Relations" offered further suggestions for cooperation and dialogue.

Discussion across the church made it plain that there are further questions that need to be explored, questions about the theological relationship between the two traditions. The 1999 ELCA Churchwide Assembly took an action calling for the creation of study materials on theological aspects of Christian-Jewish relations from a Lutheran perspective. The task was undertaken by the Consultative Panel on Lutheran-Jewish Relations, the advisory body that had also worked on the two previous statements; "Talking Points" is the result. The Panel appreciates the comments received from Jewish colleagues and ELCA staff during the writing process.

These Talking Points do not constitute an official ELCA statement about Judaism and Jewish-Christian relations. In the Consultative Panel's judgment, formulating such a statement would be premature, since there is no clear consensus on many of the issues involved. Lutherans need time to live into the new reality in Jewish-Christian relations, open to the Holy Spirit's continuing work of illumination. We very much desire feedback from your study and discussion, which will help clarify where we are and where we are headed.

PROCEDURAL SUGGESTIONS

The Talking Points begin with an introduction dealing briefly with some ways in which Judaism has changed and developed since biblical times, with the aim of trying to understand Jews today not through our stereotypes but as they define themselves. The sequence of topics ends with the question of how Jewish-Christian relations pertains to the broader realm of interfaith relations today. Between those two points, the topics can be taken up in any order.

No special preparation is needed to lead a discussion based on the Talking Points. However, the "Resources for Further Study" at the end of this appendix includes many items that will be of value to the leader as well as to any participant. It may be well first to read the Talking Point aloud, with its explanation and commentary. Clarify any terms or concepts that may be unfamiliar, and then launch into discussion. The suggested questions can guide the discussion, and others may arise from the group.

Most of the Talking Points involve theological questions that are not bound to any particular time and place. Point 6 is an exception, in that it pertains to a topic that is very much in the news day by day. It should be understood that this is not an attempt to shape a comprehensive statement on the Middle East situation in all its complexity. Rather, the point is intended to explicate why the State of Israel is so important to our Jewish neighbors, and some of the factors that make their attachment to it so profound. As with all of the Talking Points, views will differ—among both Jews and Christians—on the issues involved.

Some possible contexts for discussion of "Talking Points" include adult forums in local congregations, conferences of clergy and other church leaders, synodical assemblies, colleges, and seminaries. The Panel's intention and prayer is that discussion of these topics will foster discernment and growth in our understanding of Judaism and Jewish-Christian relations. We hope that reflection on these and related topics will contribute to contemporary formulations of Lutheran theology and practice in light of the new realities of Jewish-Christian relations.

Up to ten copies of this packet are available free of charge from the Office of Ecumenical and Inter-Religious Relations. Additional copies are $2.00 each plus postage. The contents of the packet are also available in downloadable form at www.elca.org/ecumenical/interreligious/jewish/talkingpoints.html. For use in settings specifically intended to include both Christians and Jews, such as Living Room Dialogues, the Office of Ecumenical and Inter-Religious Relations recommends the "Interfaith Circles" program, a set of discussion guides. To order, see http://www.elca.org/ecumenical/resources/lujwrsce .html or telephone 1-800-638-3522, est. 2610.

THE CONSULTATIVE PANEL ON LUTHERAN-JEWISH RELATIONS

OFFICE OF ECUMENICAL AND INTER-RELIGIOUS RELATIONS, EVANGELICAL LUTHERAN CHURCH IN AMERICA

The following were members of the Consultative Panel during the preparation of the Talking Points, and are available as consultants and resource persons.

The Rev. Barbara Gazzolo

St. James Lutheran Church

Lake Forest, Illinois

Prof. Esther Menn, Ph.D.

Lutheran School of Theology at Chicago

Chicago, Illinois

The Rev. Peter A. Pettit, Ph.D*

Institute for Jewish-Christian Understanding

Muhlenberg College

Allentown, Pennsylvania

The Rev. John Stendahl*

Lutheran Church of the Newtons

Newton Center, Massachusetts

The Rev. George P. Mocko

Retired Bishop

Delaware-Maryland Synod

Evangelical Lutheran Church in America

The Rev. Darrell Jodock, Ph.D.

Gustavus Adolphus College

St. Peter, Minnesota

The Rev. Franklin Sherman, Ph.D.*

Department for Ecumenical Affairs

Evangelical Lutheran Church in America

Chicago, Illinois

*member of drafting team

TALKING POINT #1: *JUDAISM THEN AND NOW*

Modern Judaism is a vibrant community with much to offer us in faith, ethics, and piety. Christians err if we dismiss Judaism as a misguided relic of the past.

No one who reads the New Testament can escape the fact that Jesus was a Jew, as were all of his original followers. The early Christians viewed their faith as continuous with and a fulfillment of the Jewish heritage in which they had been reared. The Jewish faith, however, found another continuation in rabbinic Judaism, taught and led by those known—as Jesus once was—as rabbis.

Christianity soon became predominantly Gentile, and the Roman Empire eventually became officially Christian. The majority of Jews, though experiencing great tribulations, continued in faithfulness to their ancient covenant ("I shall be your God, and you shall be my people"), shaped by observance of the biblical and rabbinic commandments.

A complete and self-governing Jewish culture grew around strong families and communities, study of the Hebrew Bible and the Talmud (a compilation of legal, moral, and religious traditions codified by the rabbis between the second and sixth centuries that remains a central source of Judaism to this day), a distinctive way of life, and the hope of ultimate redemption, including the vision of an eventual return to Jerusalem. The Hebrew language was nurtured in worship, and great literary traditions developed in ethnic languages such as Yiddish. The Jewish philosopher Moses Maimonides was a major influence on the Christian theologian Thomas Aquinas, and great rabbinic scholars such as Shlomo ben Isaac of Troyes ("Rashi") were cited frequently in Luther's biblical commentaries. Jewish thinkers, writers, artists, and activists have also been prominent in many modern intellectual and cultural movements.

The living Jewish community of today—in North America, in Israel, and around the world—continues the heritage of biblical Israel and rabbinic Judaism in new and vibrant ways. While diversity has led to denominational differences among Jews, there remains a core communal identity and loyalty to the ancient faith. Often giving leadership in philanthropy and social justice causes, the Jewish community is a powerful partner with the church in living out God's call to be stewards of healing for the world.

> I will make of you a great nation, and I will bless you . . . and in you all the families of the earth shall be blessed. (Gen 12:2, 3)

> They are Israelites, and to them belong the adoption, the glory, the covenants, the giving of the law, the worship, and the promises . . . (Rom 9:4)

QUESTIONS FOR DISCUSSION

1. What does it mean that both Christianity and Judaism claim to continue the heritage of biblical Israel?

2. In what arenas are you aware of Jewish contributions to community life in your locality, in this country, and on the world scene?

3. How might you learn more about the living community of Judaism in your locality? Consider setting up a discussion group with members of a local Jewish congregation, and ask both the Christians and Jews present to express what is most meaningful to them about their faith. (The "Interfaith Circles" program, listed under Resources in this packet, offers help in setting up such discussions.)

4. What can you find out about the four denominations of Judaism and what their respective emphases are? Try doing an Internet search for Orthodox, Conservative, Reform, and Reconstructionist Judaism.

TALKING POINT #2: COVENANTS OLD AND NEW

Living in the new covenant given by God in Jesus Christ, we also affirm God's continuing faithfulness to the covenant with the Jewish people.

While most Lutherans think of our relationship with God in terms of faith, forgiveness, and salvation, we also know this relationship to be one of covenant. Indeed, the apostolic witness to Jesus Christ comes to us in the Scriptures known as the "New Testament" or "New Covenant." Likewise, Jesus comes to us in the Lord's Supper with the words of promise, "This cup is the new covenant in my blood." Guaranteed by God's faithfulness, a covenant brings a promise that helps to define the life of God's people. In this it goes far beyond any mere legal contract.

From ancient Israel to our own day, Jews have lived in covenant with God as well. This is seen not only in the circumcision of Abraham and his offspring, but also, for example, in the kingship of David, the gift of the Torah at Sinai, and the appearance of the rainbow in the heavens. Israel's prophets were the ones who proclaimed God's faithful intent to establish a new covenant with the people, a living covenant "written on their hearts" (Jer 31:33), even embodied in a "new heart" (Ezek 36:26). This would not have to supersede the existing covenant understandings, but in continuity with them it would renew and extend Israel's hope and confidence in God's loving commitment.

Encountering Jesus, some Jews of the first century saw in him the power and presence of God renewing the world and including Gentiles among the people of God. They proclaimed that the promised new covenant had come into being. It was the witness of Paul that this new covenant now brought Gentiles and Jews into one people, so that in and through Christ, Gentiles too can now become "Abraham's offspring" (Gal 3:29).

So we now live in the new covenant established by God in Jesus Christ, joined in continuity to those who have already been made God's people in the covenant of Sinai,

and rejoicing with them that God's covenant, new and old, is a gift that is "irrevocable" (Rom 9:4, 11:29).

> For as the new heavens and the new earth, which I will make, shall remain before me, says the Lord, so shall your descendents and your name remain. (Isa 66:22)

> I ask then, has God rejected his people? By no means! (Rom 11:1)

QUESTIONS FOR DISCUSSION

1. What do you think of when you reflect on your life of faith as lived in covenant with God? How is a "covenant" different from a "contract"?

2. What other relationships in your life would you describe as being "covenants"? Why?

3. If we can be in multiple covenants simultaneously, can God also? What does that mean for Jews and Christians in their relationship with God and with one another?

TALKING POINT #3: *LAW AND GOSPEL*

The meaning of "law" for Jews is positive, in a way quite different from what it has usually meant to Lutherans.

What is meant by "law," in the sense in which we often speak of the Word of God as including both "law" and "gospel"? To Lutherans, "law" usually means God's demand that we live completely in accord with God's will. Since in our bondage to sin we cannot do that, we are condemned by the law and must be saved by the gospel. In this view, the law always accuses us.

We are often surprised, then, to find that Jews embrace the law more as a gift than a demand. Thus the psalmist exclaims, "O, how I love thy law [Torah]" (Ps 119:97), and the rabbis emphasize that Israel received the commandments (*mitzvot*) not to be condemned but "to live by them" (Lev 18:5)—"live" and not die. The Israelites do not receive the law in order to earn God's favor; they were saved from bondage in Egypt before they ever came to Mt. Sinai to receive the Torah. So they are already God's people when God gives them the Torah to know how to live out their divine calling.

Torah embraces the Five Books of Moses, scriptural teaching as a whole, and the rabbis' interpretation. Beginning with the Ten Commandments, which many Christians also use as a positive guide for living, it is a powerful mentor more than a legalistic taskmaster. Indeed, the Hebrew term *Torah* is better translated as "teaching" or "instruction," rather than "law."

The New Testament describes a vigorous debate between Jesus and the Pharisees, who led a lay renewal movement within Judaism, over some issues of Torah interpretation. Although this conflict has been wrongly interpreted as pitting "Christianity" against "Judaism," in fact both Jesus and the Pharisees were seeking to discern how God's will applied to the details of daily life in the Jewish community. Jews know the Pharisees as the precursors of the great tradition of rabbinic Judaism, in which this effort to perceive the meaning of

Torah teaching for each new generation was continued, and continues to this day.

The commandment against false witness calls on us to avoid negative caricatures of Jewish life and thought. Christians today are learning to pay attention to the Jewish understanding and experience of Torah in its multiplicity and its graciousness.

> Oh, how I love your law! It is my meditation all day long. . . . How sweet are your words to my taste, sweeter than honey to my mouth. (Ps 119:97, 119:103)

> So the law is holy, and the commandment is holy and just and good. (Rom 7:12)

QUESTIONS FOR DISCUSSION

1. Psalm 119 celebrates the law as God's gracious guidance in innumerable ways. Does this emphasis inevitably lead to "works righteousness" (the expectation that salvation must be "earned" by obeying the law)?

2. The Christian sacraments involve commands ("Do this . . ."), yet are experienced as a profound source of grace. Does this help us understand how, for Jews, *mitzvot* (commandments) can serve not as legalisms but as blessings?

3. Must "law and gospel" always be the interpretive principle by which Lutherans approach Scripture and preaching? If so, how does the principle relate to the broader sense of Torah in living Judaism?

4. Recent historical study of the Gospels has developed a more positive view of the Pharisees not as hypocritical legalists, but as part of a reform movement stressing (as Jesus did) piety and faithfulness in daily life. How can the strong criticism of "the Pharisees" in the Gospels be read and preached without breaking the commandment against bearing false witness?

TALKING POINT #4: *PROMISE AND FULFILLMENT*

Christians affirm that God's promises to Israel are fulfilled in Jesus Christ and in the life of the church. We need to be aware that Jews also have experienced God's continuing faithfulness in rabbinic Judaism and in the contemporary reality of Jewish faith and life.

The writers of the New Testament speak of Jesus as the fulfillment of God's promises to Israel. In doing so, they build upon a well-established pattern of promise and fulfillment that characterizes God's actions in the Old Testament (promises of offspring and land to Abraham and Sarah; promise of a dynasty to David). Using richly diverse images from Israel's heritage—Jesus as the New Moses, the Son of David, the Son of Man—they bequeath this pattern to Christian thought. What we experience in Christ is a fulfillment of the expectation God has given us through the Torah and the prophets.

God's promises are often fulfilled in unexpected ways, however. Even as the church found in Jesus the fulfillment of messianic hope, it described his role and actions in bold and distinctive combination with other scriptural themes. The new Moses is also the Suffering Servant; the Son of David is also the Paschal Lamb.

We also believe that God has yet more to accomplish in the redemption of humanity and of all creation; we still live in anticipation, praying, "Thy kingdom come." As we are grateful for what God has already done and at the same time look forward in hope to what God yet will do, we have much in common with faithful Jews. They, too, rejoice in the blessings of the covenant while still looking forward to the fullness of redemption.

God has more than one way of being faithful to God's promises. The promise and fulfillment pattern should not imply that Christianity and Judaism are mutually exclusive fulfillments. Rather, each faith community has experienced God's grace and guidance in ample measure.

Promise and fulfillment is not a once-and-for-all event, but rather a recurring pattern of God's action. Both the life of the church and the vitality of contemporary Judaism are vivid testimonies to God's power and constancy. In every generation, church and synagogue are mutual tokens of God's faithfulness. Together we await the ultimate fulfillment of all God's promises.

> Know therefore that the LORD your God is God, the faithful God who maintains covenant loyalty with those who love him and keep his commandments, to a thousand generations. (Deut 7:9)

> How can I give you up, Ephraim? How can I hand you over, O Israel? (Hos 11:8)

QUESTIONS FOR DISCUSSION

1. Of the various images used in the New Testament to depict Jesus as the fulfillment of God's promises (such as those mentioned above), which are the most meaningful to you?

2. Can a promise find fulfillment in more than one way? What are some examples?

3. Can God, or can a person, make the same promise to different people, and fulfill it differently?

4. What do you think of the idea that contemporary Judaism, in its own way, fulfills God's promises to ancient Israel?

TALKING POINT #5: *DIFFICULT TEXTS*

Christians are morally obligated to understand the New Testament's harsh words against Jews and Judaism in their original contexts, without translating those polemics into antisemitism.

The documents of the New Testament were written in a time of great controversy. The Jesus movement had begun as one among several forms of Judaism. While departing from some aspects of strict Torah observance as it spread among Gentiles, it continued to assert its identity as a legitimate inheritor of God's promises to Israel. The main body of the Jewish community, however, strove to distance itself from those who acclaimed a Galilean rabbi as Messiah, Savior, and Son of God.

The intensity of the conflict is reflected in many places in the New Testament. Scribes and Pharisees are vehemently denounced, and in the Fourth Gospel the collective term "the Jews" designates the enemies of Jesus, even though Jesus and his disciples were, of course, all Jews. The Gospel narratives minimize the role of the tyrannical Roman authorities in Jesus' death, depicting the Jews as fundamentally responsible for the crucifixion. The polemic continues in the book of Acts, and Paul contributes his own harsh words in passionate attacks on those opponents who would impose strict Jewish observance on Gentile converts. Often the New Testament writers selectively appropriated the words of Israel's prophets to shape their invective.

In subsequent history, such texts have often been linked to feelings of hostility and contempt toward Jews, giving apparent biblical warrant to violence against them. Such words—"You are from your father, the devil" (John 8:44), "His blood be on us and on our children!" (Matt 27:25)—still evoke the memory and threat of such hatred.

To remedy this, Christian must make every effort to interpret the texts with a fuller awareness of their historical contexts. Various Jewish groups in the first century C.E., including the early Christians, were struggling to understand Scripture and history as revealing God's will for Israel and the world. Later Christians, alienated from the synagogue, employed the language of those early, internal debates to condemn Jews and Judaism as a whole. We today cannot properly continue to use these texts in this way.

Christians also need to bear in mind the vast changes that have taken place since New Testament times. Originally a minority movement, Christianity soon became the dominant faith in the Roman Empire, and all too often misused its power to oppress its fellow heirs of the covenant, the Jews. Moreover, Judaism has undergone many creative developments, so that Jewish faith and practice today, while in continuity with biblical Israel, is by no means identical with it.

The reader of the New Testament needs to guard against transferring what is said there about Jews to our actual Jewish neighbors today. The gospel of love must not become a pretense for prejudice or hatred.

> You shall not bear false witness against your neighbor. (Exod 20:16)

> If I have all faith, so as to remove mountains, but do not have love, I am nothing. (1 Cor 13:2)

QUESTIONS FOR DISCUSSION

1. Do you think that texts such as those referred to above can lead to hostility against Jews today? Has this happened in your experience?

2. Before lessons such as these are read in worship, commentary can be offered to avoid any antisemitic or anti-Judaic implications. What do you think of this possibility?

3. Does it help us Christians to ask: "What if my Jewish neighbors heard this text? Does it slander them? What impression would it give them of Christians and Christianity?

TALKING POINT #6: JEWISH CONCERN FOR THE STATE OF ISRAEL

The State of Israel holds a special place in the life and thought of the Jewish people. The need for Christians to understand the depth of Jewish concern for Israel is especially urgent as we seek to participate faithfully in the quest for peace and justice for all peoples in the Middle East.

For much of its existence, the Jewish people has lived in diaspora, that is, dispersed among the nations. Although the land of biblical Israel was home to some Jews throughout this history, most lived as minorities within other nations. At times they enjoyed cordial relations with the majority population, but often they became scapegoats for social problems and were subjected to vilification and violence. Always they kept alive the memory of their biblical homeland, and classic Jewish liturgy makes repeated reference to the Land of Israel, even concluding its two major festivals—Passover and the Day of Atonement—with "Next year in Jerusalem!"

This hope bore new historical fruit in the 1880s and 1890s, when Jews fleeing persecution in eastern Europe moved to the Holy Land. Their movement was connected to the scriptural promise of a return to Zion, Jerusalem's holy mountain. (Hence the term *Zionism* is attached to various Jewish nationalist movements, though they have interpreted the scriptural promise in different ways.) In many places, Jewish and Arab neighbors lived in harmony, but tension and conflict were present from the first and grew over time. A plan developed by the United Nations to partition the land was accepted by the Jewish leadership but opposed by the Arab governments, and the establishment of the State of Israel in 1948 was met with an invasion by the surrounding nations. In this and later conflicts, Israel defended itself and, in the process, expanded its territorial control. Palestinian aspirations for an independent state and Israeli concern for national security have been the themes of both continuing conflict and approaches to peace. However, extremist elements, mutual distrust of intentions, and cycles of resentment over Israeli policies and Palestinian responses have repeatedly undermined initiatives from both sides. Efforts to achieve a just and peaceful coexistence in the region have also been complicated by the dynamics of the Cold War and other international conflicts.

Contemporary American Jews have differing views regarding the policies of the Israeli government, but the continued existence of the State of Israel is very important to them. The ability of Jews anywhere in the world to claim Israeli citizenship is especially valued as a safeguard against the tactic used by the Nazis of declaring Jews "stateless" and thereby removing them from the protection of international law.

Christian hope has not usually focused on any specific land, but on a new heaven and a new earth where God's rule will bring peace and justice to all people. This vision sets the standard for all nations; governments serve under God's blessing or judgment depending on whether they promote such peace and justice or undermine it. From this standpoint, the State of Israel, with its democratic ideals and cultural achievements, has been a blessing and a haven for Jews in a world where one-third of their people were annihilated in the Holocaust. At the same time, as a sovereign state, Israel has the moral obligation to use its power responsibly in a situation in which a displaced Palestinian population also seeks independence, security, and a peaceful future in its own land.

Assessments of the Arab-Israeli-Palestinian situation will differ, not only between Jews and Christians but also within each group. Both Israelis and Palestinians can at various times be especially vulnerable, eliciting appropriate Christian concern, advocacy, and action. Efforts to contribute to peaceful coexistence will be most effective when they are grounded in serious study of the history of the conflict, respect for the rights and grievances of all parties, and prudent concern for the use of power in a highly charged and delicately balanced situation. Solutions will not be found by the direct application of biblical prophecies or apocalyptic scenarios, but by prayerful reflection on practical possibilities, guided by an ethic of faith active in love. In the quest for a just peace, Christians will seek to maintain open dialogue with all participants and to help bear the pain of more than a century of conflict.

QUESTIONS FOR DISCUSSION

1. What similarities and differences would you see between a Jewish love for the Land of Israel and such phenomena as the nostalgic regard that many Americans have for their ethnic homelands; respect for the sacredness of church buildings; patriotism and concern for national security; reverence for the physical elements of the sacraments? What are other possible analogies?

2. What is the relation between seeing the modern State of Israel as a nation "like all the nations" and the idea of Israel as "a light to the nations"? By what standards should Israel determine its actions and policies?

3. Is the use of violence ever justified as a means to social and political ends? Under what circumstances? How can a continual cycle of retaliatory violence be broken, or avoided in the first place?

4. The conflict in the Middle East is sometimes interpreted in terms of religious warfare, with Jewish, Christian, and Muslim factions arguing polarized positions on the basis of fundamentalist readings of history and Scripture. Thus religion may be used to justify and even escalate contempt and violence. How can one envision religion playing a more constructive role?

5. How do we bring concerns for Palestinians, and our special relationship with Palestinian Lutherans in Jerusalem and the West Bank, into our dialogue and cooperation with Jews? How can we support joint Palestinian-Israeli initiatives for peace and justice?

TALKING POINT #7: TIKKUN OLAM — MENDING THE WORLD

Jews and Christians both hear the call to be active in "the care and redemption of all that God has made" and can collaborate in such efforts.

The world and human society are not what they could be. Both Jews and Christians find in the Bible a witness to the reality that something has gone wrong with God's good creation, something that God is working to remedy. Both Jews and Christians feel called to participate in that work. Christians dedicate themselves to "the care and redemption of all that God has made," and

Jews commit themselves to *tikkun olam*—mending (or healing, or repairing) the world.

For Christians, the gift of the Holy Spirit gives us power and wisdom to live rightly and be a blessing to the world. For Jews, the inborn "good impulse" of human beings offsets an opposing "evil impulse" that leads us to sin; by following the good impulse, a Jew will lead a more upright life and add to the world's betterment. For both Christians and Jews, being "a kingdom of priests and a holy nation" (Exod 19:6, 1 Peter 2:9) means bearing responsibility to use God's gifts for the good of the world.

Martin Luther spoke of God working among us in two ways—in a spiritual realm ruled by Christ and the law of love, and in a worldly realm ruled by human powers and laws of justice. Some Lutherans have misunderstood this "two-kingdoms" teaching to mean that Christians have no special role to play in the worldly realm (human society) as long as they are good citizens and proclaim the gospel for individual salvation. At its worst, this misunderstanding has allowed Lutherans to participate in the most repressive regimes and programs.

In the last century, many Lutherans and other Christians both acquiesced to and collaborated in the Nazi efforts to annihilate the Jewish people (the Holocaust, or Shoah—a Hebrew term meaning "catastrophe"). Surely this catastrophe was a grievous wound in God's creation, one for which healing must still be sought. In similar ways, the persisting problem of race relations in United States and the worldwide ecological crisis are vital arenas in which Christians and Jews can work together.

In this matter, we can learn much from Jewish teaching and heritage. In many times and places, one finds leading examples of Jews who devoted their lives to improving the society in which they lived. One stream of Jewish messianic thought envisions the Messiah coming only when Israel has fulfilled its role as witness to God's will. Such a belief ties together the task of healing the world (*tikkun olam*) with the hope of complete redemption in a very powerful way.

Lutherans and Jews can work together as partners in the tasks of social justice, ecological renewal, personal and family relationships, interfaith reconciliation, and all the other challenges of healing what is broken in our world.

> But seek the welfare of the city where I have sent you into exile, and pray to the LORD on its behalf, for in its welfare you will find your welfare. (Jer 29:7)

> Let justice roll down like waters, and righteousness like an everflowing stream. (Amos 5:24)

QUESTIONS FOR DISCUSSION

1. What brokenness in the world do you most care about healing?

2. Who are your role models for making a difference for good in the world?

3. What role does faith have in motivating people to work for a just society and healthy relationships?

4. How can Jews and Christians work together toward *tikkun olam*?

TALKING POINT #8: *CHRISTIANS AND JEWS IN THE CONTEXT OF WORLD RELIGIONS*

Christians and Jews share a special relationship within the community of world religions. Their recent experience in building mutual respect and understanding can provide a model for wider interfaith relations.

The acknowledgment of Judaism as a cocommunity of faith carries with it significant challenges for the understanding of Christian faith and identity. These have to do both with our unique relationship with the Jewish people, to whom we are so closely bound by our shared history, and with the broader issues of religious pluralism.

Our relationship to contemporary Judaism requires both sensitivity to what we have in common and a respect for the independent right of Jews to define themselves as a community. A mature Christian respect for the work of God in Judaism thus affirms the faith and practice of Jews as more than a foil, a footnote, or a problem for our own identity.

Our two communities share historical and scriptural origins. We have also influenced one another in various ways over the centuries. Yet as Christianity has developed within diverse cultures and as Judaism has lived through its own rich history, both have grown beyond the terms of their original relationship. Christianity has often been called a "daughter religion" of Judaism; alternatively, the two have been viewed as siblings, both sprung from the ancient faith of Abraham and Sarah. In fact, however, both communities have matured to be separate and fellow "adults" within the diverse world of human faiths.

Recognizing the independent integrity of Judaism, moreover, reminds us that there are other such adult faiths in that diverse world—other communities of faith and practice that also encounter the sacred. The growing reconciliation between Christians and Jews in our time may thus become an example of the way in which we might live together with people of other commitments and experiences.

Have we not all one father? Has not one God created us? (Mal 2:10)

Then Peter began to speak to them: "I truly understand that God shows no partiality, but in every nation, anyone who fears him and does what is right is acceptable to him." (Acts 10:34)

QUESTIONS FOR DISCUSSION

1. What do Christianity and Judaism have in common, and how do they differ? Are Jewish-Christian relations different than our relationships to other world religions?

2. What does the special relationship between Christians and Jews imply for our relationships to Muslims, who share the same monotheistic faith? What can we do in our local communities to foster understanding among all three groups?

3. How can one maintain a loyalty and commitment to one's own faith while at the same time respecting people of other faiths, and protecting their equal rights in civic life?

Prepared by the Consultative Panel on Lutheran-Jewish Relations of the Office of Ecumenical and Inter-Religious Relations, Evangelical Lutheran Church in America.

Your ideas about these topics are very welcome and will be considered by the Panel in its further work. To submit personal reflections or the results of a group discussion, please send a letter to the Office of Ecumenical and Inter-Religious Relations at the address below, or send an e-mail to erinfo@elca.org.

Further information on Jewish-Christian relations, including a downloadable form of these Talking Points, may be found at http://www.elca.org/ecumenical/interreligious/. See also the comprehensive set of resources on the ecumenical Web site http://www.jcrelations.net.

RESOURCES FOR FURTHER STUDY

1. HELPFUL REFERENCES AS YOU STUDY *TALKING POINTS*

About Judaism: A Guide to Beliefs and Practices. 16 page booklet with text and illustrations. Single copy $1.10; discount for bulk orders. Channing L. Bete Co. (800-628-7733)

Essential Judaism: A Complete Guide to Beliefs, Customs, and Rituals. By George Robinson. Pocket Books, 644 pages, $18.00. A comprehensive survey of Jewish life in history and today.

2. LEARNING MORE ABOUT JUDAISM

Settings of Silver: An Introduction to Judaism. By Rabbi Stephen M. Wylen. Paulist Press, 408 pages, $19.95. Thorough exposition of Jewish history, beliefs, practices, and contemporary life.

Judaism: An Introduction for Christians. James Limburg, translator and editor. Augsburg Fortress, 285 pages. A classic. Out of print, but may be available in church libraries or from used book sellers.

The Jewish Book of Why and *The Second Jewish Book of Why.* By Alfred J. Kolatch. Boxed set. Jonathan David Publishers, 768 pages, $44.95. An A-to-Z guide to all things Jewish.

The Earth Is the Lord's: The Inner World of the Jew in Eastern Europe. By Abraham Joshua Heschel. Jewish Lights Publishing, 112 pages, $14.95. An eloquent exploration of Jewish spirituality.

3. CHRISTIAN-JEWISH RELATIONS

Introduction to Jewish-Christian Relations. Edited by Michael Shermis and Arthur E. Zannoni. Paulist Press, 275 pages, $11.95. A collection of articles on key issues in the dialogue.

Jews and Christians: A Troubled Family. By Walter Harrelson and Randall M. Falk. Abingdon, 208 pages, $16.00. Essays by a Christian and a Jewish scholar on basic issues in the relationship.

Irreconcilable Differences? A Learning Resource for Jews and Christians. Edited by David F. Sandmel and others. Westview Press, 228 pages, $23.00. Deals with questions such as "How Do Jews and Christians Read the Bible?" and "How Do Jews and Christians Understand Salvation and Repentance?"

4. GUIDES TO LOCAL INTERFAITH DIALOGUE

Interfaith Circles. Offers guidance on setting up a "living room dialogue" group. Includes readings and discussion guides. Six packets, each with materials for four programs. Available from ELCA Office of Ecumenical and Inter-Religious Relations (800-638-3522, ext. 2610).

Sharing Shalom: A Process for Local Interfaith Dialogue between Christians and Jews. Edited by Philip. A. Cunningham and Arthur F. Staff. Basic readings, procedural suggestions, and discussion questions for six sessions.

5. RETHINKING CHRISTIANITY IN RELATION TO JUDAISM

Has God Only One Blessing? Judaism as a Source of Christian Self-Understanding. By Mary C. Boys. Paulist Press, 393 pages, $29.95. A study of needed changes in traditional views of Jews and Judaism, and the implications for a renewed Christian faith.

A Dictionary of the Jewish-Christian Dialogue. Edited by Leon Klenicki and Geoffrey Wigoder. Paulist Press, 240 pages, $9.95. Brief articles on key theological concepts. Part of the Stimulus book series, "Studies in Judaism and Christianity."

Constantine's Sword. The Church and the Jews: A History. By James Carroll. Houghton Mifflin, 756 pages, $28.00. A thorough history of this troubled relationship, by a lay Roman Catholic writer.

A Guest in the House of Israel: Post-Holocaust Church Theology. By Clark M. Williamson. Westminister/John Knox Press, 344 pages, $24.95. A closely reasoned theological treatise.

6. SPECIAL TOPICS

Voices from Jerusalem: Jews and Christians Reflect on the Holy Land. Edited by David Burrell and Yehezkel Landau. Paulist Press, 176 pages, $9.95. Historical and contemporary perspectives.

The Holocaust and the Christian World: Reflections on the Past, Challenges for the Future. Edited by Carol Rittner, Stephen D. Smith, and Irena Steinfeldt. Continuum, 278 pages, $24.95. Documents, illustrations, historical and theological reflections.

Luther and the Jews: A Fateful Legacy. By Franklin Sherman. A five-session study guide on the historical and theological context of Luther's writings on the Jews and the need to reevaluate them in light of the current Christian-Jewish dialogue. Available from the ELCA Office of Ecumenical and Inter-Religious Relations (800-638-3522, ext. 2610).

Removing Anti-Judaism from the Pulpit. Edited by Howard Clark Kee and Irwin J. Borowsky. Chiron Publications, 140 pages $19.95. A challenge to bring Christian preaching abreast of advances in interfaith relations.

Lutherans and the Challenge of Religious Pluralism. Edited by Frank W. Klos, C. Lynn Nakamura, and Daniel F. Martensen. Augsburg Fortress, 197 pages. Essays by five Lutheran scholars, including a review of the basic teachings of the major religions.

How to Be a Perfect Stranger: A Guide to Etiquette in Other People's Religious Ceremonies. Edited by Arthur J. Magida. Jewish Lights Publishing, 2 volumes, $24.95 each. How to act, dress, and understand what is happening in the ceremonies of many faiths and denominations. See vol. 1 for Judaism.

7. VIDEOS

We Christians and Jews: How Do We Relate? Videos presenting lectures by Lutheran theologians on *Our Common Scriptures—Our Troubled History—Our Challenging Present—Our Hopeful Future.* A "Select" program of the Program Unit on Vocation and Education, Evangelical Lutheran Church in America. Set of four (two hours each), $40.00.

Jews and Christians: A Journey of Faith. A two-hour video introducing many key issues and personalities in the Christian-Jewish dialogue today, as seen on national television. Available from Auteur Productions, Potomac, MD (301-299-6554).

8. INTERNET RESOURCES

http://www.jcrelations.net. A comprehensive international resource on Jewish-Christian relations. Articles, reports, reviews, and links to numerous related web sites, institutes and organizations.

http://www.elca.org/ecumenical/interreligious/index.html. News and documentation on interfaith relations from the web site of the Evangelical Lutheran Church in America. To order printed materials on Lutheran-Jewish relations, see http://www.elca.org/ecumenical/interreligious/jewish/talkingpoints/index.html.

http://www.maven.co.il. An inventory of Jewish resources on the Web, with links to many sites dealing with Jewish life and thought.

NOTES

INTRODUCTION

1. C.E. = the Common Era. 70 C.E. = 70 A.D. In Jewish-Christian dialogue C.E. is typically used, because it is more neutral than A.D. = "the year of *our* Lord" [*anno Domini*]. Similarly, B.C.E. = Before the Common Era. 70 B.C.E. = 70 B.C.

2. Though they often overlap, "anti-Judaism" and "antisemitism" are distinguishable. *Anti-Judaism* sees no value in the religion of Judaism. For it, Judaism is out of date, is a relic of the past, and has been superseded by Christianity. The desired outcome is for Jews to convert to Christianity. *Antisemitism* is racial rather than religious. According to antisemitism, the Jewish people, whatever their religious views, are dangerous and/or racially inferior. The desired outcome is their removal from society. Antisemitism depends on racial theories developed in the latter part of the nineteenth century—theories that claimed scientific backing. Along with nationalism and fascism, racial antisemitism was a basic component in the ideology of Nazism.

3. There have been histories of the church's anti-Judaism, such as Clark Williamson, *Has God Rejected His People? Anti-Judaism in the Christian Church* (Nashville: Abingdon, 1982). There have been theological proposals, such as Paul van Buren, *A Theology of the Jewish-Christian Reality*, 3 vols. (San Francisco: Harper & Row, 1980–1988), or Clark Williamson, *A Guest in the House of Israel: Post-Holocaust Church Theology* (Louisville, Ky.: Westminster John Knox, 1993), or Mary Boys, *Has God Only One Blessing? Judaism as a Source of Christian Self-Understanding* (New York: Paulist, 2000). There have been studies of Christian origins, such as Vincent Martin, *A House Divided: The Parting of the Ways between Synagogue and Church* (New York: Paulist, 1995). There have been aids for scriptural interpretation in sermon preparation, such as Clark Williamson and Ronald J. Allen, *Interpreting Difficult Texts: Anti-Judaism and Christian Preaching* (Harrisburg, Pa.: Trinity, 1989) or Marilyn Salmon, *Preaching Without Contempt: Overcoming Unintended Anti-Judaism* (Minneapolis: Fortress Press, 2006). Materials have also been prepared for living room dialogues, such as *Interfaith Circles* (see the listing in "Resources for Further Study" in the appendix) or the *Talking Points: Topics in Jewish-Christian Relations* reproduced in the appendix to this book.

4. Printed in the appendix of this volume.

CHAPTER 1

1. John Dominic Crossan, *Jesus: A Revolutionary Biography* (San Francisco: HarperSanFrancisco, 1994).

2. The break was not a one-time event, nor did it follow a uniform pattern. There seems to have been a great deal of variation from one locality to another, but, whatever these variations, the result was two separate religious communities in the place of one.

3. During the last decade or so there has been some discussion in Reform Judaism of revising this tradition and more actively inviting people to adopt Judaism.

4. A group of students who went with me to hear Elie Wiesel speak in 2001 at Minnesota State University in Mankato expressed surprise over a statement Wiesel made that would not surprise a fellow Jew. He said he did not like the story of Noah, because Noah did not object when God asked him to build an ark. Noah just said, "Okay," and went ahead with its construction. In Wiesel's judgment, Noah should have protested the destruction of all those other people, as Abraham did and as Moses later would do.

5. In Orthodox Judaism the *minyan* requires ten adult males; in Reform Judaism and most Conservative congregations the requirement is ten adult Jews.

6. See chapter 5, on "Difficult Texts," for specific references and a careful discussion of this issue.

7. Jesus then is "the way" (John 14:6) into the covenant for those not already in covenant with God.

8. See chapter six for a more detailed discussion of the importance of the state of Israel for contemporary American Jews.

9. See, e.g., Emil Fackenheim, *God's Presence in History: Jewish Affirmations and Philosophical Reflections* (New York: New York University Press, 1970).

10. See Richard Rubenstein, *After Auschwitz: Radical Theology and Contemporary Judaism* (Indianapolis: Bobbs-Merrill, 1966).

11. See, for example, Howard R. Greenstein, *Judaism—An Eternal Covenant* (Philadelphia: Fortress Press, 1983); chaps. 10–14 of Donald Harman Akenson, *Surpassing Wonder: The Invention of the Bible and the Talmuds* (Chicago: University of Chicago Press, 2001); Raymond Scheindlin, *A Short History of the Jewish People: From Legendary Times to Modern Statehood* (New York: Oxford University Press, 2000); and Jonathan Sarna, *American Judaism: A History* (New Haven, Conn.: Yale University Press, 2005).

12. Martin Luther, "On the Third Sunday of Advent," a sermon on Matthew 11:2-10, *Dr. Martin Luthers Sämmtliche Schriften*, ed. Joh. Georg Walch (St. Louis: Concordia, 1901), 11:84.

CHAPTER 2

1. Clark M. Williamson succinctly characterizes the literature in *A Guest in the House of Israel: Post-Holocaust Church Theology* (Louisville, Ky.: Westminster John Knox, 1993), 112–17, and refers to the classic survey by A. Lukyn Williams, *Adversus Judaeos* (Cambridge: Cambridge University Press, 1935).

2. Rosemary Radford Ruether, *Faith and Fratricide: The Theological Roots of Anti-Semitism* (New York: Seabury, 1974); idem, "The *Adversus Judaeos* Tradition in the Church Fathers: The Exegesis of Christian Anti-Judaism," in *Essential Papers on Judaism and Christianity in Conflict: From Late Antiquity to the Reformation*, ed. Jeremy Cohen (New York: New York University Press, 1991) 174–89; Williamson, *A Guest in the House of Israel*, 4f.

3. Isaac first introduced the phrase in *Has Anti-Semitism Roots in Christianity?* (New York: National Conference of Christians and Jews, 1961), 57.

4. See the collections of documents in Helga Croner, *Stepping Stones to Further Jewish-Christian Relations: An Unabridged Collection of Christian Documents* (London and New York: Stimulus, 1977); idem, *More Stepping Stones to Jewish-Christian Relations: An Unabridged Collection of Christian Documents 1975–1983* (New York: Paulist, 1985).

5. See Elliot N. Dorff, "The Covenant as the Key: A Jewish Theology of Jewish-Christian Relations," in *Toward a Theological Encounter: Jewish Understandings of Christianity*, ed. Rabbi Leon Klenicki (New York & Mahwah, N.J.: Paulist, 1991), 43f., for a further and somewhat different understanding of why "the word [covenant] does not sit well with Jews."

6. This is a peculiarly modern perspective. As we will see, for New Testament writers it was the "old" that carried honor and value; hence, it could lend credibility to a "new" development. This reversal of values from antiquity to our modern society complicates our use of biblical language and imagery.

7. Only eight references lie outside these two authors. (1) At Rev 11:19, a vision of the heavenly temple includes the ark of the covenant. (2) In the deutero-Pauline letter to the Ephesians, the readers are described as previously "without Christ, being aliens from the commonwealth of Israel, and strangers to the covenants of promise, having no hope and without God in the world" (2:12). Note the plural reference, and that it is precisely estrangement from those covenants that Christ has reconciled for them (Ephesians 3–5). The three Synoptic versions of the Last Supper include parallels to the (pre-)Pauline 1 Cor 11:25 (Matt 26:28; Mark 14:24; Luke 22:20). The Lukan corpus includes three further references to covenant, each in compositions that may come from sources used by Luke. (6) In Luke 1:72 the Magnificat hails Jesus' appearance with the praise that God "has shown the mercy promised to our ancestors, and has remembered his holy covenant." In Acts both Peter and Stephen refer to covenant in a speech. (7) At Acts 3:25 Peter tells his listeners they "are descendants of the prophets and of the covenant that God gave to your ancestors," while (8) at Acts 7:8 Stephen's narration of early Israelite history recalls that God gave Abraham the covenant of circumcision. In none of these instances is there any negative connotation to the term.

8. We cannot here enter into discussion of the history of covenant language in biblical times and literature. We mean only to say that the prophets presuppose the identification of Israel as God's people which the covenant language comes to express.

9. Harold W. Attridge, "Hebrews," in *Harper's Bible Commentary*, ed. James L. Mays (San Francisco: Harper & Row, 1988), 1260.

10. In what follows, we adopt the book's language of "first" covenant, even though the Sinai covenant is neither the first one described in Jewish Scripture nor, likely, the first one known to ancient Israelites.

11. The Greek text of Jeremiah is especially useful to the writer in this regard, putting the focus on the "continuation" in the covenant rather than on the ancestors' "breaking" the covenant, as the Hebrew text of Jeremiah has it.

12. See George Wesley Buchanan, *To the Hebrews,* Anchor Bible 38 (Garden City, N.Y.: Doubleday, 1972), 139–50.

13. See Williamson, *A Guest in the House of Israel,* 108–10.

14. See Peter A. Pettit and John Townsend, "In every generation . . . ," in *Seeing Judaism Anew: Christianity's Sacred Obligation*, ed. Mary C. Boys (Lanham, Md.: Rowman & Littlefield, 2005), 95–112.

15. We might note in passing that even the issue of veiling, or the mitigation of direct encounter with divine glory, is shared by the two covenants, since Paul claims that "all of us, with unveiled faces, [see] the glory of the Lord as though reflected in a mirror" (2 Cor 3:18; see 1 Cor 13:12).

16. This is a complicated and counterintuitive argument, since Paul's teachers would have been likely to inculcate in him the identification of Ishmael with non-Jewish Semitic neighbors and of Isaac with the Jewish community.

17. Paul bases Gentile inclusion on the "faith" that Gentiles share with Abraham, thereby finessing the issue of circumcision in the Gentile community. As Krister Stendahl has noted in *Final Account: Paul's Letter to the Romans* (Minneapolis: Fortress Press, 1995), Paul's "exegetical find" was the fact that Abraham's faith was already honored by God in Genesis 15, while circumcision is only enjoined in Genesis 17 (see Rom 4:1-12, especially v. 10).

18. Although the term *covenant* does not occur in Romans 4 and the focus remains more fully on Abraham, Paul evokes Moses and Sinai by contrasting the possibilities of Abraham being justified through faith or through law (4:13). He also makes explicit the question whether the blessedness of forgiveness is only for the circumcised Jews or also for the uncircumcised Gentiles (4:9-12). Paul is focusing on the relationship between these two groups when he addresses covenant more explicitly later in the book.

19. The first quotation is from Isa 59:20. The following verse identifies the covenant in terms similar to those in Jeremiah—the spirit of the prophet and his words will be ineradicable for future generations—but there is no reference in Isa 59:21 to the forgiveness of sins; hence Paul must here be citing Jer 31:34.

20. Gal 1:14; Phil 3:4-6.

21. Among the several hundred instances of the term *berit* in the Hebrew Bible, many involve specific pacts or agreements among individuals and groups. The brief overview here focuses on those six primary instances in which God is a party to the covenant.

22. The simple imperative in Gen 17:1, "walk before me, and be blameless," may be taken as a kind of implicit global condition. However, the only explicit expectation of Abraham in this covenant text is the perpetual observance of circumcision among his male descendants, which is specifically identified as the "sign" of the covenant, not its condition (17:11).

23. Professor Dorff notes that Shalom Paul has suggested that Jeremiah's "words of the Lord" may be taken more as threat than promise. Such a reading still sets Jeremiah's understanding apart from Deuteronomy's, in that Deuteronomy calls for obedience while Jeremiah threatens that all choice about obedience will be removed.

24. There are, of course, other terms and categories with which Israel's scriptures refer to the relationship between God and the people of God. Familial models, mentor-novice images, partnership, and liege with penitent or petitioner are several that come to mind easily. We do not mean to say that covenant is the only category, but only that covenant as category admits many meanings, all alike signifying the relationship of God and Israel.

25. The Passover *haggadah* is the framework and text by which the exodus history is recited and its significance is made clear for the present time.

26. Noam Zion and David Dishon, *A Different Night* (Jerusalem: Shalom Hartman Institute, 1997), 114.

27. See especially Rom 6:17ff., 8:2f.; Heb 9:26.

28. None of the early Christian writers address the place of the Eucharist and the relationship of cross-redemption to exodus-redemption for Jews who believe in Jesus as Messiah and Son of God. The topic is pertinent to the self-understanding of the modern "Messianic Jewish" movement; see Mark Kinzer, *Post-Missionary Messianic Judaism* (Grand Rapids, Mich.: Brazos, 2005) for a helpful introduction to the movement, though Kinzer does not take up these issues in the same covenantal redemptive terms as we do.

29. Returning to liturgical practice where we began, it is worthwhile to note that the language of covenant occurs in the Lutheran liturgical tradition at essential points of identity, redemption, and forgiveness: in the rites for baptism and the affirmation of baptism, in the Words of Institution at the eucharistic altar, and in the benediction following burial of the dead (*Lutheran Book of Worship* [Minneapolis: Augsburg, 1978], 69, 121, 201, 214 and *Evangelical Lutheran Worship* [Minneapolis: Augsburg Fortress, 2006], 108, 228, 236, 285).

30. So the characterization of this era in the title of John Oesterreicher's book, *The New Encounter Between Jews and Christians* (New York: Philosophical Library, 1986) and the subtitle of Irving Greenberg's *For the Sake of Heaven and Earth: The New Encounter between Judaism and Christianity* (Philadelphia: Jewish Publication Society, 2004).

CHAPTER 3

1. In addition I extend my heartfelt thanks to Kurt Hendel, Darrell Jodock, David Sandmel, and Frank Sherman for their comments and suggestions after reading drafts of this essay. The views expressed and any remaining errors are my own.

2. For the theological position that the law always accuses (*lex semper accusat*), even though it can and does have other functions as well, see Werner Elert, *Law and Gospel*, trans. Edward H. Schroeder, Facets Books-Social Ethics series 16 (Philadelphia: Fortress Press, 1967). For additional Lutheran discussions of law and gospel, see Herman G. Stuempfle Jr., *Preaching Law and Gospel*, rev. ed. (Mifflintown, Pa.: Sigler, 1991); Gerhard Forde, *The Law-Gospel Debate: An Interpretation of Its Historical Development* (Minneapolis: Augsburg, 1969); and Carl E. Braaten, "The Law/Gospel Principle," in *Principles of Lutheran Theology* (Philadelpha: Fortress Press, 1983).

3. For a description of Simhat Torah and other Jewish festivals and practices, see Alfred J. Kolatch, *The Jewish Book of Why* and *The Second Jewish Book of Why* (Middle Village, N.Y.: David, 1981, 1985); Arthur I. Waskow, *Seasons of Our Joy: A Handbook of Jewish Festivals* (New York: Summit, 1986); and Stephen M. Wylen, *Settings of Silver: An Introduction to Judaism* (New York: Paulist, 1989).

4. For accessible treatments of basic issues in the Jewish-Christian relationship, see Walter Harrelson and Randall M. Falk, *Jews and Christians: A Troubled Family* (Nashville: Abingdon, 1990); Michael Shermis and Arthur E. Zannoni, eds., *Introduction to Jewish-Christian Relations* (New York: Paulist, 1991); and David F. Sandmel, Rosann M. Catalano, and Christopher

M. Leighton, eds, *Irreconcilable Differences? A Learning Resource for Jews and Christians* (Boulder, Colo.: Westview, 2001).

5. For different scholarly perspectives on Paul's attitude toward Jewish law, see Stephen Westerholm, *Israel's Law and the Church's Faith: Paul and His Recent Interpreters* (Grand Rapids, Mich.: Eerdmans, 1988); and Mark D. Nanos, ed., *The Galatians Debate: Contemporary Issues in Rhetorical and Historical Interpretation* (Peabody, Mass.: Hendrickson, 2002).

6. For more on the relationship between salvation and Torah within Judaism itself, see below.

7. For further discussion of this matter, see Franklin Sherman, "Difficult Texts," chap. 5 in this volume. For the style of argumentation within the Greco-Roman world that influenced the New Testament's presentation of Christian origins, see Luke Timothy Johnson, "The New Testament's Anti-Jewish Slander and the Conventions of Ancient Polemic," *Journal of Biblical Literature* 108, no. 3 (1989): 419–41; and George M. Smigma, *Pain and Polemic: Anti-Judaism in the Gospels* (New York: Paulist, 1992).

8. See Jeremy Cohen, "Medieval Jews on Christianity: Polemical Strategies and Theological Defense," in *Interwoven Destinies: Jews and Christians through the Ages*, ed. Eugene J. Fisher, Studies in Judaism and Christianity (Mahwah, N.J.: Paulist, 1993). The chapters of this book provide an accessible overview of the history of Jewish-Christian relations from the first century of the common era to the Enlightenment.

9. The text of this Declaration is available on the Web at http://www.elca.org/ecumenical/interfaithrelations/jewish/declaration.html. For a study guide on the historical and theological context of Luther's writing on the Jews and the need to reevaluate them in light of the current Christian-Jewish dialogue, see Franklin Sherman, *Luther and the Jews: A Fateful Legacy*, available from the ELCA Office of Ecumenical and Inter-Religious Relations (800-638-3522, ext. 2610).

10. Resources that aim to bring Christian preaching abreast of advances in interfaith relations include Howard Clark Kee and Irwin J. Borowsky, eds., *Removing Anti-Judaism from the Pulpit* (New York: Continuum, 1996); Ronald J. Allen and Clark M. Williamson, *Preaching the Gospels without Blaming the Jews: A Lectionary Commentary* (Louisville, Ky.: Westminster John Knox, 2004); and Marilyn J. Salmon, *Preaching without Contempt: Overcoming Unintended Anti-Judaism*, Fortress Resources for Preaching (Minneapolis: Fortress Press, 2006). For more about the Pharisees, whom Jews today regard as the founding figures of rabbinic Judaism, see below.

11. For further discussion of the Pharisees within the context of early Judaism, see Shaye J. D. Cohen, *From the Maccabees to the Mishnah* (Philadelphia: Westminster, 1987), esp. chaps. 5 (124–73) and 7 (214–31). For an earlier Jewish perspective on the Pharisees, see Leo Baeck, "The Pharisees," in *The Pharisees and Other Essays* (New York: Schocken, 1947), 3–50.

12. For the significance of Torah within the covenantal relationship established at Sinai, see Jon D. Levenson, *Sinai and Zion: An Entry into the Jewish Bible* (San Francisco: Harper & Row, 1985), 23–86.

13. For more on the Jewish New Year and Yom Kippur, see the sources listed above, n.3.

14. See Gustav Aulén, *Church, Law, and Society* (New York: Scribner's, 1948); and Paul Althaus, *The Divine Command: A New Perspective on Law and Gospel*, Facet Books-Social Ethics series 9 (Philadelphia: Fortress Press, 1966).

15. Martin Luther's contributions to Christian ethics are discussed in Robert Benne, "Lutheran Ethics: Perennial Themes and Contemporary Challenges," and Reinhard Hutter, "The Twofold Center of Lutheran Ethics," in *The Promise of Lutheran Ethics*, ed. Karen L. Bloomquist and John R. Stumme (Minneapolis: Fortress Press, 1998), 11–30, 31–54.

16. For resources, see Carol Rittner, Stephen D. Smith, and Irena Steinfeldt, eds., *The Holocaust and the Christian World: Reflections on the Past, Challenges for the Future* (New York: Continuum, 2000); and Clark M. Williamson, *A Guest in the House of Israel: Post-Holocaust Church Theology* (Louisville, Ky.: Westminster John Knox, 1993).

17. See Cynthia D. Moe-Lobeda, *Healing a Broken World: Globalization and God* (Minneapolis: Fortress Press, 2002).

18. See Krister Stendahl, "Judgment and Mercy," in *Paul among Jews and Gentiles and Other Essays* (Philadelphia: Fortress Press, 1976), 97–108.

19. *Lutheran Book of Worship* (Minneapolis: Augsburg, 1978), 74.

CHAPTER 4

1. In some respects, a better title might be "Prophecy and Fulfillment."

2. The term "Old Testament" goes back to Melito of Sardis in the second century C.E. Jews call these books *Tanakh*, an acronym formed by the first letters of the Hebrew words for the three divisions in their canon: Torah (Pentateuch), Prophets, and Writings. For Jews the Tanakh is itself the Bible, while in Christianity the same books are one of two testaments.

3. See also Gen 13:15-17; 15:5, 7, 18-21; 17:2-8; 22:17-18; 24:60; 26:2-4; 28:3-4, 13-15.

4. As a result the LORD considered Abram righteous. The text can also be construed to mean that Abram considered the LORD's renewed promise as evidence of divine righteousness.

5. According to Exod 12:40-41 the Israelites lived in Egypt for 430 years.

6. Gen 23:19; 25:9; 49:31; 50:13.

7. These additional words express the force of the Hebrew imperfect verb form.

8. The New Testament writers accepted traditional designations of authorship (Moses, Isaiah, etc.) and read the Bible synchronically. My training in historical criticism means that I usually read the Bible diachronically, recognizing various layers in the texts, often stemming from different writers.

9. Within the canon itself Malachi promises the return of the prophet Elijah before the day of the LORD (Mal 4:5).

10. See also John 7:40, 7:52; Acts 7:37.

11. Note the play on words between "raising" someone as prophet and raising Jesus from the dead.

12. In Deut 15:11, the text grants that there will always indeed be needy people, and therefore urges readers to open their hands in generosity toward the poor. This may be another occasion where a secondary hand adds a corrective addition.

13. Jeremiah invoked this principle against the false prophet Hananiah, who prophesied that within two years the temple vessels captured by Nebuchadnezzar would be returned and Jeconiah would be restored to the throne. Jeremiah appealed to the tradition of his

predecessors who customarily announced judgment and said that a prophet who announced good times would only be proven true when this happened. Jeremiah did not wait for this eventuality, however, and returned a few days later and renounced Hananiah as a person whom the LORD had not sent. Jeremiah said that Hananiah was under a divine death sentence and he did indeed die within a year, proving the word of Jeremiah true (Jer 28:1-17).

14. The postexilic territory called Yehud was about as big geographically as the city of Chicago, with a total population possibly of less than twenty thousand.

15. The New Testament citations of this passage misconstrue the Hebrew poetry. Second Isaiah did not speak of a voice crying in the wilderness, but rather a voice cried out with a message in poetic parallelism: In the wilderness prepare the way of the LORD // make straight in the desert the superhighway of our God.

16. See also Isa 26:19 (raising of the dead); 29:18 (the deaf hear); 42:7, 42:18 (blind and deaf see and hear); 61:1 (good news to the oppressed and brokenhearted).

17. If by messianic hope we mean the expectation of a new or eschatological king who is a descendant of David, there is no messianic promise in the Pentateuch. The same could be said for a number of other Old Testament books. Second Isaiah democratizes the promise made to David by reapplying it to all members of the community (Isa 55:3). There were expectations of other eschatological figures in the Old Testament that are often merged with the messianic hope in Christian thinking. We have already discussed the expectation of a prophet like Moses in Deuteronomy, and the coming Son of Humanity is mentioned in Daniel 7. The servant figure in Second Isaiah (cf. Wisdom of Solomon 2 and 5) played a prominent role in early Christian attempts to understand the significance of the death of Jesus, but the servant is *not* a messianic figure in the biblical text itself.

18. For recent studies of this issue see Richard S. Hess and M. Daniel Carroll, eds., *Israel's Messiah in the Bible and the Dead Sea Scrolls* (Grand Rapids, Mich.: Baker, 2003), and John Day, ed., *King and Messiah in Israel and the Ancient Near East*, Journal for the Study of the Old Testament Supplement 270. (Sheffield, UK: Academic Press, 1999).

19. Cf. the similar Jewish Publication Society translation: "The Mighty God is planning grace; The Eternal Father, a peaceable ruler."

20. Isa 9:1-2 is cited as fulfilled in Matt 4:15-16, where Matthew sees the Galilean ministry as a fulfillment of the word of Isaiah.

21. Ezekiel shared this doubt about the legitimacy of Zedekiah since he dates his oracles not to the reign of Zedekiah, but to the reign of his predecessor Jehoiachin.

22. New names for Jerusalem are also cited in the last verse in Ezekiel ("The name of the city from that time on shall be, the LORD is there") and in Third Isaiah, 62:4, where Zion/Jerusalem is renamed Hephzibah ("my delight is in her").

23. Other messianic passages can be found in Ezekiel, Haggai, and perhaps Zechariah. A restoration of the Davidic line is also included in Amos 9:11-15. In this short essay, I make no pretense of referring to every possible messianic promise. In intertestamental times the notion of the Messiah was very prominent. See Psalms of Solomon 17; 2 Esdras 11–12; Testament of Judah 24; and Testament of Dan 5:10-13. The latter two texts *in their present form* are Christian, but were originally Jewish texts.

24. It is usually noted in the Dead Sea Scrolls that two messiahs, one of Aaron and one of David/Israel, were expected by those who wrote the scrolls. For the messianic expectations at Qumran, see James VanderKam and Peter Flint, *The Meaning of the Dead Sea Scrolls* (San Francisco: HarperSanFrancisco, 2002), 265–73.

25. Cf. already Exod 4:22, 23, for the LORD designating Israel as "my son."

26. Italics added.

27. Rudolf Bultmann, "Prophecy and Fulfillment," in *Essays on Old Testament Hermeneutics*, ed. Claus Westermann (Richmond: John Knox, 1963), 73–75. Antonius H. J. Gunneweg stated that the definition of the relationship between the Old and New Testaments is the most difficult historical and theological question faced by Christians. See Isaac Kalimi, "Die Bibel und die klassisch-jüdische Bibelauslegung. Eine interpretations- und religionsgeschichtliche Studie," *Zeitschrift für die Alttestamentliche Wissenschaft* 114 (2002): 594.

28. See in detail Isaac Kalimi, *Early Jewish Exegesis and Theological Controversy: Studies in Scriptures in the Shadow of Internal and External Controversies*, Jewish and Christian Heritage 2 (Assen, Netherlands: Royal Van Gorcum, 2002), 144–45.

29. See in detail, Isaac Kalimi, "The Place of the Book of Esther in Judaism and Jewish Theology," *Theologische Zeitschrift* 59 (2003): 193–204.

CHAPTER 5

1. "Talking Points," No. 5 (Chicago: Department for Ecumenical Affairs (now the Office of Ecumenical and Inter-Religious Relations), Evangelical Lutheran Church in America, 2002). See appendix, print edition, or online at http://www.elca.org/ecumenical/interreligious/jewish/talkingpoints/.

2. The days on which these texts occur and the general subject of each are as follows:

- John 20:19: Second Sunday of Easter, Years A/B/C; also Pentecost, Year A (the risen Jesus appears to the disciples).
- Mark 7:6: Fifteenth Sunday after Pentecost (= Sunday 22), Year B (controversy with some Pharisees about the clean and the unclean).
- John 10:8: Fourth Sunday of Easter, Year A (Jesus as "the gate of the sheep").
- Matt 27:25: Sunday of the Passion, Year A (the Passion according to Matthew).
- Luke 23:20-21: Sunday of the Passion, Year C (the Passion according to Luke).

3. With regard to the phrase "at last," a footnote in the NRSV suggests "completely" or "forever" as alternative translations. In either case, hardly a happy alternative!

4. "No Religion Is an Island," in *Moral Grandeur and Spiritual Audacity: Essays by Abraham Joshua Heschel*, ed. Susannah Heschel (New York: Farrar, Straus, Giroux, 1996), 242.

5. See, for an overview of these developments, William Nicholls, *Christian Antisemitism: A History of Hate* (Northvale, N.J. and London: Jason Aronson, 1993) or James Carroll, *Constantine's Sword: The Church and the Jews, A History* (Boston and New York: Houghton Mifflin, 2001). Most contemporary church bodies have repudiated these teachings; for example, the ELCA in its 1994 "Declaration to the Jewish Community," http://www.elca.org/ecumenical/interreligious/jewish/declaration.html.

6. Norman A. Beck, *The New Testament: A New Translation and Redaction* (Lima, Ohio: Fairway, 2001). He also puts passages reflecting a subordinationist view of the role of women into smaller type, and presents the New Testament documents in the order of their probable date of composition rather than the usual order. Beck is also the author of the most substantial effort to identify and analyze the "difficult texts" regarding the Jews and Judaism in his book, *Mature Christianity in the 21st Century: Recognizing and Repudiating the Anti-Jewish Polemic in the New Testament* (New York: Crossroad, 1994), a revised and expanded version of his original 1985 edition.

7. George M. Smiga, *Pain and Polemic: Anti-Judaism in the Gospels* (New York: Paulist, 1992). Smiga defines "polemic" as "an aggressive attack on the beliefs of another party" (3). He acknowledges his indebtedness for the three-part classification to an essay by Douglas Hare, though he has changed the terminology.

8. Adopting an alternative translation in the NRSV footnote at this point.

9. Thus, for example, a text such as the one cited above from John 20:19, "And the doors where the disciples had met were shut for fear of the Jews," is puzzling, terminologically at least, if one considers the fact that those *inside* the house were also Jews.

10. Matt 27:27 (cf. John 18:28).

11. The article, "Population," in the *Encyclopaedia Judaica* estimates that "shortly before the fall of Jerusalem the world Jewish population exceeded 8,000,000, of whom probably not more than 2,350,000–2,500,000 lived in Palestine."

12. As cited in Philip A. Cunningham, ed., *Pondering the Passion: What's at Stake for Christians and Jews* (Lanham, Md.: Rowman & Littlefield, 2004), 55. Also available in many other sources.

13. Despite its lack of general acceptance, the rendering "the Judeans" has been used in at least three translations known to the present writer:

> a. *Lectionary of the Christian People*, 3 vols. (New York: Pueblo; and Philadelphia: Fortress Press, 1986–88), a retranslation of the texts of the three-year lectionary by Gordon Lathrop and Gail Ramshaw. Also translates *hoi Ioudaioi* as "the Jewish people."
> b. The translation by Norman A. Beck cited above (n. 6). In addition to "the Judeans," Beck also uses other renderings of *hoi Ioudaioi* as he deems them situationally appropriate, e.g., "Jesus' own people."
> c. *The Five Gospels: The Search for the Authentic Words of Jesus*, trans. Robert W. Funk, Roy W. Hoover, and the Jesus Seminar (New York: Macmillan, 1993; reprinted in 1997 by HarperSanFrancisco). (This volume includes the apocryphal Gospel of Thomas). The reason given here for using "Judeans" rather than "Jews," however, is historical, unlike Lowe's geographical rationale. The editors propose the following use of terms (italics added): "The religion of the first Jerusalem temple was practiced by *Israelites*. The religion of the second temple (520 B.C.E.–70 C.E.) was practiced by *Judeans*. The religion of the rabbis and synagogues (90 C.E. and continuing) was and is practiced by *Jews*" (545). Thus they deem the term "the Jews" inappropriate for the earlier period.

14. New York: American Bible Society, 1995. Not to be confused with the Bible Society's earlier "Today's English Version" (TEV).

15. Eugene H. Peterson, *The Message: The New Testament in Contemporary Language* (Colorado Springs: NavPress, 1993, and subsequent editions).

16. A classic text on the Pharisees from an appreciative standpoint is Ellis Rivkin, *The Hidden Revolution: The Pharisees' Search for the Kingdom Within* (Nashville: Abingdon, 1978).

17. *The New Interpreter's Study Bible*, Walter J. Harrelson, gen. ed. (Nashville: Abingdon, 2003).

18. Ronald J. Allen and Clark M. Williamson, *Preaching the Gospel without Blaming the Jews: A Lectionary Commentary* (Louisville, Ky.: Westminster John Knox, 2004).

19. Gerard S. Sloyan, *Preaching the Lectionary: An Exegetical Commentary with CD ROM* (Minneapolis: Fortress Press, 2004); *The Crucifixion of Jesus: History, Myth, Faith* (Minneapolis: Fortress Press, 1995); *Why Jesus Died*, Facets (Minneapolis: Fortress Press, 2004).

20. All Philadelphia or Minneapolis: Fortress Press.

21. New York: Viking Compass.

22. Jewish scholarship on Jesus down to the early 1980s was summarized by Donald A. Hagner in *The Jewish Reclamation of Jesus: An Analysis and Critique of Modern Jewish Study of Jesus* (Grand Rapids, Mich.: Zondervan, 1984). A survey to a later point is offered by the present writer in his essay "The Quest for the Jewish Jesus," in Oliver Rafferty, SJ, ed., *Reconciliation: Essays in Honour of Michael Hurley* (Dublin: Columba, 1993). Some of the most accessible works on the subject are Jacob Neusner's *A Rabbi Talks With Jesus: An Intermillennial, Interfaith Exchange* (New York: Doubleday, 1993), and his companion volume, *Children of the Flesh, Children of the Promise: A Rabbi Talks With Paul* (Cleveland: Pilgrim, 1995). See also the symposium edited by Arthur E. Zannoni, *Jews and Christians Speak of Jesus* (Minneapolis: Fortress Press, 1994), and the more recent collection of essays edited by Paula Fredriksen and Adele Reinhartz, *Jesus, Judaism, and Christian Anti-Judaism: Reading the New Testament After the Holocaust* (Louisville, Ky: Westminster John Knox, 2002). For detailed expositions of the Gospels in the light of rabbinic literature, see Samuel Tobias Lachs, *A Rabbinic Commentary on the New Testament: The Gospels of Matthew, Mark and Luke* (New York: KTAV, 1987) and Rabbi Michael Hilton with Fr. Gordian Marshall, O.P., *The Gospels and Rabbinic Judaism: A Study Guide* (New York: KTAV, 1988). On Paul, see Alan F. Segal, *Paul the Convert: The Apostolate and Apostasy of Paul the Pharisee* (New Haven, Conn.: Yale University Press, 1990), and the symposium edited by Hayim Perelmuter and Wilhelm Wuellner, *Paul the Jew: Jewish/Christian Dialogue* (Berkeley, Calif: Center for Hermeneutical Studies, 1992).

23. Episcopalian biblical scholar Marilyn Salmon offers helpful ideas for preachers in her book *Preaching without Contempt: Avoiding Unintended Anti-Judaism,* Fortress Resources for Preaching (Minneapolis: Fortress Press, 2006).

Chapter 6

1. W. D. Davies, "Jewish Territorial Doctrine and the Christian Response," in *Renewing the Judeo-Christian Wellsprings*, ed. Val A. McInnes (New York: Crossroad, 1987), 2. Davies notes that there are two terms in the Hebrew Bible which might be translated as "land": *aretz* and *adamah*. While *adamah* generally means soil or earth, the term *aretz* contains the sense of a politically defined territory. Generally, as early as the rabbinic tradition, the rabbis referred to the land that God promised to Abraham and his descendents as *ha-aretz* (the land).

2. Betsy Halpern-Amaru, "Land Theology in Philo and Josephus," in *The Land of Israel: Jewish Perspectives*, ed. Lawrence A. Hoffman (Notre Dame, Ind.: University of Notre Dame, 1986), 66. These categories, as outlined by Halpern-Amaru, are just one way of thinking about the different ways that the Land of Israel is conceived in the Hebrew Bible, and they are particularly useful for our purposes in this brief survey.

3. Ibid., 66–67.

4. Harry M. Orlinsky, "The Biblical Concept of the Land of Israel: Cornerstone of the Covenant between God and Israel," in Hoffman, ed., *The Land of Israel*, 40.

5. Halpern-Amaru, "Land Theology," 74.

6. Orlinsky, "The Biblical Concept of the Land of Israel," 52.

7. Dewey Beegle, "The Promise and the Promised Land," *Sojourners* 6, no. 3 (March 1977): 24.

8. Richard Sarason, "The Significance of the Land of Israel in the Mishnah," in Hoffman, ed., *The Land of Israel*, 115, 120.

9. Rabbi Ed Snitkoff, "Always Live in the Land of Israel," *MyJewishLearning.com*, http://www.myjewishlearning.com/ideas_belief/LandIsrael/early_landisrael/Rabbinic_LandIsrael.htm (accessed September 28, 2007).

10. Davies, "Jewish Territorial Doctrine and the Christian Response," 6.

11. Charles Primus, "The Borders of Judaism: The Land of Israel in Early Rabbinic Judaism," in Hoffman, ed., *The Land of Israel*, 107.

12. Sarason, "The Significance of the Land of Israel in the Mishnah," 126.

13. Bradley Shavit Artson, "The Earth is God's: Holiness & Land," Judaism at American Jewish University, http://judaism.uj.edu/Content/ContentUnit.asp?CID=1526&u=5404&t=0 (accessed September 28, 2007).

14. Marc Saperstein, "The Land of Israel in Pre-Modern Jewish Thought," in Hoffman, ed., *The Land of Israel*, 204.

15. Ibid., 195.

16. Shalom Rosenberg, "The Link to the Land of Israel in Jewish Thought: A Clash of Perspectives," in Hoffman, ed., *The Land of Israel*, 146.

17. Ibid., 157.

18. Moshe Idel, "The Land of Israel in Medieval Kabbalah," in Hoffman, ed., *The Land of Israel*, 178.

19. Saperstein, "The Land of Israel in Pre-Modern Jewish Thought," 197.

20. Ibid., 198.

21. *Talking Points: Topics in Christian-Jewish Relations* is available in the appendix or on the Internet at http://www.elca.org/ecumenical/interreligious/jewish/talkingpoints/index.html.

22. A number of studies of the history of the Zionist movement could be recommended. A particularly good resource is Arthur Hertzberg, ed., *The Zionist Idea: A Historical Analysis and Reader* (Garden City, N.Y.: Doubleday, 1959). Moreover, a classic Christian appreciation of the historical gift of the return to the Land may be found in the recently republished James

Parkes's 1954 book, *End of an Exile: Israel, the Jews and the Gentile World,* 3d ed. (Marblehead, Mass.: Micah, 2005).

23. Many in our Christian congregations, even clergy, have been shielded from exposure to the sort of virulent antisemitism associated with the Dreyfus affair. The hate-filled caricatures and calumnies of that literature might frequently be thought artifacts of discredited crackpot Nazism or crazed Islamist demagogues. It is important to recognize that such material was widely circulated in many Christian publications and found an audience in both Catholic and Protestant communities. Like the anti-Jewish diatribes of Luther from an earlier period, this invective and slander should obviously not be appropriated and endorsed, but it does need to be "owned" by Christians. It is a family secret, the shame and sin of our own kin in the faith. Most Jews know of it only too well even while most of us have never experienced it as something in our own midst. The humbling truth is that here is not only a sin of "the children of the church": the guilt lies with its fathers as well.

24. The 1958 best-selling novel (later a film) by Leon Uris, *Exodus,* shaped or reinforced the heroic and inspiring narrative of Israel's founding for a mass audience in America and throughout much of the non-Muslim world. Sadly when, in 1984, Uris published *The Haj,* a novel intended similarly to describe a narrative of Arab experience, many readers found instead a prejudicially negative presentation of his characters and their culture, an apparent denial of the kind of value and nobility the earlier book had found in the Zionist struggle.

25. Among the amazing details in the apocalyptic scenario that involves the Temple Mount for some religious Israeli nationalists and some "Christian Zionists" is the need to have the ashes of a flawless red heifer in order to purify the Jews who would go to pray at the site of the Temple once it is reclaimed for Israel. The lack of such a heifer was thus cause for gratitude for those who pray for peace, but in 1997 a Texas Christian cattle breeder succeeded in producing for Jewish nationalists a rust-colored female calf intended for the fulfilling the imagined plan of God and of speeding the day of Armageddon and Christ's return. See Gershom Gorenberg, *The End of Days: Fundamentalism and the Struggle for the Temple Mount* (New York: Diane, 2000).

26. "Christian Zionism" of this sort has participated in the increasing ascendancy of conservative and often fundamentalist evangelicalism in American political life. Right-wing Israelis have found in these dispensationalist Christians eager and effective allies. At the same time, these Christian Zionists have shown little sympathy for, or awareness of, the suffering of Palestinians, Christian or Muslim.

27. Bernard Avishai, *The Tragedy of Zionism* (New York: Farrar, Straus, Giroux, 1985), is a particularly powerful discussion of the kinds of dilemmas facing modern Israel since the 1967 war. His title should not be taken to mean that Zionism or the State of Israel was a mistake. Avishai is explicitly committed to that endeavor and ideal. Incisively and movingly, however, he reflects on the tragic costs and dangerous choices entailed by the present. Twenty-some years later, many of his words seem even more pertinent.

Naim Stifan Ateek, *Justice, And Only Justice: A Palestinian Theology of Liberation* (Maryknoll, N.Y.: Orbis, 1989), presents a similar set of concerns about Israel but does so as an open representative of and advocate for the Palestinian population. Ateek's account of Zionism is from a Palestinian perspective but not altogether unsympathetic. His call is not for the eradication of Israel but for Jews and Palestinians alike to heed the call of the prophets for justice in the land.

28. Mitri Raheb's *I Am a Palestinian Christian* (Minneapolis: Fortress Press, 1995) gives a powerful account of the reality of life in the Holy Land from the perspective of a Palestinian committed to both coexistence and justice. Raheb's family has lived in Bethlehem for centuries and he serves as pastor of the Lutheran church there. With eloquence and generosity toward others, he tells the story of his people in a time of great difficulty. It is a book that deserves and needs reading alongside the positive accounts of Israel's meaning for Jews.

29. With our strong awareness of terrorist acts committed by Palestinians, we Americans have generally been unconscious of the role that such acts also played in the Jewish war for Israel, both against the British authorities and against Arabs. That story is not one to dwell on—it can become just one more debating point—but our almost total one-sidedness when it comes to the perception and memory of violence should be recognized and challenged.

30. Some Jews have argued forcefully that Jewish preoccupation with the Shoah has become harmful to Jewish identity and moral vision. There is a sacred duty to honor and remember and to confront the obscenity of what was perpetrated, but a focus upon one's history and heritage so insistently in terms of one's own victimization can be immensely destructive, both disempowering a sense of agency and absolving from moral accountability. There are multiple ways in which such self-understanding can lead to either activity or passivity that subverts the good of Zion and the making of peace God ordains. Strikingly, a similar problem exists in much Palestinian rhetoric and in the construction of identity on that side of the struggle in the Holy Land. How can *shalom* be known when both sides see themselves prototypically as the recurrent victims of the other's cruel and immense power?

31. Charles P. Lutz and Robert O Smith, *Christians and a Land Called Holy: How We Can Foster Justice, Peace, and Hope* (Minneapolis: Augsburg Fortress, 2006), is a highly commendable resource for that quest.

32. The appeal to American Christians by Palestinian church leaders seeking support and advocacy for their suffering people has been met by a counteroffensive by some in the Jewish community who consider that appeal inimical to Israel's interests and even survival. The ugly characterization of conscientious people whom we personally love and know to be persons of integrity and compassion, the misrepresentation of their views and the maligning of their motives both saddens and angers us. This offensive against Palestinian Christian leadership on the American scene does little to advance the cause of understanding and coexistence but rather undermines the kind of conversations that are needed. But let us Christians not be drawn by our anger into despairing withdrawal from engagement with the Jewish community by one passionate faction who think they are defending Israel from her enemies. Too often, not least within and in regard to the Holy Land, the hard-edged few have controlled the agenda through the reactivity of the many.

33. A 1993 Jewish, Christian, and Muslim colloquium on the spiritual significance of Jerusalem gave a fascinating opening into this kind of stimulated reflection. Unfortunately, such discussions will tend to be of interest among Christians just for what they say about the issues of the Middle East rather than also for what they might teach us about ourselves. See Hans Ucko, ed., *The Spiritual Significance of Jerusalem for Jews, Christians, and Muslims* (Geneva: World Council of Churches, 1994).

CHAPTER 7

1. Gerald Blidstein, "Tikkun Olam," in *Tikkun Olam: Social Responsibilities in Jewish Thought and Law*, ed. D. Shatz, C. Waxman, and N. Diament (Northvale, N.J.: Jason Aronson, 1997), 54.

2. Arnold Wolf, "Repairing Tikkun Olam," *Judaism* 50, no. 4 (Fall 2001): 479–82.

3. Hayim Soloveitchik, "Confrontation," *Tradition* 6, no. 2 (1964): 20–21.

4. David Bleich, "Tikkun Olam: Jewish Obligations to Non-Jewish Society," in Shatz, Waxman, and Diament, eds., *Tikkun Olam*, 71.

5. Jack Bieler, "A Religious Context for Jewish Political Activity," in Shatz, Waxman, and Diament, eds., *Tikkun Olam*, 146.

6. Ibid.

7. Marc Stern, "Jews and Public Morality," in Shatz, Waxman, and Diament, eds., *Tikkun Olam*, 165.

8. Ibid., 159.

9. Ibid., 160–64; Bieler, "A Religious Context for Jewish Political Activity," 148.

10. Adat Shalom Reconstructionist Synagogue at http://www.jrf.org/adatsmd/tikunola .html (accessed October 5, 2007).

11. Blidstein, "Tikkun Olam," 27.

12. Ibid., 1.

13. Ibid., 26.

14. *Sotah* 37a on Exod 14:15, cited by Bieler, "A Religious Context for Jewish Political Activity," 151.

15. Blidstein, "Tikkun Olam," 42–43.

16. Ibid., citing Maimonides, 29.

17. See also Lawrence Fine, "Tikkun: A Lurianic Motif in Contemporary Jewish Thought," in *From Ancient Israel to Modern Judaism: Intellect in Quest of Understanding—Essays in Honor of Marvin Fox,* ed. Jacob Neusner, vol. 4 (Atlanta: Scholars, 1989).

18. Howard Schwartz, *Reimagining the Bible: The Storytelling of the Rabbis* (New York: Oxford University Press, 1998), 140–41.

19. Blidstein, "Tikkun Olam," 26.

20. Schwartz, *Reimagining the Bible,* 114.

21. Ibid.

22. Stern, "Jews and Public Morality," 166.

23. Charles Liebman and Steven Cohen, *Two Worlds of Judaism: The Israeli and American Experiences* (New Haven, Conn.: Yale University Press, 1990), 112.

24. Ibid., 110.

25. Ibid., 110–11.

26. Ibid.

27. David Elcott, *A Sacred Journey: The Jewish Quest for a Perfect World* (Northvale, N.J.: Jason Aronson, 1995), 92.

28. Ibid., 89.

29. Ibid., 93.

30. Ibid., 94.

31. Abraham Heschel, *The Prophets* (New York: Harper & Row, 1962), 253.

32. Emil Fackenheim, *To Mend the World: Foundations of Post-Holocaust Jewish Thought,* reprint ed. (Bloomington: Indiana University Press, 1994), xxii.

33. Elcott, *A Sacred Journey,* 94.

34. See Fine, "Tikkun: A Lurianic Motif."

35. Blidstein, "Tikkun Olam," 1.

36. Liebman and Cohen, *Two Worlds of Judaism,* 110–11.

37. "A Statement of Principles for Reform Judaism," adopted at the 1999 Pittsburgh Convention, Central Conference of American Rabbis, May 1999/Sivan 5759; and "A Commentary on the Principles for Reform Judaism," Central Conference of American Rabbis, 2000.

38. Temple Israel Synagogue at http://www.templeisrael.com (accessed October 5, 2007).

39. Brooklyn Heights Reform Synagogue at http://www.bhsbrooklyn.org/bhstik.htm (accessed October 5, 2007).

40. Adat Shalom Reconstructionist Synagogue at http://www.jrf.org/adatsmd/tikunola .html (accessed October 5, 2007).

41. Irving Greenberg, *The Jewish Way: Living the Holidays* (New York: Simon & Schuster, 1988), 127.

42. Ibid.

43. Aviezer Ravitzky, "Peace," in *Contemporary Jewish Religious Thought*, ed. A. Cohen and Paul Mendes-Flohr (New York: Scribner's, 1987), 685.

44. Ibid.

45. Joseph Healey, "Peace," in *Anchor Bible Dictionary*, ed. D. N. Freedman (New York: Doubleday, 1992), 5:206.

46. Claus Westermann, "Peace (*shalom*) in the Old Testament" trans. W. Sawatsky in *The Meaning of Peace: Biblical Studies*, ed. P. Yoder and W. Swartley (Louisville, Ky.: Westminster John Knox, 1992), 20.

47. Ibid., 39.

48. Ravitzky, "Peace," 686.

49. Wayne Muller, *Sabbath: Finding Rest, Renewal, and Delight in Our Busy Lives* (New York: Bantam, 2000), 134.

50. Abraham Heschel, *The Sabbath* (New York: Farrar, Straus, Giroux, 1951), 23.

51. Arthur Waskow, "Rest" in Cohen and Mendes-Flohr, eds., *Contemporary Jewish Religious Thought*, 803.

52. Heschel, *The Sabbath*, 19.

53. Greenberg, *The Jewish Way,* 138.

54. Heschel, *The Sabbath*, 29.

55. Greenberg, *The Jewish Way,* 139.

56. Ibid., 131.

57. Norman Beck, "Vocation and *tikkun olam:* A Lutheran Christian Perspective," March 2001, presentation at Gustavus Adolphus College during Consultation on Lutheran-Jewish Relations.

58. Marc Kolden, "Luther on Vocation," in *Word & World* 3, no. 2 (1983): 390.

59. Ibid.

60. Martin Luther, "The Freedom of a Christian," in *Martin Luther: Selections from His Writings,* ed. John Dillenberger (New York: Anchor, 1961), 73.

61. Timothy Lull, "Freedom and Vocation: Our world is full of people longing for fulfillment," in *The Lutheran* (May 2003): 6.

62. Kolden, "Luther on Vocation," 386.

63. Martin Luther, *Lectures on Genesis 45–50,* Luther's Works 8, ed. Jaroslav Pelikan (St. Louis: Concordia, 1966), 94–95.

64. Luther, "The Freedom of a Christian," in Dillenberger, ed., *Martin Luther,* 74.

65. Kolden, "Luther on Vocation," 383.

66. See Michael Strassfeld, *A Book of Life: Embracing Judaism as a Spiritual Practice* (New York: Schocken, 2002).

67. Adat Shalom Reconstructionist Synagogue at http://www.jrf.org/adatsmd/tikunola .html (accessed October 5, 2007).

CHAPTER 8

1 . Both Mark Swanson and Barry Cytron reviewed the draft of this chapter and offered helpful comments to the author, but only one, Mark Swanson, wrote a formal response. This procedure differed slightly from that followed in the other chapters. The reason for the deviation is that chapter 8 moves beyond Jewish-Christian relations to discuss Christian relations with other religions. Mark Swanson responds from the perspective of a person deeply involved in Christian-Muslim dialogue.

2. The Deists, the Baptists, and the Quakers were philosophically in favor of religious freedom. The Puritans, the Anglicans, and others accepted it as a pragmatic solution. They preferred disestablishment rather than allowing any other church to enjoy the support of the federal government.

3. Will Herberg's *Protestant, Catholic, and Jew: An Essay in American Religious Sociology* (Garden City, N.Y.: Doubleday, 1956) is usually cited as a good way to date the public acknowledgment of that acceptance. The election in 1960 of John F. Kennedy as the first Roman Catholic president was another sign of this change. The endorsement of religious liberty and of ecumenism at Vatican Council II (1962–1965) accelerated the process.

4. During the 1920s and the 1930s there was a general fear in the United States of too many immigrants from the "less advanced" peoples of southern and eastern Europe, and the more recent Jewish immigrants were thought to fit into this category. Antisemitism was fueled by the popular weekly radio broadcasts of Father Charles Coughlin and by the pub-

lication in English, with the assistance of Henry Ford, of the forgery known as *The Protocols of the Elders of Zion*. The latter alleged an international Jewish conspiracy, which seemed to some to explain the genesis of the Depression.

5. American civil religion went beyond Deism when its spokespersons claimed that God had a special purpose or destiny for the United States as a "city on a hill" or a "beacon of light" for the nations. Its divine destiny was to be a model of freedom for the peoples of the world.

6. Two things can cause confusion: (a) the Christian doctrine of the Trinity, which is not shared by Jews and Muslims. However much this Christian teaching may complicate things, the original intent of that Christian teaching was to affirm monotheism and to affirm that Christians believed in the same God as did Abraham, Isaac, and Jacob. From the standpoint of Christians, at least, there is no difference between the God they worship and the God of biblical Israel, which is the God Jews and Muslims also claim to worship. Hence the Trinity does not automatically undermine the assertion that Jews, Muslims, and Christians worship the same God. (b) The Muslim use of "Allah," which appears to distinguish them from Jews and Christians. However, "Allah" simply means "the God." Whereas the English word *god* can mean either "a god" or "the God" (of Abraham, Isaac, and Jacob), "Allah" is more precise. It refers specifically to the latter and not to the former. Hence it too does not undermine the continuity and similarity regarding God.

7. Irving Greenberg, "Judaism and Christianity: Their Respective Roles in the Strategy of Redemption," in *Visions of the Other: Jewish and Christian Theologians Assess the Dialogue*, ed. Eugene Fisher (New York: Paulist, 1994), 18–19. This essay is reprinted in *For the Sake of Heaven and Earth: The New Encounter between Judaism and Christianity* (Philadelphia: Jewish Publication Society, 2004); the quotation is found on 174.

8. Observation made by Mark Swanson.

9. Greenberg, "Judaism and Christianity," in Fisher, ed., *Visions of the Other*, 9, and *For the Sake of Heaven and Earth*, 164.

10. See chapter 1 in this volume for an additional discussion of this point.

11. One example is that the Jewish practice of a *bar mitzvah* ceremony for thirteen-year-olds was adapted from the Christian practice of confirmation.

12. Greenberg, "Judaism and Christianity," in Fisher, ed., *Visions of the Other*, 11, and *For the Sake of Heaven and Earth*, 166.

13. To cite a rather unusual example, one of my neighbors in Allentown, Pennsylvania, was the president of a local synagogue even though he considered himself an atheist. He explained that, although he did not believe in God, he considered Jewish teachings the most profound interpretation of life available, and so he actively and energetically supported synagogue activities. What is significant here is that particular beliefs were not requisite for membership or leadership in a synagogue in quite the same way they are for Christians who are expected to profess and to continue to profess a baptismal creed (the Apostles' Creed).

14. Anti-Judaism is a judgment that the *religion* of Judaism is without value. Antisemitism is a judgment that the *people* known as Jews are without value—whether they are religious or not religious, or even if they have converted to Christianity. Antisemitism is based on nineteenth- and early twentieth-century theories regarding the importance of racial purity. It originally claimed to be authorized by science rather than religion.

15. Paul van Buren, *A Theology of the Jewish-Christian Reality*, Part 1: *Discerning the Way* (San Francisco: Harper & Row, 1980), 42.

16. I recognize that this may oversimplify the complexity of the claims made in the New Testament. I hope the advantages of clarity and brevity render this flaw excusable.

17. Greenberg, "Judaism and Christianity," in Fisher, ed., *Visions of the Other*, 26, and *For the Sake of Heaven and Earth*, 182.

18. Van Buren, *A Theology of the Jewish-Christian Reality*, 20.

19. Clark Williamson makes a similar point when he says, "The *adversus Judaeos* [against the Jews] tradition is an ideology which contradicts the theological claim that God justifies us. We cannot justify ourselves, no matter how hard we try. . . . God alone is sovereign, ultimate, absolute. We—our faith, hope, and convictions—are not." *Has God Rejected His People? Anti-Judaism in the Christian Church* (Nashville: Abingdon, 1982), 143.

20. Note Luther's opposition to a "theology of glory." He criticized some scholastic theologians for trying to climb up to the back door of heaven and peek in to see what God was thinking. A theologian of the cross lives within the limitations of creatureliness.

21. Van Buren, *A Theology of the Jewish-Christian Reality*, 64.

22. The phrase is from Emil Fackenheim.

23. For a discussion of the cultural issue, see, for example, James Davison Hunter, *Before the Shooting Begins: Searching for Democracy in America's Culture War* (New York: The Free Press, 1994).

24. And on that standard—that is, the standard set by this, the most Jewish of teachers, fulfilling the most Jewish of hopes—contemporary Jewish teaching measures up very well.

CASE STUDY

1. Even so, this case study is not a comprehensive strategy for addressing that concern, focusing as it does on the particular insights that emerge in these "covenantal conversations" rather than on the host of elements that would need to be taken into account in articulating a comprehensive strategy. It would be presumptuous, at best, to attempt such a strategy statement in the brief compass of this chapter.

2. Rufus E. Miles, "The Origin and Meaning of Miles' Law," *Public Administration Review* 38 (September/October 1978): 399–403.

3. Accompaniment in a technical sense has characterized Lutheran mission work for more than a decade as an earlier model of first-world patronage to third-world churches has given way to partnership and now mutual accompaniment among churches from around the world. In the accompaniment model, the experiences and ministries of indigenous local churches are received as gifts in the more established churches just as much as those churches provide their own gifts in turn. It is just this emphasis on the distinctive local contexts of different churches that makes the accompaniment model so helpful to my efforts here. See *Global Mission in the 21st Century: A Vision of Evangelical Faithfulness in God's Mission* (GM21, http://www.elca.org/globalmission/policy/gm21full.pdf, accessed December 18, 2007; esp. 5–6, 12) for a fuller description of accompaniment and the FAQs of ELCA Global Mission for

a brief overview (http://www.elca.org/globalmission/policy/faq.html, accessed December 18, 2007).

4. Since the accompaniment model developed in the global mission arena, the language of the church's relationship with the Jewish people has not been used. In describing the accompaniment model, GM21 speaks of "walking together in a solidarity that practices interdependence and mutuality" (p. 5), "walking together . . . in companionship and in service in God's mission" (p. 6), "the mutual respect of the companions" (p. 6). These phrases ring in close harmony with several phrases from the 1994 "Declaration of the ELCA to the Jewish Community" and *Talking Points*. The ELCA has expressed an "urgent desire to live out our faith in Jesus Christ with love and respect for the Jewish people" (1994 Declaration; accessed at http://www.elca.org/ecumenical/interreligious/jewish/declaration.html, on December 18, 2007). The Talking Points suggest that "the Jewish community is a powerful partner with the church in living out God's call to be stewards of healing for the world" (*Talking Point* #1), "we live in the new covenant . . . , joined in continuity to those who have already been made God's people in the covenant of Sinai" (*Talking Point* #2), "church and synagogue are mutual tokens of God's faithfulness" (*Talking Point* #4), "for both Christians and Jews, being 'a kingdom of priests and a holy nation' (Exod 19:6, 1 Pet 2:9) means bearing responsibility to use God's gifts for the good of the world" (*Talking Point* #7), "we can learn much from Jewish teaching and heritage (*Talking Point* #7), and "Judaism as a co-community of faith" and "our relationship to Judaism requires both sensitivity to what we have in common and a respect for the independent right of Jews to define themselves as a community" (*Talking Point* #8). As we consider the implications of the Talking Points for our life as a church, then, I cannot help but ask whether this language does not suggest a kind of accompaniment of the church with the Jewish people. An approach to this suggestion is already made by GM21, in fact, which recognizes that "mission is also lived out in respectful and listening relationships with those with whom we would proclaim the gospel and share the life of God: people of all living faiths" (p. 12).

5. If there is a "side" with which churches in the United States must identify, it is the role that the United States plays in the conflict. There is ample opportunity for engagement in advocacy on behalf of peace in the halls of the U.S. Congress and among multinational corporations based in the United States. It is these powers to whom U.S. churches are called first to speak truth, with as much courage and creativity as Middle Eastern partners use in prophetic critique of their own leaders.

6. Several Jewish thinkers have suggested that it was the establishment of the State of Israel, more than the Shoah (Holocaust), that confronted Christianity with the crisis of recognition and reformulation. See Irving Greenberg, "The New Encounter of Judaism and Christianity," *Barat Review* 3, no. 2 (June 1967); reprinted in *For the Sake of Heaven and Earth* (Philadelphia: Jewish Publication Society, 2004), 115. See also Eugene Korn and Tzvi Marx in oral presentations to the Christian Scholars Group (Boston, June 6, 2004) and to the Lutherische Europäische Kommission Kirche und Judentum (Amsterdam, May 20, 2005), respectively.

7. The same inference can be drawn when there are references to "occupied territory" regarding areas within "green-line Israel"—the territory stipulated as Israeli under the UN partition plan.

8. October 26, 2005, with extensive worldwide media coverage.

9. *The Oslo Syndrome: Delusions of a People under Siege* (Lyme, N.H.: Smith and Kraus, 2005), excerpted at http://mideastoutpost.com/archives/000143.html (accessed October 3, 2007).

10. "An Arab-Israeli's Theological Reflections on the State of Israel After 40 Years," *Immanuel* 22/23 (1989): 111–12.

11. "What is the Holy Land without the baptized people of the land?" (Ann E. Hafften, ed., *Water from the Rock: Lutheran Voices from Palestine* [Minneapolis: Augsburg Fortress, 2003], 26); and, "[Palestinian Christians] believe that we represent the continuity of the Old Testament and New Testament peoples' existence on the land. . . . The land is holy only with the continued existence of the living body of Christ" (Munib A. Younan, *Witnessing for Peace: In Jerusalem and the World* [Minneapolis: Fortress Press, 2003], 64f.); see also Mitri Raheb, *I Am a Palestinian Christian* (Minneapolis: Fortress Press, 1995), 15–16.

12. In the "additional" (*musaf*) prayer on holidays the Jewish community also acknowledges God's hand in their scattering: "in light of our sins we were exiled from our land"; this is not, however, the only theological interpretation of the destruction of the Temple.

13. Space does not permit a full accounting of all those events; indeed, the work of reinterpretation is far from completed. For a brief example of this sort of work, see Peter A. Pettit and John Townsend, "'In Every Generation': Judaism as a Living Faith," chap. 9 in *Seeing Judaism Anew*, ed. Mary C. Boys (Lanham, Md.: Rowman & Littlefield, 2005), 95–112.

14. Helmut Gollwitzer, "What is the Theological Implication?" *Christian News from Israel* 12:1–2 (1958): 38.

15. For a 1989 review of the limited theological activity in this regard, see Petra Heldt and Malcolm Lowe, "Theological Significance of the Rebirth of the State of Israel: Different Christian Attitudes," *Immanuel* 22/23 (1989): 133–45, who comment in their conclusion on "the slow rate of change of Christian attitudes—and in many quarters the absence of change—regarding the very idea of renewed Jewish sovereignty in the biblical homeland" (145).

16. To be sure, the sixth-century B.C.E. experience of exile led those who shaped the Torah in Babylonia to assert that Israel could live as God's people outside the land (see James A. Sanders, *Torah and Canon* [Philadelphia: Fortress Press, 1972], 47–53). Yet even they provided the Torah with a climactic scene—the first-fruits offering and covenantal recital that takes place "when you enter the land that the LORD your God is giving you as a heritage" (Deut. 26:1)—to which "Israel in dispersion could cling for as long and as often as need be [in] the unifying hope of returning home" (Sanders, *Torah and Canon*, 48).

17. For one window into this way of thinking, see my article, "Christian Zionism from a Perspective of Jewish-Christian Relations," *Journal of Lutheran Ethics* 7, no. 5 (May 2007), accessed December 19, 2007, at http://www.elca.org/jle/article.asp?k=723.

18. See the campaign Web site at http://www.elca.org/peacenotwalls/ and the strategy statement at http://www.elca.org/peacenotwalls/downloadable/strategyfull.pdf (both accessed December 23, 2007).

19. Recall "The Dividing Wall," the title of the Mennonite Central Committee video.

20. Jefferson Morley cites the July 8, 2004, report in the Israeli daily, *Ma'ariv*, that construction of the barrier had reduced suicide attacks within Israel by 90 percent from one

year to the next ("As World Court Deliberates, Israel Seethes," *Washington Post*, July 8, 2004, at http://2www.washingtonpost.com/wp-dyn/articles/A36381-2004Jul18.html, accessed October 3, 2007).

21. The liturgy begins at Lifta, "an ethnically cleansed and destroyed village." The narrative regarding this "Station 1" of the Via Dolorosa recalls the biblical portrayal of Jesus' condemnation by the Jewish leaders and crowd, "to retain the friendship and good will of mortal men, his accusers cry out, 'Crucify him!' and condemn the man . . ." The liturgy then begins:

> Just as Jesus is condemned to die by the authorities to protect their own power, status and ideals, so the Palestinians suffer as the result of the fear and ideology of the founders of the State of Israel.

> Just as Jesus is condemned to die so the actions of 1948 passed a death sentence on historic Palestine and 418 villages . . .

Note that Israel's offense is not expansionist policies or administrative abuses subsequent to the 1967 war, but "the initial devastation caused by the founding of Israel," as the liturgy put it.

22. Naim Ateek, "Who Will Role [*sic*] Away the Stone (Mark 16:3)," sermon at Notre Dame Chapel, Jerusalem, February 24, 2001, at http://www.sabeel.org/old/conf2001/ateekser.htm (accessed October 3, 2007).

23. See http://www.tomgrossomedia.com/img/italy_Imhyjesus.jpg (accessed December 22, 2007).

24. See http://www.aish.com/jewishissues/mediaobjectivity/World_Turned_Upside-Down.asp (accessed December 22, 2007).

25. The circumstances under which many Palestinians became refugees from their homelands in the State of Israel in 1948 are a matter for consideration in another context; wartime conditions, the UN sanction of Israeli statehood, and the actions of neighboring Arab states all have bearing on the 1948 refugee question. In Israel's administration of the lands occupied during the 1967 War, there has been neither policy nor practice of population transfer.

26. New York: Simon & Schuster, 2006. See, for example, Alan Dershowitz in *The Huffington Post* (http://www.huffingtonpost.com/alan-dershowitz/the-world-according-to-ji_b_34702.html, accessed December 22, 2007), and Joseph Lelyveld in *The New York Review of Books* (54, no. 5 [March 29, 2007], http://www.nybooks.com/articles/19993, accessed December 22, 2007) for a range of the criticism that Carter's book received.

27. Raheb, *I Am a Palestinian Christian*, 12.

28. Recounted by the Rev. John Stendahl in personal conversation, most recently in Chicago, November 10, 2007.

29. "Healing the World—Working Together: Religion in Global Society," 10 (http://rabbidavidrosen.net/Articles/Christian-Jewish%20Relations/Healing.doc, accessed December 22, 2007).

30. See Raheb, *I am a Palestinian Christian*, 13, especially footnote 31.

31. Expressed variously by Samuel Johnson and U.S. Senator Hiram Johnson, and widely attributed to Aeschylus.

32. The legitimacy of this use is contested especially among Lutheran theologians because of the ease with which it could bind the believer back into a system of works righteousness. Luther certainly emphasized the freedom that comes with faith, but it is not a freedom from conscientious engagement in the world. Oswald Bayer points to Luther's exposition of "the passage in Romans 13:8-10 in which Paul refers to love as the fulfilling of the law. With faith we receive freedom for service in love 'so that we have no law nor owe anyone anything except love [Rom. 13:8]. We are to do good things for our neighbors just as Christ has done for us through his blood. Hence all the laws, works, and commandments that are required of us to serve God do not come from God. . . . Yet these laws, works, and commandments that are required of us to serve our neighbors are good and we should do them . . .'" (*Living by Faith: Justification and Sanctification* [Grand Rapids: Eerdmans, 2003], 39–40; quoting Luther in the German edition, *Luthers Werke*, 60 vols., ed. J. F. Knaake, et al. [Weimar: Böhlau, 1883–1996] 12:157, 6-14). Bayer also notes Luther's description of the "inner heart" from which spring a Christian's good works "is given only by God's Spirit who fashions a [person] after the law, so that [the person] acquires a pleasure in the law" (op. cit., 39, quoting Luther in the American edition, *Luther's Works*, 55 vols., ed. J. Pelikan and H. Lehmann [St. Louis and Philadelphia: Concordia and Fortress Press, 1955ff.], 35:367).

33. This is the paraphrase most closely associated with the Reverend Dr. Martin Luther King Jr., a student of Parker's sermons. According to Joshua Cohen, "the phrase . . . or variants on it occur throughout King's writings and speeches. See Martin Luther King Jr., *A Testimony of Hope: Essential Writings of Martin Luther King, Jr.*, ed. James Washington (San Francisco: Harper & Row, 1986), 141, 207, 230, 277, 438. According to Taylor Branch, the phrase came from Theodore Parker. See *Parting the Waters: America in the King Years, 1954–1963* (New York: Simon & Schuster, 1988), 197n. ("The Moral Arc of the Universe," *Philosophy and Public Affairs* 26, no. 2. [Spring, 1997]: 93, n. 5). Parker's statement, without a specific source, takes the form, "I do not pretend to understand the moral universe; the arc is a long one, my eye reaches but little ways; I cannot calculate the curve and complete the figure by the experience of sight; I can divine it by conscience. And from what I see I am sure it bends towards justice" (at http://thinkexist.com/quotation/look_at_the_facts_of_the_world-you_see_a/339283.html, accessed December 28, 2007, and other sites).

34. Rabbi Melissa Klein, Allentown, Pa., in personal conversation, May 18, 2005.

35. Hayim Halevy Donin, *To Be a Jew* (New York: Basic, 1972), 45.

BIBLICAL INDEX